GROSSMAN'S CYCLOPEDIA

The Concise Guide to Wines, Beers, and Spirits

GROSSMAN'S CYCLOPEDIA

The Concise Guide to Wines, Beers, and Spirits

BY HARRIET LEMBECK

RUNNING PRESS
PHILADELPHIA • LONDON

This edition is abridged from *Grossman's Guide to Wines, Beers, and Spirits*, 7th edition.

Published by arrangement with Hungry Minds, Inc.

Printed in China

9 8 7 6 5 4 3 2 1
Digit on the right indicates the number of this printing

Library of Congress Cataloguing-in-Publication Number 2001094424

ISBN 0-7624-1210-0

Cover and interior design by Frances J. Soo Ping Chow
Edited by Michael Washburn
Illustrations by permission of Hungry Minds, Inc.
Typography: Adobe Garamond Titling, Trade Gothic, and Goudy

This book may be ordered by mail from the publisher.
Please include $2.50 for postage and handling.
But try your bookstore first!

Running Press Book Publishers
125 South Twenty-second Street
Philadelphia, Pennsylvania 19103-4399

Visit us on the web!
www.runningpress.com

Table of Contents

Introduction 7

Wines of Bordeaux 16

Wines of Burgundy 56

Wines of Champagne 93

Wines of Alsace 121

Rhône Wines 129

Wines of Austria 179

Wines of Hungary 184

Wines of Canada 193

Wines of Argentina 197

Wines of Australia 207

Wines of New Zealand 220

Wines of China 225

Wines of Japan 228

Brandies 235

Whiskies 272

Vodkas 318

Gins 328

Rums 343

Other Spirits 362

Cocktails and Other Mixed Drinks 379

Glossary 470

Appendix A 527

Appendix B 576

Appendix C 604

Appendix D 611

Appendix E 621

Appendix F 634

Appendix G 635

INTRODUCTION

The liquor "industry" is almost as old as man himself, and our knowledge of it is made up of widely scattered information in every language written or spoken. The subject is continually developing and consequently is always intriguing.

The development and improvement of the quality of alcoholic beverages have been the natural results of the advance of science and civilization. The role of science has been limited to ensuring uniformity of quality and sound products year in and year out, for nature still insists on having something to say in the matter, even when it comes to distilled spirits.

The vine, the brewing kettle, and the still have accompanied the spread of Christianity, establishing certain honorable traditions that the trade proudly upholds today. It is also interesting to note the esteem in which the wine trade is held abroad. It was the first "trade" considered sufficiently honorable and dignified for a member of the aristocracy to engage in, and many of the leading European firms are directed by members of noble families.

In England a wine merchant is consulted in matters pertaining to wines, beers, or spirits just as a lawyer is in legal matters. The confidence thus placed in him gives the merchant a keen consciousness of his responsibility. Also, as he knows that his descendants will continue the business he builds, family pride leads him to pass on an impeccable reputation. It is not unusual to find firms that have been doing business under the same name in the same place for hundreds of years—in some cases more than four hundred years. This is the European custom, and we are happy to note that it is beginning to take hold in the United States.

One of the leading Champagne shippers illustrated this point when he told us: "When I ship my wine, my name appears on the label. It is I who guarantee the quality. My reputation is more important to me than any pecuniary profit I may derive from the sale. It took my forebears two hundred years to establish this reputation for shipping wines of quality, and rest assured that I am going to pass on as good a name to my successors as I received." It is men of this type who have placed the wine and spirit trade on the high plane that has become traditional.

Based on these traditions, certain firms have established their brands so well that the public asks for their product by the name of the shipper. This has been particularly true in the case of Cognac and whiskies, but since the American public is "age conscious," many people buy dates rather than brands in whose names we have confidence. This has happened in the case of wines, as well. It is true that certain wines do improve with age—up to a point—but there are other wines that are more pleasant if drunk when young, as in the case with light white wines, whose charm lies in their freshness.

The industry as a whole today is a most important part

of our business life, employing, directly or through allied enterprises, millions of men and women. It is one of the three most important sources of tax revenue for the federal and state treasuries.

Just as prohibition is bad, so is excess, and in no case is this more evident than in the use of alcoholic beverages. There is no better word of advice on this point than that which Lord Chesterfield gave to his son in a letter from London, dated March 27, 1747: "Were I to begin the world again with the experience I now have of it, I would lead a life of real, not imaginary, pleasures. I would enjoy the pleasures of the table, and of wine; but stop short of the pains inseparably annexed to an excess of either."

The leaders of the industry unanimously prefer that more people drink and enjoy beverages, rather than that individuals drink more.

It is gratifying to note the moderation exercised by the public in the use of alcoholic beverages. A per capita consumption in the United States of slightly over two gallons of wine per year indicates an average of three-quarters of an ounce per day. Wine has recently surpassed spirits consumption, which averages seven-tenths of an ounce per day, but this amount of wine consumption is still extremely low when compared with other countries. Beer consumption has increased to slightly more than ten times that of wines or spirits, averaging eight and one-half ounces per capita per day. The new low-alcohol and low-calorie wines and beers most likely account for much of these increases, while enabling the public to maintain its standards of moderation.

The *Guide* has been divided into five main sections: wines, beers and ales; spirits; uses, merchandising, and control; and, finally, the appendices, which contain useful, quick-reference data. All of the material has been carefully indexed to make the book easier to use for reference purposes.

Condensed information on the entire industry is given, including the description of a product, its method of production, selling, care, and uses in public and private places. The practices described are those generally used in the United States, unless otherwise specified.

It is our hope that libraries will find the *Guide* a comprehensive source of information on all phases of the subject; that producers, vintners, distillers, and brewers will find it valuable as a general reference and as a means of equipping their sales representatives with information about the other phases of the industry; and that the wholesale distributor will find it invaluable as a training manual for his staff and as a reference book. The various appendices also have been compiled with a view to practical use.

Particular care has been taken to provide information on every phase of the industry for retail establishments, whether off-premise (stores) or on-premise (hotels, restaurants, or clubs).

After reading the book, it may be useful for store owners to review certain chapters when promoting particular products. For example, during the Christmas season there is an opportunity to sell liqueurs in their fancy bottles. It is good business to be aware of these details and to refer to the *Guide* if one is asked, for example, for a liqueur whose style or character may have been forgotten.

It is also advisable for the hotel, restaurant, or club manager to keep his service personnel well informed. They are his sales staff and cannot be expected to increase the sale of beverages if they are not familiar with them. This applies equally to the wholesaler and distributor. The sales staff that is trained and can give information will become salesmen instead of order takers.

While the *Guide* has been designed primarily to be of use to the trade, it is our earnest hope that it will be read by the person who is most important to the entire industry: the consumer. It is to please and serve him that the industry constantly strives. A greater familiarity with the beverages discussed in this book, we believe, not only would aid him in purchasing with assurance, but would, perhaps, point out to him many intriguing qualities he may have overlooked and therefore increase his enjoyment.

To provide the reader with practical information, to increase his knowledge and enjoyment, and, above all, to impart something of the fascination of the subject are the purposes of this *Guide*.

WINES OF BORDEAUX

If France is the most famous wine-producing country, then the Bordeaux district (Gironde) is the most famous in the production of great red wines. The district produces three distinct varieties of wines, equally distinguished: magisterial clarets; clean, dry, white Graves; and luscious, golden Sauternes.

Fifty years before the birth of Christ, Burdigala (Bordeaux) was the chief history town and commercial center of Biturigis Vivisi. Later, in the fourth century, it was made the capital of Aquitanica Secunda. Its fame, then as now, was irrevocably linked with the excellence of its wines, which were praised by Columella, renowned Roman writer of the first century.

Through his marriage to Eleanor of Aquitaine in 1152, Henry of Anjou acquired the Senechaussee of Bordeaux (Gascony) and the vast Duchy of Guyenne. Two years later he became King Henry II of England, and for three hundred years Gascony belonged to the English crown. Its wines enjoyed wide popularity in the British Isles, a taste that exists to this day.

The history of the famous wines of Bordeaux began more than two thousand years ago. We do not know who first produced a wine of the claret type, but the poet Ausonius sang of its charms and virtues during the Roman occupation. The famous Château Ausone is supposed to have been his vineyard.

What is claret? The term was originally used by the English when they referred to the red wines of Bordeaux. The English made up a large part of the market for Bordeaux wines, and many English words have gained common usage in the wine world, not only in Bordeaux. The word *claret* has definite geographic origins in Bordeaux, but it is not a legal term in France. Many other countries use the term to describe a red wine they feel is similar to the type made in Bordeaux. This usage, unfortunately, has detracted from the elegant connotation of a château-bottled red wine.

The Bordelais (Bordeaux country) viticultural region is divided into five main (left) and four lesser (right) districts:

Médoc (includes Haut-Médoc)	**Premières Côtes de Bordeaux**
Graves	**Côtes de Bourg**
Saint-Émilion	**Côtes de Blaye**
Pomerol	**Entre-deux-Mers**
Sauternes	

There is a further subdivision, the commune, or parish. The parish is a geographical, political, and, formerly, religious subdivision, as a parish priest and church were required to administer to the spiritual needs of a community. The Church worked out such a perfect geographical subdivision that the state saw no reason to change it and took it over.

The most important district is the Médoc, a triangular peninsula stretching north some fifty miles from Bordeaux to Soulac and varying in width from six to ten miles. It lies between the Gironde River on the east and the Atlantic Ocean on the west and is divided into Médoc and Haut-Médoc. Of the appellation wines produced in the area, Médoc accounts for 25 percent and Haut Médoc produces 75 percent. With few exceptions (for example, the dry white wines of Pavillon Blanc du Château Margaux, Château Loudenne, and Château La Dame Blanche), only red wines are produced in the fifty-three communes that make up the entire Médoc. The four most important—Pauillac, Saint-Julien, Margaux, and Saint-Estèphe—are all located in the Haut Médoc, which extends thirty miles from Bordeaux to just north of Saint-Estèphe.

The Graves takes its name from the gravelly or pebbly quality of the soil. The district stretches for twenty-five miles in the southwest corner of Bordeaux and is for the most part level plain that becomes hillier to the south.

Here are produced both red and white wines. The

most important communes of the Graves are Pessac, Léognan, and Martillac.

Saint-Émilion and neighboring Pomerol are in the eastern part of Bordeaux, north of the Dordogne River in the vicinity of the town of Libourne. Saint-Émilion can be considered as two distinct sections: the Graves section (not the Graves region previously discussed) on a plateau that extends into Pomerol, and the Côtes to the southeast, around the town of Saint-Émilion. The main grape is the Merlot, which ripens earlier than other Bordelais grapes, and which produces wines that are fruity, scented, and mature earlier than their Médoc counterparts. Pomerol, a single commune northwest of Saint-Émilion, boasts many famous vineyards for its small size.

In the southern portion of the Graves we come to a district smaller than the island of Manhattan but viticulturally favored as are few regions in the world. The rich, luscious, highly perfumed wines of the Sauternes are entirely distinct from all the other wines of Bordeaux and have an excellence all their own. The Sauternais (Sauternes country) lies in the southeast of Graves and on the left bank of the Garonne River. Five communes compose Sauternes country: Sauternes, Barsac, Bommes, Fargues, and Preignac. The wines from any of these communes are known by the regional names of Sauternes. Barsac, however, even though it is a Sauternes, has its own appellation, and many of its châteaus prefer to use it rather than the larger Sauternes appellation.

In these districts are produced useful wines, both red and white, that are generally shipped as Bordeaux Blanc or Bordeaux Rouge. Some petite châteaus travel under their own names, but many are blended into branded, commercial wines.

One would think that rich soil would be required to produce fine wine.

Nothing could be further from the truth. In fact, the

soil of the Bordeaux wine region is mainly gravel, limestone, or sand with a clay subsoil. More unfriendly soil for agriculture would be difficult to find, and yet the vine flourishes best in just these types of soil. Where no other crop can be grown successfully, the vine gives the best quality of wine grape. This is equally true in the other famous viticultural regions of the world.

The principal vine used in the production of the great clarets of the Médoc and Graves is the Cabernet Sauvignon. Growing in small, close-set bunches, its violet-scented grapes are small and sweet and give the wine its vinosity. Other vines, such as Merlot, Petit Verdot, and Carmenère, are planted to give special qualities to the wines. In Saint-Émilion and Pomerol, however, the principal grape is the early-ripening Merlot, the balance being mostly Cabernet Franc (also called Bouschet). The best white wines of Graves and Sauternes are made from the Sémillon and Sauvignon Blanc grapes.

The vine in Bordeaux is not allowed to grow wild; in fact, it is cut back close to the ground after the vintage, so that the winter appearance of a vineyard is that of a bare field dotted with an orderly series of stumps. The vines are not allowed to grow more than 2½ to 3½ feet high so that what strength they derive from the soil will go into producing grapes of quality.

There are more than thirty thousand vineyards in the Bordeaux wine region, most of which are called *château*, meaning "castle." In many cases the property boasts a medieval castle, but when the term is used as generally as it is in Bordeaux, the majority of these "castles" are simply farmhouses used only for pressing grapes and storing wine.

Obviously, if each of the vineyard owners were to attempt to sell his wines directly to buyers from all over the world, there would be no end to the confusion. Hence there evolved many generations ago clearinghouses in the form of Bordeaux wine merchants, brokers who buy the wine from the different vineyard owners, sometimes bottled, but more often in larger quantities in the wood. The broker ships the wine as he receives it, or he blends it with wine from other vineyards and bottles it, not under the château or vineyard name, but under his own proprietary brand name. With few exceptions the vineyard owner never markets his own wines but depends on the wine merchant to do it for him.

The Bordeaux wine trade has developed five types of labels:

1. Château bottled
2. Château wine bottled by a cooperative or by a wine merchant
3. *Monopole* or trademark
4. Commune or regional
5. Varietal

There are two distinct types of labels used on château

wines. The first, château bottled, indicates that the wine has been produced, cared for, and bottled at the vineyard property where the grapes were grown. It has on the label, or sometimes on the capsule, the phrase *mis en bouteille au château*, which means "bottled at the château." The vineyard owner delivers this wine, bottled, labeled, and cased, to the wine merchant or shipper. The cork is always branded with the château name and the vintage year. Examples are Château Lafite-Rothschild, Château Latour, and Château d'Yquem.

The second type of label, château wine bottled by the wine merchant, indicates that the wine has been produced at the château named on the label but has been purchased in the cask and bottled by the shipper in his Bordeaux cellars. The shipper's name appears on the label.

There are some châteaus that do not practice château bottling at all; they have found it more profitable to sell their wines in cask to the different wine merchants who bottle them. On these and other A.O.C. wines the following phrases may be found: *mis en bouteille à la propriété*, *mise d'origine*, and *mis en bouteille dan la région de* . . . , followed by the name of the specific region.

Whereas château bottling guarantees authenticity of origin, it does not have to guarantee quality. Because of changing vintage conditions, château-bottled wines vary in quality from year to year. This has a direct influence on the price governing each vintage and explains why a younger vintage will sometimes fetch a higher price than an older one of the same wine. A good example is the 1978 Château Lafite-Rothschild, which costs more than three times as much as the less desirable 1977.

In order to take care of his customer's needs in every part of the world, the Bordeaux shipper must always have a wide assortment of château wines. Although there is no wine "stock market" in Bordeaux, châteaux bottlings are traded in somewhat the same manner as stocks and bonds.

Through the centuries the trade has evolved a system that is eminently fair and satisfactory, both to the vineyard owner and to the shipper.

Suppose, for instance, that the 1978 vintage of Château Latour totaled 300,000 bottles, all château bottled. Eight wine merchants agree to buy up the entire vintage and split it among themselves. Each of them would then have the same wine to offer to the trade, identical in every respect as to labeling, capsules, cases, and so forth, and their prices would be more or less the same. Along comes a ninth merchant who needs this wine for one of his customers. As the eight merchants have cornered the market on this wine, he must buy from one of the original purchasers and pay him a profit, and he must also make a profit for himself on the sale. Therefore, when buying château-bottled Bordeaux wines, shop for the lowest price, since it is all the same wine, assuming it has been properly stored.

The third type of label is the *monopole*, or private brand. A *monopole* wine is almost invariably a blend of various wines from different parts of a region that the shipper maintains year in and year out at the same standard of quality. It is a plentiful, everyday wine. There are many shippers who have these brands. Examples are: Grande Marque, Fonset-Lacour, La Cour Pavillon, and Mouton-Cadet.

The fourth label is the commune, district, or regional label. A bottle so labeled contains wine produced in the commune, district, or region named, for example, Médoc (wine in this bottle was produced in the Médoc district). This wine does not necessarily come from one vineyard but may be from several in the commune, district, or region named. It probably is a blended wine, bottled by the shipper at his Bordeaux cellars. For this reason it is possible to obtain wines of widely varying quality and price bearing identical place names and vintages from different shippers. One shipper may use better-quality wine in his blend, while another feels that price is more important than quality. The Bordeaux shipper, like any other businessman, tries to satisfy his customers' needs. Beware of bargains, compare prices, and taste a bottle before you buy a case.

The varietal label is the fifth type. This term has been used in the United States to indicate that the grape variety named on the label predominates in the wine itself. The purpose was to break away from generic names that were not definitive and to identify more precisely the nature of a wine. This practice was formerly used only in Alsace, Switzerland, Italy, and a few other regions in Europe, but recently the shippers of Bordeaux, Burgundy, and the Loire have also used varietal labels. The French authorities require the use of 100 percent of the grapes named; the E.E.C. minimum is 85 percent, while the U.S. minimum is 75 percent. For France, this is a departure from the traditional style of winemaking, which usually uses more than one grape variety.

There seems to be some confusion as to the exact meaning of the word vintage in reference to wines, whether they are imported or produced in the United States. The word has two meanings:

1. *Vintage* means gathering the grapes, pressing them, and making wine. There is a vintage (harvest) every year.
2. The date (or *millésime*) on a bottle of wine signifies the year in which the grapes were harvested. Some vineyards bottle and date every year's production. Certain regions, such as Champagne, date only the wines of exceptional years. Since this is not done every year, the dated wines are known as vintage wines.

A vintage chart, judiciously used, can be helpful, but it is important to remember table wines change constantly. No two wines, even from the same district, develop at a constant rate. Furthermore, not all wines made in a great year are great, and not all wines made in a relatively poor year are poor.

Sweeping generalities of this kind cannot be applied when one considers the thousands of vineyards involved. However, the chances are better for good wines when conditions are generally favorable, and with these reservations in mind, a vintage chart can be useful (see Appendix B).

Classified Growths

In 1855 a number of Bordeaux wines were to be established at the Exposition in Paris. There was some question about the order in which the wines should be shown as, inevitably, there was rivalry among the best-known vineyard owners as to who produced the finest wine. In order to settle the matter once and for all, a jury of wine brokers was selected to classify the outstanding clarets and Sauternes in order of merit. Although this was done over a century ago, for the most part these classifications still hold and are accepted the world over.* Fifty-seven red wines of Médoc and one from Graves were chosen and classified in five classes or groups, while twenty Sauternes were grouped in two main classes, and one Sauternes was placed in a special class. After 1855 some vineyards were sold and subsequently divided. This accounts for the different number of classified châteaus found in different source books, depending on when the vineyards were counted, but at present the generally accepted number is sixty-one (see Appendix C). Below the fifth growth in the Médoc and the second growth in the Sauternes are further classifications: *grand crus bourgeois exceptionnel*, *grand crus*

*In 1787, sixty-eight years before the Bordeaux classification of 1855, Thomas Jefferson wrote, "The cantons in which the most celebrated wines of Bourdeaux are made are Médoc down the river, Grave adjoining the city, and the parishes next above; all on the same side of the river. . . . Of red wines, there are four vineyards of the first quality, *viz.*, 1. Château Margau, . . . 2. La Tour de Ségur, . . . 3. Hautbrion, . . . 4. Château de la Fite. . . ."

bourgeois, and *bourgeois*.

In 1953 the leading wines of Graves were officially classified. In 1959 the list was revised, and this time thirteen red and eight white wines were selected. In 1955 an official classification was made of the top clarets of Saint-Émilion. Twelve were chosen as first classified great growths (two rated "A" and ten rated "B") and seventy-two as great classified growths. Both of these classifications have been adopted by the *Institut National des Appellations d'Origine des Vins et Eaux-de-Vie* (see Appendix C). Because of the demand and the high prices of the great classified growths, more and more wines with regional labels and proprietary brands are being sold.

To differentiate between a classified claret and a *cru bourgeois* is easy. To tell the difference between a second and a third growth is very difficult. Most of the sixty-one vineyards produce excellent wines whose main differences lie in nuances of nose (bouquet), body, and delicacy apparent to the connoisseur, but not necessarily to the layman. However, certain basic, distinguishing marks are apparent in wines from different parishes or sections. For example, the wines of Pauillac (Château Lafite-Rothschild, Château Latour, Château Mouton-Rothschild, and so on) have more body than those of Margaux (Château Margaux), which have finesse and delicacy, while the red wines of the Graves (Château Haut-Brion, Château La Mission Haut Brion, and so on) are fuller than the Médoc wines mentioned. Even fuller and more fruity are the Pomerol (Château Pétrus) and Saint-Émilion (Château Ausone, Château Cheval Blanc, and so on).

Château Lafite-Rothschild. Lafite is spelled with one *f* and one *t* and should not be confused with similar names such as Laffite or Laffitte. According to a document dated 1355, Château Lafite belonged to a certain Jean de Lafite. In 1868 Baron James de Rothschild acquired it at private auction for the reputed sum of 165,000 pounds, and it is still held by his heirs. In a good year Château Lafite-Rothschild has a magnificent deep color, a softness and delicacy of flavor, and a violet bouquet.

Château Latour, also a first growth, takes its name from an ancient tower. This, according to legend, is the only remaining vestige of the original castle of Saint-Lambert, supposedly destroyed by Du Guesclin when the English were driven out of Gascony. The retiring English, say the ancient tales, left a vast fortune buried in or near the tower. But the fortune, as we well know, was buried not below but above the ground, for the great wines of Château Latour have more body and a more pronounced flavor than those of either Lafite or Margaux.

Château Margaux, in true medieval splendor, once boasted a stout fortress surrounded by moats a hundred feet wide, which were connected to the Gironde by canals so boats could sail up to its gates. In 1447 it was the property of Baron François de Montferrand. After him it passed through many hands until, in 1879, it came to Count Pillet-Will. Today it is owned by Mme. André Mentzelopoulos, widow of a financier. The wines of Château Margaux are generous without being too full bodied, are elegant, and have a delightfully fragrant bouquet. In one of the best parts of its vineyard a limited quantity of fine wine is produced from the Sémillon and Sauvignon Blanc grape varieties. It is labeled Pavillon Blanc due Château Margaux.

Château Haut-Brion, in the parish of Pessac in the Graves, is the last of the original 1855 listing of first growths and the only wine of the sixty-one to be chosen from outside the Médoc. It is, in fact, in the suburbs of Bordeaux. Haut-Brion, pronounced *o-bree-ohn*, is according to some chroniclers, the French spelling of O'Brien; this is possible, as there must have been some Irishmen in Gascony during the English period. As far back as the fourteenth century, at the court of Pope Clement V, these wines were highly regarded. Lacking the softness and lightness of their fellow first growths, these wines are renowned for their full, generous body and beautiful, deep color. This superb vineyard has been the property of the family of Clarence Dillon, the American financier, for a number of years.

Château Mouton-Rothschild, whose owners were outspoken against the 1855 classification, did not accept tamely having their wine rated below the first four growths and as a result adopted this challenging motto:

Premier ne puis	**First I cannot be**
Second ne daigne	**Second I do not deign to be**
Mouton suds.	**Mouton I am.**

In 1973, after much work by Baron Philippe de

Rothschild, the vineyard was classified in Bordeaux as a first growth. (The 1855 classification remains unchanged.) The Baron then wrote a new motto:

> **First, I am**
> **Second, I was**
> **But Mouton does not change.**

Judging by the prices Mouton usually fetches, this move was more than justified. Over the years Mouton has consistently equaled the prices of the four first growths. Although the 1855 classification is still amazingly accurate, many inequities have developed however. On the basis of market prices, Château Pétrus of Pomerol and Château Cheval Blanc of Saint-Émilion, which were not included in the 1855 classification, are among the top clarets of Bordeaux.

Well-known second growths in the American market are the wines of Châteaus Léoville-Lascases, Léoville-Barton, Léoville-Poyferré, Gruaud-Larose, Ducru-

Beaucaillou, Lascombes, Rausan-Ségla, Brane-Cantenac, Pichon-Longueville (Baron), Pichon-Longueville-Comtesse de Lalande, Cos d'Estournel, and Montrose.

Among the third growths, Châteaus Giscours, Palmer, Kirwan, and Calon-Ségur are well known in America, while among the fourth growths, the wines of Châteaus Prieure-Lichine, Talbot, and Beychevelle are often sold in the United States.

Finally, there are the fifth growths, of which the better known in the United States are Châteaus Pontet-Canet, Grand-Puy-Lacoste, Grand-Puy-Ducasse, Lynch-gages, Mouton-Baron-Phillipe, and Batailley. There are too many people who turn up their noses at fifth growths, considering them poor or even inferior. What they forget or overlook is that fifth growths are still part of that special group of sixty-one wines that were selected from among thousands of the better red wines of Bordeaux. The fact is that they are still great wines, though perhaps not peers of the first growths.

The fine clarets of the Graves region were not classified officially in 1855. It was not until 1953, and again in 1959, that official classifications were at last made and published (see Appendix C). From the Graves come such outstanding wines as Châteaus La Mission Haut Brion, Pape-Clément, Haut-Bailly, Smith-Haut-Lafitte, Bouscaut, and Domaine de Chevalier. They are fuller bodied and not quite as delicate as the wines of the Médoc, but Graves clarets make up in richness what they lack in finesse.

Politics or jealousy must have had something to do with the 1855 classification, as the wines of Châteaus Ausone and Cheval-Blanc in Saint-Émilion, and Pétrus, L'Evangile, and Vieux Château Certan in Pomerol, were not included. These wines, because of their high percentage of Merlot grapes, have a deep color, rich bouquet, and fullness of body. They also mature earlier than wines made with more Cabernet Sauvignon grapes. Because of all these factors, the wines made of Saint-Émilion and Pomerol are often called the Burgundies of Bordeaux. Ausone, whose average yield is quite small, Cheval Blanc, and Pétrus all produce magnificent wines that almost invariably command prices equal to the great Médoc clarets. Saint-Émilion clarets were finally classified in 1955 (see Appendix C). Still other wines of great repute are Châteaus Figeac, La Gaffelière, Canon, Magdelaine, Pavie, and Clos Fourtet in Saint-Émilion. In Pomerol famous wines include Petit-Village, La Fleur-Pétrus, Nenin, and Trotanoy.

White Wines of Bordeaux

More white wine than red is made in the Graves (pronounced *grahv*). The white wines are clean, dry, and fresh and have a pleasant, fruity bouquet of their own.

Most of the Graves wines are shipped by the Bordeaux houses under private brand labels as standard blends, each house having several brands varying in quality and dryness in order to please the tastes of their several world markets. There are several outstanding château-bottled white Graves: Châteaus Olivier, Carbonnieux, and Laville Haut Brion. Of these, well known in this country is Château Olivier, from an estate whose castle and vineyards were renowned in the twelfth century. Here the Prince of Wales, known as Edward the Black Prince, had a hunting lodge during the time when Aquitaine was an English domain and he was governor general of Gascony.

The ancient legends of these old châteaus have the perfume and enchantment of the wines themselves. It is related of Château Carbonnieux that, in order to convince a certain sultan of Turkey of the merits of French wine (wine being prohibited to the Faithful by the Koran), Château Carbonnieux was shipped to him labeled

"Mineral Water of Carbonnieux." So impressed was the Commander of the Faithful upon drinking the wine that he exclaimed, "When they have water that is so pure and so agreeable, how can the French drink wine?"

Other well-known white wines of the Graves are Châteaus Bouscaut, Domaine de Chevalier, and Haut-Brion Blanc.

The grape varieties in the Graves are the Sémillon and the Sauvignon Blanc. The Sémillon gives wine finesse, velvetiness, color, and aroma. The predominant Sauvignon Blanc produces a wine that is full and rich in bouquet. Sauvignon Blanc has the acidity to stand on its own as a varietal wine. Although the same grape varieties are used in the Graves as in the Sauternes, where the Sémillon predominates, the Graves produces a dry wine because the grapes are gathered when they are ripe. They are not left to hang on the vine until overripe, as is done in Sauternes, where climatic conditions are different.

There are five communes in the Sauternes area: Sauternes (which gives the regional name to the entire section), Barsac, Bommes, Fargues, and Preignac. Wine produced from grapes grown in any of these five communes is legally permitted to be called Sauternes.

There is a pronounced difference in the way Sauternes are made as compared with the Graves. In fact, the wine originally resembled the Graves. But many years ago, it seems, the owner of a château in this district, reputedly Yquem, was away on a hunting trip. He was delayed and therefore did not return in time to order the gathering of the grapes when they were ripe. As his men had no authority to start this work, they waited for the master to appear some four weeks later. The grapes were overripe, shriveled, and covered with mold, but the owner decided to gather them nonetheless and see what could be done. To his own surprise as well as that of everyone else, the wine that developed from these overripe grapes was unlike anything they had tasted before. It was delicious—very rich, luscious, and highly perfumed.

Today we understand what happened. When the grapes reach a certain stage of maturity beyond the full stage of ripeness, a special mold settles upon them, known technically as *Botrytis cinerea.*

When gathering grapes in Sauternes, skilled workers do not begin until the sun is high, about half past eight in the morning, and they stop before the sun goes down because the dew washes off some *Botrytis cinerea*. The French call this condition of overripeness *pourriture noble*, meaning "noble rottenness." The grapes are not, of course, rotten, as rotten grapes are removed lest they spoil the wine; they are merely overripe. Only bunches in a perfect condition of overripeness are picked, and therefore a vineyard may be gone over as many as eight times before all the grapes are gathered, a procedure that naturally adds to the cost of production.

Leaving the grapes on the vine until they attain *pourriture noble* makes their skins become porous and the water in the grapes evaporates, thus concentrating the sugar, increasing glycerine, and reducing acidity. This gives a smaller yield of juice, or must, per acre, but it ensures richness. Sauternes, consequently, are always rich, sweet wines. There is no such thing as a dry Sauternes.

Because these wines are rich in sugar, it is difficult to keep them from refermenting during unseasonably warm weather. The only preventive is to sulfur the casks well before they are filled. The sulfur fumes sterilize the cask, destroying any bacteria that might be present, and, when the wine is poured in, the sulfur acts as a deterrent to the yeasts remaining in the wine, as they are ready to continue their fermentation job at the least provocation.

The wines of the five Sauternes communes are all very similar in character, and they are all sweet. Sweetness and dryness, of course, are relative qualities. Some Sauternes are sweeter and richer than others, but compared with white wines from the Graves or any other section of the Bordeaux wine region, they are much softer, sweeter, and fuller bodied.

This does not mean that dry white wine cannot be produced. The Appellation of Origin law and its *Appellation Contrôlée* regulations do not prevent production of such a wine in Sauternes, but they forbid its being labeled Sauternes or Barsac. It can only be labeled Bordeaux Blanc.

Many châteaus in Sauternes are producing dry white wines from the Sauvignon Blanc grape alone. Since these are not in the famous sweet, rich style of Sauternes, they may not use the name of the château on the label. They are sometimes called "Bordeaux Sauvignon Sec."

Of the five communes entitled to use the regional term Sauternes, Barsac is the most enterprising. While the vintners in Sauternes, Bommes, Fargues, and Preignac are content to market their wines simply as Sauternes, those of Barsac prefer that their wines be known by the name of their commune. As far as sweetness is concerned, there is little difference between Barsac and the rest of Sauternes, at least when château-bottled wines are compared.

However, comparing Sauternes and Barsac shipped under the label of a Bordeaux wine merchant is another story. These are blended wines, and when the shipper blends he can control the result. He can blend for sweetness, relative dryness, perfume, or body. He knows perfectly well that if his Sauternes and Barsac are identical, there is no reason to buy both wines. So he blends one wine for more sweetness, establishing two different wines. There is no consistency among shippers as to which of the two wines will be sweeter.

Haut in French means "high," but it has no official significance for Sauternes and Barsac. The word is sometimes used on labels to denote the producer's level of quality. As a rule, these wines cost more than the simple Sauternes or Barsac. Haut has no geographical significance, as there is no region designated as Haut Barsac or Haut Sauternes.

In the classification of 1855 the wines of the great Sauternes vineyards were classed in order of merit in the same manner of the clarets. This classification embraced twenty-one growths, but because of the split-up of several vineyards, the number today is twenty-seven (see Appendix C).

Château d'Yquem. In the fourteenth century when Edward II was king of England, his wine merchant and buyer in Bordeaux was Pierre Ayquem (also spelled *Eyquem*). It was he or one of his descendants who gave the family patronym to the vineyard whose storied wines have evoked more and greater hyperbole than almost any other wine since the celebrated Falernians of Roman times.

A few of these are: "the extravagance of perfection," "a ray of sunshine concentrated in a glass," and "a ray more brilliant than the sun's."

In 1859 Grand Duke Constantine of Russia paid the fabulous sum of 20,000 gold francs for a tun (twelve hundred bottles) of the 1847 vintage. This was about $3.50 per bottle, an unheard-of price in those days.

There is no question about d'Yquem's wines being in a class by themselves, as demonstrated by their 1855 classification as Premier Cru Supérieur, and meriting the apparent exaggerations of poets intoxicated by such perfection.

The finer vintages of Château d'Yquem combine richness of perfume, depth of vinosity, and fullness of body in perfect balance. There are differences among vintages and some are sweeter than others. D'Yquems will vary in their luscious richness, depending on their age and the vintage.

At Yquem, the usual proportion of grapes is 80 percent

Sémillon and 20 percent Sauvignon Blanc. The Sémillon is allowed to hang on the vine until it is overripe, and has acquired the *Botrytis cinerea*. The Sauvignon Blanc is harvested at the usual time, to ensure that the wine has enough acidity.

Château La Tour-Blanche. According to ancient documents, this fine vineyard was at one time the property of Jean Saint-Marc de La Tour Blanche, treasurer general to the king. Sometime after the French Revolution its ownership passed to M. Osiris, who bequeathed the entire property to the state for a viticultural school. Its wines are elegant, full, and rich.

Note the spelling of *La Tour* as two words. Many people confuse Château La Tour-Blanche, the Sauternes, with Château Latour, the claret.

Château de Rayne-Vigneau. Property for generations of the

Vicomtes de Pontac, Rayne-Vigneau has had a glorious history. Its most notable exploit was defeating the best German wine in a blind tasting at the World's Fair of 1867 and being selected as the finest white wine of that age. The two wines in question were a Château Vigneau 1861 and a Rhine wine of the same vintage.

Château Suduiraut, bordering Château d'Yquem, was formerly controlled by the crown. Today its wine labels bear the legend *ancien cru du Roy* ("former property of the king"). The wine is vigorous, with a rich aroma, and commands very high prices.

Château Guiraud (formerly Bayle) is a beautiful property that includes a fine vineyard—about 150 acres in extent—a park of 350 acres, and a lovely old château. The wine of Château Guiraud is famed for its delicacy, perfume, and body.

Châteaus Coutet and **Ceimens**. The wines of these vineyards, situated in the commune of Barsac, are first growths and possess the typical firmness and elegant bouquet of Sauternes. They are rich Sauternes like the other growths of Bommes, Fargues, Preignac, and Sauternes.

Châteaus LaFaurie-Peyraguey, **Clos Haut-Peyraguey, Rieussec**, **Rabaud-Promis**, and **Sigalas-Rabaud**. These other first growths are all excellent wines that are sometimes available in the United States.

Among the second growths the best known on our market are Château Filhot, in the commune of Sauternes, and Château Myrat, in the commune of Barsac. Château Caillou, also from Barsac, ages gracefully. Although classed as second growths, they are nonetheless excellent wines possessing a fine, rich bouquet and body.

There are districts other than the major ones discussed previously that produce distinguished, useful, and usually less expensive wines. For example, Entre-deux-Mers, "between two seas," a large section lying between the Garonne and Dordogne rivers before they meet, produces a vast quantity of white wine, some dry and some sweet. Bourg and Blaye, across the Gironde from the Médoc, produce clean, dry white wines as well as robust, fruity red wines, some of exceptional quality.

See Appendix B for notes on the Bordeaux vintages, and Appendix C for the Classifications of Bordeaux.

WINES OF BURGUNDY

"None other will I have," said Duke Philip the Good of Burgundy when he set his heart on marrying the beautiful Princess Isabella. This thoroughly typical phrase was adopted as the ducal motto of the House of Burgundy. It represents the attitude of Burgundians then and now, proud of their race, their lineage, and their wines lineage, and their wines. It was their wont to style themselves "Dukes of Burgundy and Lords of the finest wines in Christendom."

The history of wine in Burgundy dates back to Caesar's conquest of Gaul and is almost as turbulent as the political story of the region. The Roman legions planted vines from Italy, and when the wine began competing with that of the mother country, Emperor Domitian ordered the vines uprooted and the fields planted in corn. This was in A.D. 96. Fortunately the edict was enforced only halfheartedly and was finally rescinded entirely by Emperor Probus in A.D. 278.

Long before the wine of the region was known by the regional term Burgundy, the Church—which here, as elsewhere, had a strong influence in the development of quality wines—had made famous among medieval gourmets the names of such vineyards as Clos de Bèze, Corton-Charlemagne, Romanée, Clos de Vougeot, Meursault, and Montrachet.

Wine from these vineyards—first known as wine of Auxerre, since the wine went to Paris and the outside world by boat down the Yonne River from the "port" of Auxerre, and later as wine of Beaune—did not acquire the name Burgundy until the sixteenth century. When Petrarch advised Pope Urban V to remove from Avignon to Rome, according to legend His Holiness demurred because his entourage complained, "There is no Beaune wine in Italy, and without Beaune wine how unhappy we would be." This difficulty seemingly was overcome during the pontificate of Gregory XII.

Wine has always been Burgundy's chief source of fame, but, unlike wine from other regions, Burgundy wines do not all come from a small, densely cultivated geographical locale. Because of the acquisitiveness of Burgundy's dukes, who reached out on all sides for more and more land, the area known as Burgundy was created by gradually adding small parcels of land. Wine produced in every part of the duchy became known simply as Burgundy. This wine-producing region includes vineyards in four different departments: Yonne, Côte d'Or, Saône-et-Loire, and Rhône.

First is the "true Burgundy," the Côte d'Or or "golden slope," divided into the Côte de Nuits and the Côte de Beaune. The Côte d'Or is a string of low-lying hills extending thirty-eight miles from Dijon in the north to Santenay in the south; the width of the vineyards is from 550 to 600 yards. Second, farther south lie the Côte Chalonnaise and the Mâconnais, in the Department of

Saône-et-Loire. Beaujolais begins in the Saône-et-Loire but lies mainly in the Department of the Rhône. (This department should not be confused with the large, general wine-producing area called Côtes du Rhône, farther south.) Last, about halfway between Dijon and Paris, north of the Côte d'Or, in the Department of the Yonne, there are thirteen hundred acres of vineyards around the town of Chablis that may be planted to produce that famous white wine.

The soil of the Côte d'Or, rich in iron, is chalky, argillaceous (white clay), and rocky. The slopes are said to take their name from the burnished appearance they present in late fall when the leaves have turned golden.

The fine red wines come from the Pinot Noir grape, while the white wines of repute are produced from the Chardonnay. The Pinot Noir and Chardonnay are noble plants that produce quality but not quantity, and here as nowhere else is the *vigneron* tempted to increase his output at the sacrifice of quality.

The other red grape variety in Burgundy that predominates in the south is the Gamay, a more productive variety that gives a poor wine in the Côte d'Or but produces an extremely enjoyable red wine in the clay and granite soil of Macon and Beaujolais. The other white grape of Burgundy is the Aligoté, which is highly productive and makes a simple and short-lived white wine.

Pinot Blanc, which used to be grown, has virtually disappeared. The label "Pinot Chardonnay Macon" is a misnomer, since the wine is not a blend of Pinot Blanc and Chardonnay, and Chardonnay is not even part of the Pinot family.

The most famous vineyards are found on slopes with a southern exposure. They neither extend to the summit of the hills nor reach the lower plains. The fine vineyards form something like a wide, continuous ribbon laid along the gentle slopes, rarely dropping below the eight-hundred-foot elevation or rising above the thousand-foot level. The plain is seven hundred feet above sea level, and the higher hills are fifteen hundred feet.

It is on these slopes that the Pinot Noir seems to do best and the Gamay is rarely found. On the plains and summits, however, the Gamay is most in evidence. Wines from a mixture of the two varieties are known as Bourgogne Passe-Tout-Grains and contain at least one-third Pinot Noir grapes.

In Burgundy, as in other viticultural regions, *Phylloxera* did its devastating work, and today the vineyards have been replanted with American *Phylloxera*-resistant roots on which the native Chardonnay, Pinot Noir, Gamay, and other varieties have been grafted. The last native stocks were removed in the early 1950s.

The laws controlling the origin and labeling of wines limit the production of the vineyards that are capable of producing fine wines in order to ensure the highest quality possible, thus forcing the *vigneron* to prune his vines properly. As the quantity is strictly limited, he does everything in his power to aid the vine in giving quality.

The system of vineyard ownership in Burgundy is different from that in any other viticultural region of France and is duplicated to any extent only in Germany. To begin with, the vineyards are all very small. The largest, Clos de Vougeot, is only 126 acres, and Romanée is just about 2 acres, the average being under 25 acres. Not only are the vineyards extremely small, but with rare exceptions they are held by anywhere from three to sixty or more owners, each proprietor having title to a small parcel of the vineyard.

At Clos de Vougeot, for example, there are sixty-six owners who cultivate their individual parcels of the vineyard, gather the grapes from their own vines, press them, and vinify the resulting must. As the human element enters into production, it is understandable that, although the same Pinot variety is planted in the entire vineyard, and all the operations of making the wine take place at the same time, there may be sixty-six different wines produced, all legally entitled to the appellation Clos de Vougeot.

This may be contrasted with the system in Bordeaux, where even the largest and most famous châteaus are owned by just one person or corporation who controls the entire product that appears under the château's label.

Since Burgundy often has many owners of a vineyard, there cannot be château-bottled wines. However, "estate bottling" received great impetus after Repeal in the United States. American connoisseurs began to demand château-bottled Burgundies, and there simply was no such thing. Estate-bottled Burgundies have been grown, vinified, and bottled by a specific producer, whose name appears on the label, and are the equivalent of château-bottled Bordeaux. Estate-bottled wines are labeled *mis en bouteille au domaine*.

While this is good merchandising and benefits the consumer, since in theory the Burgundians would strive to offer only the very best quality, estate bottling guarantees only the authenticity of vineyard origin and that the wine comes from the grapes of a single producer and has not been blended with wines from any other producer or from any other vineyard. The practice of estate bottling has proliferated so since World War II that it is not uncommon today to see estate bottlings of wines labeled Gevrey-Chambertin, Chambolle-Musigny, Vosne-Romanée, and so forth, which contradicts the entire meaning and objective of the system. For example, a wine labeled Gevrey-Chambertin is a blend of wines produced in any part of the Gevrey-Chambertin commune. When the label also states it is estate bottled, the blend is made entirely of wines from the producer's vineyard holdings in Gevrey-Chambertin. These can be, although they are not necessarily, parcels in the great Le Chambertin and also from the most poorly rated vineyards in the commune. We believe that estate bottling should be reserved and practiced for only the unblended wine of the great vineyards that is bottled by the actual producer who is a proprietor, no matter how small his holding.

Not all of the growers ship their own wines, and if the shippers were to keep each grower's wines separate their lists would not only be interminable but also very confusing. For this reason it has been only natural for shippers to buy, say, Clos de Vougeot from several growers, blend these wines together, and offer them as their own (the shippers') quality of Clos de Vougeot. This also tends to equalize the price.

Wines that are not estate bottled may be labeled *mis en bouteille à la propriété* or *mise d'origine*.

The most famous Burgundy vineyards have their own appellations. Wines from vineyards that are less famous, but are from famous communes, will travel under the commune's appellation. If neither is well known, the wine will go forth as Côte de Nuits, Côte de Beaune, or simply red or white Burgundy. A Burgundy wine will always bear the best-known name to which it is entitled. (In Bordeaux, on the other hand, even the largest or most famous châteaus carry the appellation of their commune.)

For example, in the commune of Gevrey-Chambertin, wine from the famous Chambertin vineyard, which has its own appellation, will invariably be labeled Appellation Chambertin Contrôlée. Wine from a vineyard in the same commune whose name might be even less well known than the commune name, will be labeled Appellation Gevrey-Chambertin Contrôlée, using the commune's appellation.

Wine from any vineyard in the communes of Comblanchien or Corgoloin will be labeled Côte de Nuits-Villages or simply Bourgogne Rouge, because neither the vineyards nor the communes are well known outside the district.

Most of the red wines of the communes of Meursault, Puligny-Montrachet, and Chassagne-Montrachet suffer the same fate and are shipped as Côte de Beaune, as these communes, while world famous for their white wines, are not too well known for their reds.

The famous vineyards of the Côte d'Or have been classified by the *Appellation Contrôlée* authorities. A hierarchy of quality of Burgundy wines has been established based upon vineyard site and wines produced. The finest vineyards have been labeled Grands Crus, and their names have become controlled appellations. Premiers Crus vineyards are a notch below. Less famous vineyards may have their names on the label along with the commune name.

Probably the most expensive wine of Burgundy is that of Romanée-Conti, a rather small vineyard in the commune of Vosne-Romanée. Like all things, its price is governed by supply and demand, since the area planted in vines is a little less than 4½ acres. In recent years, even larger vineyards in other communes that rival Romanée-Conti, such as Chambertin, Clos de Vougeot, and Musigny, also command very high prices, since actually the total amount of Burgundy produced is not enough to quench the thirst of the world.

Côte de Nuits

The red wines of the Côte de Nuits are generous and full bodied and have a deep, fruity, unique bouquet that is the result of the combination of the Pinot Noir grape and the Burgundian soil. They develop less rapidly than the wines of the Côte de Beaune. In 1882 the commune of Musigny decided that the sale of all its wines would be increased if the commune were to adopt the name of its most famous vineyard, and therefore Chambolle became Chambolle-*Musigny*. This system has been adopted by the communes of Gevrey-*Chambertin*, Flagey-*Echézeaux*, Vosne-*Romanée*, Nuits-*Saint-Georges*, Aloxe-*Corton*, Puligny-*Montrachet*, Chassagne-*Montrachet*, and others. The most important Grands Crus vineyards of the Côte de Nuits are discussed below:

Chambertin. Napoleon, so the story goes, would drink no other wine and planned all his great military and civil victories when warmed by the generous fire of Chambertin. But when he was before Moscow his supply ran out, resulting in his disastrous retreat from Russia. Knowing his penchant for Chambertin, the allies generously permitted that he be supplied with it at Saint Helena.

No one knows the date of origin for the vineyard of Chambertin, but like all ancient vineyards it is rich in legends. One story connected with it throws some light on the entire history of viticulture in Burgundy. In the year 630, according to the records, the Duc d'Amalgaire gave a parcel of vineyard, with an area of thirty-five acres, to the Abbey of Bèze. Henceforth the vineyard was known as Clos de Bèze, and in time its wines acquired much renown. Sometime later, but before 1219, when we have our next parchment record, a peasant named Bertin, who owned the field bordering Clos de Bèze, reasoned that if he planted the same grape varieties as grew in the famous Clos de Bèze vineyards, his wines would be good, too. The French word for field is *champ*, and the vineyard then must have been known as Champ de Bertin. This was finally contracted to the present Chambertin, and since 1219 the wines from the two vineyards have been confused and looked upon as one and the same. Today the total area of Chambertin and Chambertin-Clos de Bèze is sixty-seven acres. Chambertin-Clos de Bèze may be labeled either Chambertin-Clos de Bèze or simply Chambertin. Chambertin may not be labeled Chambertin-Clos de Bèze. Both wines are big, heady wines that acquire a firm roundness with age. See Appendix D for other Grands Crus vineyards in this commune.

Les Musigny and Les Bonnes Mares. These two great rival vineyards lie in the commune of Chambolle-Musigny, but Les Bonnes Mares, which has 34 acres in Chambolle-Musigny, also has 4½ acres in the commune of Morey-Saint-Denis. Both wines are known for their finesse, suppleness, and elegance, but, although they are similar in character, Les Musigny, with only 14 acres, is the more famous of the two.

Clos de Vougeot. These are fruity wines, having rich flavor, color, body, bouquet, and infinite grace and character. The elegance of its wines has merited Clos de Vougeot, in the commune of Vougeot, an honor that is today traditional.

It is said that Napoleon, the Little Corporal and now

all-powerful emperor, heard of the excellent wines made at Vougeot. He sent word to Dom Gobelet, the last clerical cellar-master at Clos de Vougeot, saying that it would please him to taste these superlative wines. "If he is that curious," replied the venerable Cistercian haughtily, "let him come to my house."

The beautiful, imposing Château du Clos de Vougeot is situated on the upper slopes in the very center of the vineyard. For many centuries it belonged to the Cistercian Abbey of Cîteaux. The earliest available records of the abbey vineyard ownership date back to 1110. The present château was begun in the thirteenth century and completed sometime in the sixteenth. Its primary function was to serve as the pressing house and cellars for the wine-production activities of the Cistercian Order, who owned it until the French Revolution, when it was secularized. Today the château is the property of the Confrérie des Chevaliers du Tastevin, the "brotherhood of gentlemen of the tasting cup." The great ceremonies, functions, and dinners of the Confrérie are held there.

Romanée-Conti, in Vosne-Romanée, is the generally accepted king of Burgundy, always having all the qualities of great wine: body, vinosity, bouquet, and character. The wines are rich and long lived.

Romanée, **Romanée-Saint-Vivant**, **Le Richebourg**, and **La Tâche**. The commune richest in great vineyards is Vosne-Romanée. These vineyards vary in size from the bare two acres of Romanée, fifteen acres of La Tâche, and twenty acres of Le Richebourg, to almost twenty-four acres of Romanée-Saint-Vivant. The wines of these great growths differ, but it would take one long accustomed to drinking them to identify these differences. Suffice it to say that they all have beautiful color, a deep bouquet and flavor, body, and elegance.

Les Grands Echézeaux and **Echézeau**. The former's twenty-three acres and the latter's seventy-four acres are neighbors to the west of Clos de Vougeot, and there is a close resemblance among all of these wines. While in the commune of Flagey-Echézeaux, these wines are usually considered with the wines of neighboring Vosne-Romanée, because Les Grands Echézeaux vineyard once belonged to the Abbey of Saint-Vivant, and today belongs almost entirely to the Société Civile du Domaine de la Romanée-Conti. The wines are softer and more delicate than the famed red wines of Vosne-Romanée.

Clos de Tart, **Clos de La Roche**, and **Les Saint-Georges**. The first two vineyards, with acreages of 17¾ and 38 respectively, lie in the commune of Morey-Saint-Georges. These three fine vineyards of the Côte de Nuits have rich wines, with color, body, and character, and in good years they are comparable to any of the great Côte de Nuits.

The most northerly commune of Côte de Nuits before Dijon is Fixin. Here the wines are similar to those of Gevrey-Chambertin and are sometimes their equal. Perrière (not to be confused with Les Perrières of Meursault) and Clos-du-Chapitre produce good, strong Burgundy wines.

The appellation Côte de Nuits-Villages is restricted to the wines of the five communes of Fixin, Brochon, Prissey, Comblanchien, and Corgoloin.

Côte de Beaune

The medieval city of Beaune is the headquarters of the Burgundy wine trade. Most of the great shipping houses have their cellars in the city itself and it is in Beaune that we find the world-famous Hospices de Beaune.

The red wines of the Côte de Beaune develop more rapidly and are ready for drinking sooner than those of the Côte de Nuits. They show a pleasant, fruity bouquet, softness, and finesse and are tenderly supple, which makes them most agreeable wines at all times.

Hospices de Beaune. There are many well-preserved examples of Beaune's long history—churches, parts of the old city wall, and battlements—all still in use in one way or another; but her proudest monument is Les Hospices de Beaune, a charitable hospital built in 1443. It has rendered continuous and devoted service to the poor of the region for over five hundred years, wars and revolution notwithstanding.

The Hôtel-Dieu, or hospital, is an exquisite example of Flemish architectural style. It is a four-story-high, block-square building, surmounted by a slanting roof whose green, yellow, and black slates are arranged in a classic pattern. The cobblestone open central courtyard—the Court of Honor—was the original locale for the Hospices' annual wine auctions.

Over the centuries modern improvements have been adopted in the care of the sick, but some of the original wards, kitchens, chapels, and the museum have been preserved in their original fifteenth-century state. The museum contains many works of art, including paintings of Nicolas Rolin and his wife, Guigone de Salins, and the magnificent altarpiece of the Last Judgment, all on wood, which she commissioned the Flemish painter Roger van der Weyden (1440-1464) to paint expressly for the Hospices de Beaune.

In 1441 Pope Eugene IV authorized the creation of the Hospices de Beaune as a hospital to care for the poor and indigent people of Beaune. Nicolas Rolin, tax collector during the reign of Louis XI, and his wife donated the property and erected the building. They also gave the Hospices several parcels of vineyards so that the Hospices might be supported by the sale of its wines.

The legend of the period has it that Nicolas Rolin

could well afford to provide such a charity for the poor, as he had created so many of them. Whether or not that is true, the Hospices de Beaune has proved to be a remarkable institution. Its principal support has always come from the sale of wines produced from vineyards that devout Burgundians have willed to the Hospices. Today these comprise some thirty parcels that are known by the names of the donors (see Appendix D).

For over four centuries the Hospices' wines were sold privately, but since 1859 they have been sold at a festive public auction on the third Sunday of every November. All of the Hospices de Beaune vineyards are located in the Côte de Beaune, from Aloxe-Corton to Meursault, but because they represent the first real opportunity for buyers to taste the wines of each vintage, the prices fetched at the auction determine to a great extent the rating of the vintage for all Burgundy wines. Often the prices are more than the individual wines are really worth, but the factors of charity and publicity unquestionably influence the bidding.

Le Corton, **Le Clos du Roi**, **Les Bressandes**, and **Les Pougets**. In the commune of Aloxe-Corton lie the famous vineyards of Le Corton with an area of 28 acres, Le Clos du Roi with 26 acres, Les Bressandes with 42 acres, and Les Pougets with 24½ acres. Le Corton is the only Grand Cru red wine of the Côte de Beaune. It is usually solid and robust. With bottle ripeness it expands and possesses a wealth of bouquet, roundness, body, and breed and can be compared with the great Côte de Nuits wines. Le Clos du Roi and Les Bressandes are also big wines, but they are more like Beaune wines in character. They have a lovely color, aroma, and finesse. The wines from Les Pougets vineyard are always very fine, with excellent color, flavor, and body.

Île-des-Vergelesses and **Les Basses-Vergelesses**. These vineyards have areas of twenty-three and forty-four acres, respectively, in the commune of Pernand, and their wines are renowned for their finesse and distinction.

Les Fève and Les Grèves. These are the two outstanding examples from Beaune itself. Les Fèves, with 10½ acres, and Les Grèves, with 78½ acres, produce wines noted for their fine, rich softness and elegance.

Les Rugiens and Les Épenots. The commune name, Pommard, is probably the most famous Burgundy wine name. It is certainly far better known than that of its finest vineyard, Les Rugiens (33½ acres). For that reason most of its wine comes to our table labeled simply Pommard, and because of the demand its price is usually somewhat high. Should you come upon authentic and properly matured examples of Pommard-Rugiens of Les Épenots (27 acres), you will find them generally delicate, fruity, and well-rounded wines of character.

The red wines of the communes of Volnay and Monthélie are light red in color, elegant, and delightful. Those of the commune of Auxey-Duresses are somewhat like those of Pommard and Volnay, and the red wines of the commune of Chassagne-Montrachet have a richness and fullness that remind one of those of the Côte de Nuits.

Santenay, at the southern end of the Côte de Beaune, produces firm red wines that can age nicely. These wines have recently come on the market as good values. Les Gravières is the best known vineyard.

The appellation Côte de Beaune-Villages applies to only red wine and is restricted to sixteen communes: Auxey-Duresses, Blagny, Chassagne-Montrachet, Cheilly-les-Maranges, Chorey-les-Beaune, Dezize-les-Maranges, Ladoix, Meursault, Monthélie, Pernand-Vergelesses, Puligny-Montrachet, Saint-Aubin, Saint-Romain, Sampigny-les-Maranges, Santenay, and Savigny-les-Beaune.

White Wines of Burgundy

All of the main subdivisions of the Burgundy wine region produce white wines, each of which is of an individual character and has its following. The Department of the Yonne gives us chablis. The Côte de Nuits sends us three unique white wines, although the majority of the great white wines of Burgundy come from the Côte de Beaune. Still farther south is Macon, which produces considerable quantities of crisp white wines, including Pouilly-Fuissé and Macon Blanc, which are great favorites in the United States. In neighboring Beaujolais a small amount of Beaujolais Blanc is produced.

For making white wines the *plante noble* is the Chardonnay. Other varieties of grapes are used, but to a very minor degree, with the exception of the copious Aligoté, which produces large quantities of an agreeable but short-lived wine that is mostly consumed locally.

This wine may be labeled varietally, as Bourgogne Aligoté, and it may have some Chardonnay or Pinot Blanc in it.

The wine the world knows as Chablis comes from the northernmost part of Burgundy. Its distinguishing characteristic, not to be found in every vintage, is an austere, flinty quality, much prized by those who have had the good fortune to encounter it. Chablis is, perhaps, the driest and palest of table wines. Its color should be a pale straw yellow.

The flinty quality is known as *pierre-à-fusil* ("gun flint"), and the taste is like a sharp, metallic tang. Added to this effect is the wine's delicate, fruity bouquet, and herein lies its cooling, refreshing quality. Although in good years Chablis is a long-lived wine, we prefer it young and fresh. Chablis is exceptional with oysters. They were made for each other, as you will discover if you try them together.

Chablis is classified, in descending order of quality,

as follows: Chablis Grand Cru, Chablis Premier Cru, Chablis, and Petit Chablis. The best vineyards are crescent-shaped hillsides just north of the village of Chablis and make up the Grand Cru classification. They are Blanchots, Bougros, Les Clos, Grenouilles, Les Preuses, Valmur, and Vaudésir.

Chablis Premier Cru comes from twenty-nine vineyards, situated in ten communes, which are considered superior. Chablis is a blend of wine from several vineyards. Petit Chablis comes from the outskirts of the area. As with other wines of Burgundy, the reputation of the shipper is the best guarantee of quality. See Appendix D for a list of Premiers Crus vineyards.

In the Côte de Nuits, at the famous Musigny vineyard in Chambolle Musigny, about 100 cases of Musigny Blanc are produced by Comte Georges de Vogue. To the south, next to the Château du Clos de Vougeot, famous for its red wines, are five acres planted with Chardonnay grapes from which 450 cases of Clos Blanc de Vougeot are made. In the commune of Nuits-Saint-Georges some 250 cases of Nuits-Saint-Georges Blanc are produced. These are distinguished wines, possessing full flavor and body.

Moving south to the Côte de Beaune we find the greatest white wines of Côte de Beaune Burgundy in the communes of Aloxe-Corton, Meursault, Puligny-Montrachet, and Chassagne-Montrachet.

Corton-Charlemagne. This renowned white wine is made in the commune of Aloxe-Corton, at the forty-two-acre Charlemagne vineyard, so named in honor of the great emperor. It is a Grand Cru vineyard, making Aloxe-Corton the only commune with both a white and a red Grand Cru vineyard.

Les Perrières, **Les Genevrière**, and **Les Charmes**. These famous vineyards, with 42, 42, and 38¼ acres respectively, lie in the commune of Meursault. The wines are full bodied and dry, with finesse and elegance. They are said to have the perfume of hazelnuts.

At the southern end of the Côte de Beaune lie the communes of Puligny-Montrachet and Chassagne-Montrachet. Like their counterparts in the Côte de Nuits, they have affixed the name of their most famous vineyards, Le Montrachet, to their own names. Shippers' blends of wines from either of these communes will usually be very good.

Le Montrachet. There is no question that this is one of the world's great white wines. It is full bodied and robust yet possesses elegance, perfume, and dignity that are hard to match. Coming from a rather small vineyard, only 18½ acres, half of which lies in the commune of Puligny and half in that of Chassagne, the wines are in such demand that they usually fetch prices equal to those of the great red growths of the Côte de Nuits. H. Warner Allen has called Le Montrachet the Château d'Yquem of Burgundy.

Chevalier-Montrachet and **Le Bâtard-Montrachet**. Chevalier-Montrachet has 15½ acres in the commune of Puligny-Montrachet, and Le Bâtard-Montrachet, totaling 29¼ acres, is in both Puligny- and Chassagne-Montrachet, as is Le Montrachet. The wines of these two vineyards are very much like Le Montrachet, with a wealth of bouquet and finesse. They are never inexpensive. Care must be taken not to confuse the vineyard wine Chevalier-Montrachet with the commune wine of Chassagne-Montrachet.

Côte Chalonnaise

The Côte Chalonnaise lies just south of the Côte de Beaune. The soil, grapes, and wines of the Chalonnaise are quite similar to those of the Côte de Beaune, but they do not often attain the same quality. The four communes having appellations are Rully and Montagny, producing mostly white wines, and Mercurey and Givry, producing mostly reds. A considerable amount of sparkling wine is produced in Chalonnaise, especially in Rully.

Måconnais and Beaujolais

On the rolling low hills south of the Côte d'Or lie the districts of Macon and Beaujolais. Although each makes both red and white wines, Macon is more famous for its white wines and Beaujolais is better known for its reds.

The most famous white wine of Macon is Pouilly-Fuissé, named for the twin towns of Pouilly and Fuissé where the vineyards lie. Nearby Pouilly-Loché and Pouilly Vinzelles also produce crisp white wines. Saint-Véran is the appellation for wines from villages that surround Pouilly-Fuissé. All of these wines are made from the Chardonnay grape. Wines that are Macon or Pinot-

Chardonnay-Macon are made from the Chardonnay and Pinot Blanc grapes. They may be labeled as is, or Macon Supérieur, Macon-Villages, or Macon followed by the name of the community where it is produced, such as Lugny or Viré. No doubt more communes will apply for their own appellations as this wine increases in popularity. Red wines of Macon are made mainly from the Gamay grape, and are regionally named.

In Beaujolais the granitic soil brings out the best in the Gamay grape, which is not successful in the Côte d'Or. The best growth, or *crus*, in the north are limited to nine: Brouilly, Chénas, Chiroubles, Côte de Brouilly, Fleurie, Juliénas, Morgon, Moulin-à-Vent, and Saint-Amour. These may use the name Burgundy on their labels. The second classification is Beaujolais-Villages, which is limited to the wines of thirty-nine communes. Third comes Beaujolais-Supérieur, whose alcohol content is the same as Beaujolais-Villages, but which comes from a larger area; and, finally, enormous quantities of plain Beaujolais.

The wines of the region have a clear, brilliant red color and a fairly light body when compared with those of the Côte d'Or. Their primary characteristic is fresh fruitiness. They are most pleasant while in the fresh vigor of youth and for this reason should not be kept for many years. In France most of these wines are drunk before they are two or three years old.

For details on the Burgundy vintages, see Appendix B.

Sparkling Burgundy

Sparkling wines may be made in Burgundy from red or white wines, but red sparkling wine is most usually seen. Because of the predominance of red juice, these wines are fuller bodied than the white counterparts, and are sometimes produced to be slightly sweeter.

At least 30 percent of the blend of sparkling Burgundy must be from Pinot Noir, Pinot Gris, Pinot Blanc, or

Chardonnay grapes. The balance may be Aligoté, Melon, Sacy, and/or Gamay à Jus Blanc.

Sparkling Burgundies are made by the approved *méthode champenoise*, which will be explained in the following section on Champagne. All sparkling wines from Burgundy, whether red or white, must qualify under the appellation Crémant de Bourgogne. They may never be called Champagne.

WINES OF CHAMPAGNE

The word *Champagne* is synonymous with happiness, gaiety, and laughter, for it is the joyous wine of festive occasions. "Champagne," said André L. Simon, "has always been, still is, and will ever be an extravagant wine and the most charming and fascinating of wines."

There is a difference between La Champagne and Le Champagne. The former is the name of the ancient French province, part of which is today the Department of the Marne; the latter is the sparkling wine produced in the delimited Champagne region, about the size of Washington, D.C., located ninety miles east of Paris.

Wine has been made in Champagne since early Roman times, when Caesar conquered Gaul. That early wine was a still wine, however, and even today a nonsparkling wine is made in the region under the appellation Côteaux Champenois. But the name Champagne is reserved for the sparkling wine of France whose qualities and unique characteristics result from climate, soil, subsoil, and grapes grown in the strictly delimited area of Champagne, from second fermentation within a tightly corked bottle, and from long aging in the cellars of Champagne.

The histories of the province and its wine are intertwined. The most important city, Reims, was named for Saint-Remi, one of its first archbishops, who in A.D. 496 converted the first Frankish king, Clovis, to Christianity and at the baptism presented Clovis with a cask of Champagne from his own vineyard.

It was not until the seventeenth century that the sparkling wine we associate with the name of Champagne came into use. Some say that Dom Pérignon (1639-1715), a blind Bénédictine monk who was treasurer and cellarer of the Abbey of Hautvillers near Epernay, is the man who put the bubbles in champagne.

Actually, the bubbles occurred naturally. Champagne is the most northerly wine-producing region of France, and the early arrival of winter often slowed down or halted fermentation before it was complete. After the wine was bottled, the arrival of warm spring weather would start a second fermentation inside the bottle. Carbon dioxide was released inside the closed bottle, which made the wine sparkle.

It was Dom Pérignon who was the first to use the bark of the cork tree as a stopper for Champagne bottles. Although cork bark had been used in other wine regions, Dom Pérignon introduced it in the Champagne region to replace the bits of tow soaked in oil that were used as stoppers, making it possible to retain the sparkle within the wine for long periods of time. Being an excellent taster, he soon observed that the wines of one vineyard were consistently dry, those of another richer and fuller bodied, while those of a third possessed more finesse. He decided to try blending these wines to produce a more balanced wine with a completeness that the component wines could not show individually. The result was that he made better wines than had been produced before, and to this day the system is followed to obtain a wine of uniformly high quality and distinctive house style.

With all this development in the bottle, there was the problem of removing sediment that had collected so the wine would be clear. Removing the sediment was time consuming, and effervescence was lost in the process. It wasn't until the nineteenth century that the system of *remuage*, which is still used today, was developed.

From 1927 to 1937 the *Appellation Contrôlée laws* were being developed in France. A separate clause dealing with Champagne processes defined the *méthode champenoise*, making Champagne one of the most rigorously controlled and most carefully made wines in the world.

The Champagne growing area today consists of 65,000 acres, which will be increased to 72,000 acres over the next few years. The vineyards are planted in 250 different villages, most of which are clustered around the cities of Reims and Epernay. The Marne River, which flows from east to west, forms an important line of division. North of the Marne mainly black grapes are grown, around the towns of Ay and Hautvillers and in the Montagne ("mountain") de Reims section at Mailly, Verzy, Verzenay, Bouzy, and Ambonnay. South of the river lies the Côte des Blancs, where white grapes are grown around the towns of Cramant, Avize, Oger, Le Mesnil, and Vertus.

Chalk is important to the Champagne region, both for growing the vines and for aging the wine in the deep chalk cellars. A thin top layer of earth covers a chalky, porous subsoil that extends down for hundreds of feet. The porosity allows excess water to drain, while maintaining the proper amount of moisture necessary for growth of the vines.

The three grape varieties from which Champagne

may be made are the red Pinot Noir and Pinot Meunier and the white Chardonnay. The Montagne de Reims vineyards are planted mainly in Pinot Noir, the grape that gives full flavor and body to the wine. Pinot Noir and Pinot Meunier are grown in the valley of the Marne. The Côte des Blancs, or "white slope," is so named because it is planted with Chardonnay. This grape contributes freshness, lightness, and elegance to the final blend.

All Champagne vineyards are rated for quality. The best vineyards or *crus* are rated 100 percent with the remainder anywhere down to 80 percent, dependent on such factors as exposure, drainage, microclimate, etc. When the grapes are harvested, the price for that vintage is agreed on, and the vineyards rated 100 percent get paid 100 percent of the price, and the other vineyards are compensated proportionately. The well-known Champagne houses usually buy the grapes from the vineyards rated between 90 and 100 percent.

The Champagne Method
(Méthode Champenoise)

The art of making Champagne really begins with the selection of grapes. Most of the important Champagne houses own vineyards, but to meet their needs all of them must also buy additional grapes from fourteen thousand small growers in Champagne's main vineyard areas. The vineyards are primarily family holdings averaging 3½ acres. Since Champagne is a blend of twenty to thirty still wines made from grapes grown in a number of different vineyards, no vineyard name appears on the label; consequently the name of the blender or producer, which is always there, takes on importance.

Harvesting the grapes begins at the end of September or in early October, one hundred days after the vines flower. The exact time is determined by the *Comité Interprofessionnel du Vin de Champagne* (C.I.V.C.) after the laboratory tests of grape sugar content and acidity have been made and the grapes are fully ripe. Within ten days an army of seventy thousand workers does the harvesting.

The ripe grapes are gathered in baskets, called *paniers*. When a *panier* is full it is taken to the side of the road, where experienced sorters cull out any green, overripe, or defective grapes to ensure that only perfect, sound fruit goes to the press. This selection process is called *épluchage* and is only practiced by the leading producers. After the *épluchage* the grapes are placed in *caques* or *clayettes* ("large baskets") and carried to nearby pressing houses.

The press may belong to a Champagne firm, to the local village, to a cooperative of vineyard owners, or to brokers or middlemen. To avoid coloration of the juice, wide but shallow hydraulic presses that hold eighty-eight hundred pounds are used. Each basket is weighed and marked to ensure the exact quantity being placed in the press. The amount of grapes that makes one loading of a press is called a *marc*. From each *marc* four pressings of juice are obtained, known as *cuvée*, *première taille*, *deuxième taille*, and *rebêche*. Pressure is applied twice for the *cuvée*, and after each pressure the grapes are worked toward the center of the press with wooden shovels. For the *première* and *deuxième tailles* pressure is applied only once. For the *rebêche* the *marc* is removed to a smaller press. The finest houses, or *Grandes Marques*, which pride themselves on the quality of their wines, use only the *cuvée* and *première taille* pressings and sell the wine resulting from the *deuxième taille* in cask. *Rebêche* wine cannot be used for Champagne; it is used for distillation.

As the juice is pressed from the grapes, it gushes out from the bottom of the press through a channel and is gathered in a cistern below the presses, whence it is transferred at once into vats or casks and carefully labeled with the name of the vineyard where the grapes were grown.

The first fermentation, as with all other white wines,

starts out vigorously and gradually slows down during the second week. Fermentation may take place in traditional oak barrels, glass-lined tanks, or stainless steel tanks. With modern equipment, the temperature is maintained around 70 degrees Fahrenheit for the three weeks necessary to complete fermentation.

The new wine is racked to remove large particles that have settled to the bottom, and it is now chilled. This used to be accomplished by opening the winery doors to the cold winter air. Now modern refrigeration methods are used. This chilling causes the soluble tartrates to form insoluble bitartrates, which precipitate out, leaving the wine clear and stable.

By spring the *chef de cave*, or "cellar-master," will know whether he is making vintage or nonvintage Champagne. If nonvintage, he must decide which wines, from which vineyards and in what proportions, should be married to older reserve wines to produce the characteristic house style of Champagne with the desired quality, aroma, elegance, and durability.

The new wines are then pumped, in the proper proportions, into large blending vats where they are thoroughly combined.

A small amount of sugar dissolved in old wine, together with special second yeasts, is added to the blend to ensure uniform secondary fermentation. This is fermentation called the *liqueur de tirage* or *dosage de tirage*. The quantity of sugar varies from year to year, depending on the natural sugar the new wine contains. The wine is then bottled and corked. The corks are secured by either metal clips known as *agrafes* or crown caps such as those used on soft drink bottles.

The bottles are stacked on their sides in the cellars that are hewn out of the solid chalk subsoil of the region. The yeasts discover the sugar and go to work, creating additional alcohol and carbon dioxide gas. Since the gas cannot escape it becomes a component of the wine.

During the first couple of years in the chalk cellars the stacks of bottles are examined for breakage—which is inevitable, as there are bound to be a few imperfect bottles that cannot stand the strain of about 90 pounds per square inch pressure developed by the newly created gas. In the early days the percentage of breakage was very high (sometimes as much as every other bottle), but today, with improved methods of bottle manufacture and the scientific use of the saccharometer to measure the exact sugar content of the wine, breakage has been reduced to less than 1 percent.

The action of fermentation is like a fire, and where there is fire, there are ashes. As a result of the secondary fermentation that has taken place in the bottle, "ashes," or dead yeast cells, have been left in the form of a sediment that must be removed to achieve a clear and brilliant wine. Removing the sediment is not easy, however. In this long, hard, tedious job the bottles are placed in specially built racks, called *pupitres*. At first the bottles are set at a forty-five-degree angle, and the angle is gradually increased until the bottles are standing perpendicularly, head down. A workman grasps each bottle, gives it a shake, a slight turn, and an increased tilt (*remuage*, or "riddling"), and lets it fall back into its slot on the rack with a small jolt. This is repeated every three days for each bottle. The object of this *remuage* is to move the sediment down onto the cork in a spiral movement. This operation takes about six to eight weeks. A skilled *remueur* can handle from thirty thousand to fifty thousand bottles a day.

When the wine is perfectly clear, the bottles are removed from the *pupitre* in preparation for the removal of sediment.

Since this is a very costly and time-consuming process, it stands to reason that attempts would be made to do this riddling automatically. After many years of testing, an acceptable machine has been developed, and some of the houses in Champagne are now using it.

Dégorgement is the process of removing the collected sediment from the corked bottle. The neck of the bottle is dipped into a very cold brine or glycol solution that freezes a little wine on the cork into a sludge with the sediment. Traditionally, a skilled workman, wearing a leather apron and often a wire-covered mask to protect his face in case of a bursting bottle, grasps the bottle. Standing opposite a barrel and protected by a shield, he releases the *agrafe* with a pair of pliers or removes the crown cap and at the same time turns the bottle right side up. The cork flies out, taking the frozen bit of sediment with it. He gives the neck of the bottle two sharp raps to loosen any bit of sediment that may have adhered to it. A small amount of the wine foams out. He examines this foam to be sure the wine has a perfectly clean bouquet, and then he hands the bottle to another workman sitting nearby, who adds the *liqueur d'expédition*, or *dosage*.

Today the disgorging process is automated in many houses.

The wine that has been lost during the *dégorgement* must be replaced. This is done by adding wine from previously disgorged bottles. Simultaneously some sweetening liqueur is added, the amount varying with the desired sweetness of the final product. This *liqueur d'expédition*, or *dosage*, is a concentrated solution of the finest sugar, dissolved in mature wine.

The shipping cork, which must say *Champagne*, is now driven in by machine and tightly wired down. During disgorgement some of the gas is lost, and the final pressure after recorking is reduced to about seventy-five pounds per square inch. The bottle goes back to the cellars for further rest before the labels and the plastic or lead-foil capsules are put on. When this is accomplished, the Champagne is ready to start its journey to our tables.

Because tastes vary, and some people prefer a dry and others a sweet Champagne, shippers have adopted a simple system of labeling to indicate how sweet the wine in the bottle is. The following list should serve as a general guide to denote the varying degrees of sweetness. All shippers use these descriptive terms. There is, however, some variation. Thus, while a Brut is always drier than an Extra Sec, one shipper's Brut may be slightly drier than another's.

Type	Description	Sugar Content/Liter
Brut	very, very dry	less than 15 grams
Extra Dry	somewhat sweeter but fairly dry	from 12 to 20 grams
Sec or Dry	medium sweet	from 11 to 35 grams
Demi Sec	quite sweet	from 33 to 50 grams

As in other wine-producing regions, the quality of Champagne grapes and the resultant wine varies greatly according to summer weather conditions. Two qualities of vintage are possible: fairly good wines, which can be enhanced by blending with wines of a previous vintage;

and fine, well-balanced wines that need no assistance and can stand on their own merit. The latter happens two, three, or possibly four times in a decade, and bottles of wine in this category are dated with the year in which the grapes that produced them were grown. These are known as vintage wines. Vintage wines are usually Brut. Wines in the first category, blends of several vintages, are not dated and are known as nonvintage wines.

The minimum standards specified under the existing *Appellation Contrôlée* regulations establish that non-vintage Champagne must be matured in bottle one and one-half years, and vintage Champagnes three years. Leading producers usually age their wines longer before they are shipped, especially the *tête de cuvée* wines, which are considered by the house to be their best.

A Champagne label carries a vintage year only when the *chef de cave* feels vintage it is warranted. This decision is made by the individual house, based on the Champagne merits of the harvest. Fine old vintage Champagne is one of the most delicate of all wines, and keeping vintage Champagne longer than ten years is risky. A fine vintage develops and matures nobly with the years if it is properly stored and undisturbed, but it becomes oxidized with age. On the other hand, young wines have a light, fruity freshness that is their most charming characteristic. Late-disgorged Champagnes are the only exception to these general comments. Many of the fine French Champagne producers store small quantities of various vintages undisgorged in their cellars for their personal use on great occasions. The House of Bollinger, however, has marketed late-disgorged Champagne labeled *R. D., Récemment Dégorgé* ("recently disgorged"). The label shows both the vintage date and the date of disgorgement. Late-disgorged Champagnes not only retain all their qualities but also benefit considerably from greater maturity.

Tête de cuvée, *cuvée speciale*, or *prestige cuvée* is a top-of-the-line Champagne that accounts for about 15 percent of Champagne sales in the United States, with about twenty different producers represented. While not specifically defined by the *Appellation Contrôlée* regulations, these Champagnes are made with the first pressings of grapes grown in the top-rated villages in vintage years, are aged longer on the yeasts than standard Champagnes, and are frequently bottled in replicas of antique bottles. They are very expensive.

Champagne is produced every year. In a vintage year, no more than 80 percent of the harvest may be sold, so that there will be sufficient reserve wines to blend with wines produced in lesser years. Nonvintage Champagne has no date on the label, and is always less expensive than vintage. This does not mean that the quality is necessarily less. These are the Champagne house's standard wines, and most houses will readily agree to be judged on the basis of their nonvintage bottlings.

The first Champagne salesman was the Marquis de Sillery, of the seventeenth century. He was one of the richest vineyard owners of the region and in great favor at court. He introduced sparkling Champagne there and was the first to ship it to England.

What the Marquis de Sillery did for sparkling Champagne in France, Saint Evremond did in London. Soldier, writer, philosopher, and courtier, he was last but not least a gourmet and a connoisseur. Having incurred the displeasure of his king, he left France and settled in London, where he became one of the brightest lights of London society. He made it the fashion to drink Champagne, and the English ever since have been recognized as the most discriminating connoisseurs of fine Champagne and are the region's best customers outside France.

In those early days Champagnes were generally sweet to appeal to the tastes of the period. In the nineteenth century, however, Veuve Pommery reasoned that the sweetness masked the lively, delicate taste of Champagne and that Champagne might prove more enjoyable if the *dosage* was reduced.

Her experiments led her to dry and extra dry Champagnes, which she introduced commercially. These became especially popular in London, and the term *English market* has since come to mean very dry Champagnes.

Recently, Americans have developed a taste for very dry Champagnes as well. Not only has the United States become the most important export market for Champagne, but about two-thirds of the Champagne shipped to this country is Brut. There are some Champagnes on the market that have no *dosage* at all.

A unique development in Champagne production was established by Pierre Taittinger, who felt that many people would prefer a light and more delicate Champagne. Knowing that Chardonnay grapes could impart these qualities to the *cuvée*, he departed from the usual proportions of two-thirds red grapes and one-third white, which is the traditional *cuvée*. Pierre Taittinger made a wine of 100 percent Chardonnay grapes from extensive holdings in vineyards south of Epernay in the Côte des Blancs. This Champagne is marketed as Blanc de Blancs and is dry, elegant, and expensive. Many houses produce this style of Champagne today.

Several firms offer Rosé or Pink Champagne, a wine that is currently in vogue. It is usually produced by adding the desired proportion of still red table wine from the Champagne district, generally from the villages of Bouzy or Ambonnay, at the time of assembling the *cuvée* or just before the second fermentation in the bottle. It can be obtained in nonvintage, vintage, and *tête de cuvée* bottlings. It is usually quite dry.

When the pressure in the bottle is between 3-4 atmospheres, rather than 5-6 atmospheres in a bottle of Champagne, the wine is called *crémant*, a Champagne with a light foam. Few houses export this quality, particularly since the sparkling wine taxes levied by the U.S. government are the same as for the product with higher pressure. Mumm's exports a *crémant* from the 100 percent village of Cramant.

Since 1975, French laws allows the word *crémant* on *vins mousseux* from other regions, *i.e.*, Crémant de Bourgogne, Crémant d'Alsace, and Crémant de Loire. These are full pressure sparkling wines, but should not be confused with those produced in the delimited Champagne region, even if made by the Champagne method.

Côteaux Champenois is an appellation under which still wines of Champagne may be shipped. The wines are made from the same grapes, under the same regulations as Champagne, but they do not go through the blending, aging, or second fermentation in the bottle. This explains why they may not be called Champagne. Bollinger,

Laurent-Perrier, and Moët & Chandon, among others, export these fresh, dry wines.

Once a bottle of Champagne is uncorked, it generally should be consumed in its entirety. A Champagne recorker, however, will help to preserve the bubbles for about forty-eight hours, especially if the Champagne is kept very cold.

For convenience, Champagne producers bottle their wine in various sizes.

The following are permitted in the U.S. under metric bottling regulations:

Name	**Size**	
	Metric standard *(liters)*	U.S. measure *(fluid ounces)*
Split	0.187	6.3
Half-bottle	0.375	12.7
Bottle	0.75	25.4
Magnum (2 bottles)	1.5	50.7
Jeroboam (4 bottles)	3.0	101.4
Methuselah (8 bottles)	6.0	204.8
Salmanazar (12 bottles)	9.0	307.2

Champagne, as is the case with most wines, develops better in a large container than in a small one, but it is important to know that the shippers rarely develop their Champagnes in sizes other than the half-bottles, bottles, magnums, and sometimes jeroboams. Methuselahs and Salmanazars are filled by decanting from bottles under pressure. While those are very festive for large parties, they should not be held too long in one's wine cellar. The magnum is the best practical size to use, followed by the bottle.

Champagne is one of the most delicate and delightful of all wines, but because it takes so long and is so costly to produce, it can never be cheap. This puts it in a class by itself as the "glamor" wine. It is indispensable at weddings, receptions, and formal banquets, but it is not limited to special occasions. Champagne is just as much at home with oysters as it is with ham or dessert, if a Champagne of the proper sweetness is chosen. Most people would not enjoy an extremely dry Brut with strawberry mousse, but a Demi Sec would be very pleasant. A chilled glass of Champagne makes a delightful apéritif to a wine-accompanied meal. Champagne also has its uses in the kitchen.

We have already spoken on page 16 about the general guidelines for tasting wines, noting the appearance, the bouquet, the taste, and the aftertaste. When one evaluates Champagne, however, there is an additional factor to be considered—and that is the bubbles. What is desired is an indication of good bonding of gas to liquid, and that is demonstrated by the presence of numerous, long lasting bubbles. Small-size bubbles are more desirable than larger bubbles for the same reason. Incidentally, a glass with a bowl that comes to a point, such as a flute or a tulip, will produce better bubbles than a saucer glass.

Vin mousseux refers to all sparkling wines, although the name Champagne may be used only for sparkling wine made in the delimited district of Champagne. Almost every wine region of France produces a *vin mousseux*. In addition to Champagne, there are only sixteen other French *vins mousseux* that are entitled to carry an *Appellation Contrôlée*.

The finer producers of *vin mousseux* use the *méthode champenoise*, although other methods of production may be used.

Vin Mousseux-Produit en Cuve Close is the designation for sparkling wines made by the Charmat or bulk process.

WINES OF ALSACE

The vineyards of Alsace are the most northern of France, extending from Strasbourg south to the border of Switzerland. The Vosges Mountains create a protective western border, with the Rhine River completing the boundaries to the east. Since it was easy to travel between France and Germany across the Rhine River, Alsace was often caught in a struggle between the two countries.

Despite the use of grape varieties more common to Germany, the people of Alsace, their grapes, and their wines are proudly French, producing bone dry wines, often vinified in oak, that offer contrast to neighboring German wines.

Alsace has been an important wine-producing region since the Roman conquerors occupied the valley of the Rhine. Undoubtedly they planted the vine in Alsace before they did in Germany. The vines they brought from Italy were not the same as those that flourish there today, but the records do not show when the change occurred. During the half-century of German authority, the Alsatian identity of these fine wines was submerged, and while much wine was made, it was all consumed in Germany or used for blending purposes. Quantity rather than quality was the order.

". . . a fertile country," wrote Julius Wile, "fields and valleys waving with grain, hillsides covered with symmetric rows of vines marching up and up until they merge with the orchards, bearers of the fruits from which are distilled the famous *eaux-de-vie d'Alsace*, Quetsch and Mirabelle [plum brandies] and Kirsch [cherry brandy]; and the orchards finally give way to the mighty forests which top the hills and cover the Vosges Mountains. . . .

"There is an atmosphere in Alsace—one of close alliance between man and soil, an aura of maturity combined with a freshness of spirit, of physical youngness that one finds even in the aged, of a people that has known the past, lives in the present, and does not fear the future."

Growing the vine and harvesting in Alsace do not differ radically from other white-wine regions in France except that, because of Alsace's more northerly location and cooler climate, the vines are trained high and allowed to reach for the sun. The grape varieties do not ripen at the same time, and since many vineyards are planted with three, four, or more varieties they must be picked over several times during the vintage.

From the north southward the towns whose surrounding vineyards are famous are:

Barr. This is the home of the famous Clos Gaensbroennel ("little goose fountain") vineyard.

Ribeauvillé and **Riquewihr**. Located in the center of the region, they have long enjoyed a reputation for producing excellent Alsatian wines.

Ammerschwihr. The important vineyard here is Kaefferkopf.

Guebwiller and Thann. Almost in the shadows of Switzerland, these are the southernmost towns of the region. There is a hill at Guebwiller called Kitterle, or "leg cutter." These leg-cutter wines are said to have been among Napoleon's favorites.

The grapes permitted in the production of *Appellation Contrôlée* Vin d'Alsace are Riesling, Gewürztraminer, Sylvaner, Muscat d'Alsace, Pinot Gris (Tokay d'Alsace), Pinot Blanc (Klevner), and Pinot Noir. When these grapes appear on the label, there must be 100 percent of the variety used to make the wine.

The Riesling is considered the most notable of the grapes of Alsace, making wines that are rich, dry, and austere. The Gewürztraminer has a unique, spicy and flowery bouquet, with full flavor and a dry finish. In some very ripe years the Riesling and Gewürztraminer are affected by the "noble rot," and the wines produced are rich and luscious. The Pinot Noir, incidentally, makes a light rosé wine in Alsace.

In Alsace, the name of the wine is usually the name of the grape from which it is produced, sometimes in conjunction with the name of a village. For many years, the names of famous vineyards were seen on labels, such as Clos Ste. Hune and Clos Gaensbroennel. Since many of these vineyards date back to the fourteenth century, their names were permitted to be used.

New regulations now state that the term *Grand Cru* may be used on labels with vineyard or vineyard-area designations if the wines have come from classified vineyards, have been produced from Riesling, Gewürztraminer, Pinot Gris, or Muscat d'Alsace, and have been approved by a tasting panel. If the panel rejects the wine, the vineyard name may not be used—only the grape name.

Vineyard areas are being defined and classified. These place names are called *Lieu-Dit*. Fifteen vineyard areas have been listed so far. Phrases such as *Grande Réserve* or *Réserve Exceptionnelle* are no longer allowed.

The phrase *Vendange Tardive* is used for late-harvest wines. The rich, ripe wines, incidentally, need longer aging than the normally harvested wines.

Wines from Alsace also appear on the market under a shipper's trademark name, and are usually blends of grapes. These have generally replaced Edelzwicker. No grape name or classified place name will be on the label. The shipper's name is of utmost importance, since is usually a wine grower and winemaker as well. As in Champagne, grapes are purchased to supplement the grower's own vineyards to create the final blend.

All Alsace wines must be bottled in the green Alsace flute, which is a tall, slim bottle. The wines must be bottled in the region and cannot be shipped in casks.

Sparkling wine is also produced in Alsace, carrying the *Appellation Contrôlée* designation of *Crémant d'Alsace*. White sparkling wines may be produced from white or black grapes. Rosé sparkling wines may only be produced from Pinot Noir.

RHÔNE WINES

The viticultural Rhône Valley stretches 130 miles, from the gastronomic center of Lyon to the ancient and historic city of Avignon. Here northern and southern vineyards produce two different styles of wines.

The Rhône River has been a means of transportation and communication, and the area has had historical and religious importance. South of Lyon, near the ancient Roman city of Vienne and across the river from Condrieu, lie the vineyards of the Côte Rôtie ("roasted slope"). The wines from this district were highly praised by Pliny the Younger, Plutarch, and Columella.

Thirty miles south of Côte Rôtie on the left bank of the Rhône near Tain, the renowned hill of Hermitage rises up majestically. Sir Gaspard de Sterimberg, a Crusader returning from the Albigensian Crusade, in southern France, decided to settle on these heights in 1209 and live the contemplative life of a hermit at the Chapel of Saint-Christophe at Hermitage. From the south he had brought a vine cutting, which he planted on the hill. According to legend it was the first Syrah brought to the Rhône. He tended his vine patiently and eventually it bore fruit, from which he made a fine wine that, ironically, brought him fame.

For seventy-two years, 1305–1377, the papacy was occupied by Frenchmen, who, fearful of the perils of Rome, maintained the Holy See at Avignon, to the south. This period is sometimes called the Babylonian Captivity of the popes. The first of the Avignon popes was Clement V, who, as a native of Bordeaux and archbishop of Bordeaux, was familiar with viticulture and left us the legacy of that grand Graves claret—Château Pape-Clément, the vineyard which he is said to have owned.

When Clement V decided to settle the Holy See at Avignon, he built a fortress-palace just outside the town. This edifice was dubbed the new château of the pope, Châteauneuf-du-Pape. Since wine is important to a man from Bordeaux, Clement had vines planted, and they still produce the wine that is known as Châteauneuf-du-Pape.

Flowing southward, the turbulent Rhône River cuts its swath to the Mediterranean. Along its route there are two widely separated sections that produce red, rosé, and white wines of repute.

The northern part has terraced cliffs, giving the vines good exposure to the sun. The soil contains granite and shale. The southern part is covered with large round stones that hold the heat, and the climate is more typically Mediterranean. Throughout the Rhône Valley the growing season is long and hot, creating robust, alcoholic wines that take time to develop.

The principal red grape variety of the Côtes du Rhône is the Syrah (sometimes called Sirah, Sirrac, or Serine). While some true Syrah is also grown in California, it is unrelated to California's Petite Sirah. The Syrah is the only red grape permitted in Côte Rôtie and Hermitage. Of twenty-three grapes grown in the area, other important red grapes are the

Grenache, Clairette, Bourboulenc, Mourvèdre, Cinsaut, and Carignan. White grapes include the Viognier, Roussanne, Marsanne, and Picpoul. These are used both for making white wines and for softening some red wines.

At Châteauneuf-du-Pape the wine may be the result of judicious blending of as many as thirteen grape varieties. Baron P. Le Roy Boiseaumarié, president of the Syndicate of Vineyard Owners of Châteauneuf-du-Pape and proprietor of Château Fortia, stated in 1932 that the choice of grapes to produce a perfect Châteauneuf-du-Pape was as follows (percentages and grape varieties vary today, with Grenache predominating):

1st group	For warmth, richness, and roundness	Grenache and Cinsaut	20 percent
2nd group	For solidity, keeping power, color, and the right flavor	Mourvèdre and Syrah	40 percent
3rd group	For vinosity, agreeableness, freshness, and bouquet	Counoise and Picpoul	30 percent
4th group	For finesse, fire, brilliance	Clairette and Bourboulenc	10 percent

The red wines of Châteauneuf-du-Pape traditionally have been big and slow to develop. After a brief period where the wines were vinified to be drinkable sooner, winemakers have now returned to the traditional fuller style. Some white wine is also produced at Châteauneuf-du-Pape. It has good body, flavor, and character, although not as fine as the red.

The wines of Côte Rôtie are very deep in color and have a rich headiness and a roughness that takes some years to throw off. The wines spend three years in wood before bottling. As they grow older they lose some of their color, throw a rather heavy deposit, and rid themselves of their youthful harshness. Twelve to fifteen years is the youngest at which Côte Rôtie should be drunk.

Some white wine is produced at nearby Condrieu and at Château Grillet from the Viognier grape. Production from both is very small and it is rare to find these wines in commerce. If you are fortunate enough to come across any

Château Grillet, you will find it to be pale in color and medium bodied, but with a wealth of character and a magnificent bouquet. It will be expensive. Château Grillet is one of France's smallest *Appellation Contrôlée* areas.

The vineyards of Hermitage are fewer than four hundred acres and produce both red and white wines. The red wines, which Professor Saintsbury called the "manliest of wines," are big, full bodied, strong, and deep colored and have marvelous keeping qualities. The white wines are full and medium dry and have a deep bouquet. When mature they have an amber gold color and a lovely mellowness.

The appellation Crozes-Hermitage has been in effect since 1952; it applies to wines produced in eleven townships around the famous hillside of Hermitage. They are similar to Hermitage wines but have somewhat less character. Comas and Saint-Joseph are not as well known but are enjoyable and well priced.

The Côtes-du-Rhône appellation applies to wines

made in over one hundred communes, which can be white, rosé, or red. Much of this wine is made in large cooperatives. Côtes-du-Rhône Villages, a more recent appellation, applies to wines made from the best seventeen communes, whose name may appear on the label. Beaumes de Venise, one of these communes, produces both dry red wines, labeled Côtes-du-Rhône Beaumes de Venise, and sweet Muscat wines, labeled simply Beaumes de Venise.

Across the river from Avignon is the town of Tavel, which gives its name to one of the most delightful of all the rosé wines. Tavel combines the dryness of a red wine with the fresh lightness of a white. Several grapes are used, including not more than 60 percent Grenache and at least 15 percent Cinsault. It has a delightful coral color; is clean, fresh, and dry; and usually has a lovely, fruity bouquet and flavor. Tavel is best when young, no more than five years old. Neighboring Lirac also produces rosé wines that are similar to Tavel. They are coral in color; clean, fresh, and very dry. They should be drunk young. Rosé wines from the Rhône are usually shipped in clear, flute bottles.

Rhône wines, both red and white, are bottled in the same type of bottle used in Burgundy. They are more like Burgundy in character than any other wines. For these reasons many people have been confused, and on many a wine card Châteauneuf-du-Pape is erroneously listed as a Burgundy.

Piedmont

Piedmont produces the majority of Italy's most regal red wines, while being one of the most austere regions in the country. From the glaciers of the Alpine banks the land descends in a series of charming valleys and fertile plains to the Po River, from which it again rises gradually to the hills of Monferrato, where the vine is cultivated with religious fervor. Piedmont's name is derived from "*a pie del monti*," meaning "at the foot of the mountains." The famous red wines are full, rich, travel well, and improve with age. They include Barolo, Barbaresco, and Gattinara.

The region is ruled by Turin (Torino), the home of vermouth and the center of industry. It is the richest market for wines in the region. The Piedmontese are tenacious, industrious, and faithful to their land. Their vineyards are neat and symmetrical.

Barolo is the name of a town as well as the name of the surrounding area fully planted to its limits with over two thousand acres under vine. The area is situated on a hill of porous rock, which undoubtedly is an extinct volcano. On this hill Nebbiolo grapes grow best, and they give one of the finest and most justly celebrated red wines Italy has, also called Barolo. The proud growers call it the wine of kings and king of wines. In good years Barolo is a big, full-bodied wine, with a ruby-red color that takes on a brownish shade as it ages. It is generous yet austere, rich in alcohol, but, with age, always soft and velvety, with an unmistakable violet bouquet. All Barolos must spend at least two years in barrels of oak or chestnut. Barolo must be at least three years old before release, Barolo Riserva four years, and Barolo Riserva Speciale five years of age.

Northeast of Barolo is the town and district of Barbaresco, which produces Barbaresco wines. The hillside vineyards surround the old red-towered remnant of Barbaresco Castle on the crest of the hill, overlooking the stone houses below. The hills are also planted with Nebbiolo vines, but different soils create different wines. Barbaresco's minimum age is two years, with the Riserva aged for three, and the Riserva Speciale aged four. Both Barolo and Barbaresco have been granted D.O.C.G. status.

It is interesting to note that in Julius Caesar's *Commentaries* there is a reference to these wines, which he greatly appreciated and wanted to introduce to Rome. The particular wine to which he referred came from the little village of Morra (Murra). "From Murra," he wrote, "we brought the best wine to our city of Rome."

The third most important red wine from Piedmont is Gattinara, principally made from the Nebbiolo grape, with some Bonarda permitted. Gattinara is a small D.O.C. area, with about eighty acres under vine, in the northeast part of Piedmont that borders on Lombardy. The Sesia River flows through Gattinara. The wine is aged at least four years, after which it begins to get a velvet quality.

Adjoining the D.O.C. area of Gattinara, are vineyards planted with the same grapes, often producing similar styles of wine, but without the D.O.C. classification. The wine is named for the colloquial name of the Nebbiolo grape, which is "Spanna."

Nebbiolo also appears as a varietal wine, when the place names of either Alba or Carema appear on the label.

The most widely planted grape in Piedmont is the Barbera, producing 50 percent of the red wines of this region. These varietally labeled wines always have a place name affixed to the grape name, such as Barbera d'Alba, Barbera d'Asti, Barbera dei Colli Tortonesi, and Barbera del Monferrato. The wine is usually drunk young, but can take moderate aging.

Many of the premium red wines mentioned thus far from Piedmont are now appearing on the market with single vineyard designations.

Grignolino, made from the grape of the same name, is a light, fruity, rather dry wine that sometimes has a slight natural effervescence. Dolcetto is another varietal red wine that is light and makes an excellent carafe wine. Another grape variety, Freisa, is so named for its raspberry bouquet. It makes both a dry red wine and a sweet, slightly sparkling, or "crackling," wine. Grignolino, Dolcetto, and Freisa have a place name after the grape variety name.

Boca, Fara, Ghemme, Lessona, and Sizzano are five other red wines made from the Nebbiolo, Vespolina, and

Bonarda grapes. These are good red wines with limited production.

From the Cortese Bianco grape is produced Cortese, usually a delicate, straw-colored wine with a greenish cast, and a pleasant, fresh aroma. Cortese produced around the town of Gavi, however, is quite distinctive, and has been granted D.O.C. classification.

Asti, the sparkling wine center of Italy and the home of the famous sparkling Asti Spumante, is a town with a great historical background. Bismarck showed such predilection for it that he exclaimed: "I want one good bottle for each of my officers. It will serve to keep their heavy heads awake."

The actual production zone of Asti Spumante lies south of the town. The vineyards of San Stefano along the rugged banks of the Belbo River, and vineyards around Canelli produce the most highly prized Moscato Bianco grapes, which go into making this sparkling wine of Asti.

Asti Spumante is the most popular Italian sparkling wine. It is a delicious wine with a pleasant, decidedly sweet Muscat flavor and low alcohol (7.5 to 9 percent) that gives it a lovely, fresh fruitiness. Most of the shippers have changed over from bottle fermentation to Charmat fermentation. Aside from the time and expense savings, the fragrance of the Muscat grape is captured much better by this method. Some of the Italian sparkling wine producers do use the *méthode champenoise* in years of exceptional heat and sugar content. A sparkling wine that used to be made in Piedmont was Lacrima Christi, but this is no longer permitted. The wine is now made in Campania, the best coming from the province of Avellino. It may or may not be sparkling.

A sweet dessert wine, Caluso Passito, is produced north of Turin from the white Erbaluce grape in the area of Caluso. These grapes undergo a drying process (Passito) that raisins them and leaves them rich in sugar. When the wine is lightly fortified, it becomes a Passito Liquoroso.

LOMBARDY

Lombardy has three main wine regions: the northern lake region framed by the Swiss Alps with breathtaking beauty, the southwestern portion next to Piedmont, and the eastern sections separated from the western half by the Adda River, which borders on the Veneto. The Po River, Italy's longest river, flows through the southern part of the region. Milan, Italy's industrial capital, is situated in central Lombardy.

Some of the best wines of Lombardy come from an area known as the Valtellina, in the northernmost province of Sondrio on the Swiss border. The vineyards are carved out of the mountains and are tended by hardy individuals. Both red and white wines are made, but the Sassella, Grumello, Inferno, and Valgella reds are the most famous and are made from at least 95 percent Nebbiolo grapes, known locally as Chiavennasca. Differences in soil and altitude give these wines a different character from the Nebbiolo wines of Piedmont. A wine labeled Valtellina may come from any of the four named areas, and must be aged for one year minimum. With two years of aging it may be called Valtellina Superiore, and Riservas must have a minimum of four years age. A unique, high-alcohol, rich red wine, made with semidried grapes, is called Sforsato (Sfursat), which means "forced" in Italian.

In southwest Lombardy, the Oltrepò Pavese area, once part of Piedmont, is considered by many to be an excellent wine-producing district. Many good, inexpensive wines are made for local consumption, as well as for export, primarily from the Barbera and Bonarda grapes. One proprietary brand, Frecciarossa, is produced by the Odero family, whose château bottling dates back to the last century. Frecciarossa is made from different grape varieties, many brought from France, and appears as red, white, and rosé wine.

Many of the spumante producers buy grapes from this area, especially Pinot Bianco and Pinot Nero. Some white wines are produced from the Riesling, Cortese, and Pinot Bianco, and a rosé is made from Pinot Nero.

In the east, near charming Lake Garda, is produced a pleasant, light white wine called Lugana, made from the Trebbiano grape. It is most enjoyable when young, especially so with a freshly caught trout from Lake Garda. The most famous wine from this area is the Riviera del Garda Rosé. Called Chiaretto, which means "light red," it is a ruby-hued rosé with a gentle flavor, soft texture, and a hint of bitterness.

Slightly to the west of Lake Garda is the province of Brescia, where wines are produced in the Franciacorta zone. Light, flavorful reds are made from a mixture of Cabernet Franc, Barbera, Nebbiolo, and Merlot grapes, as are the red Cellatica and Botticino. The white Franciacorta Pinot Bianco makes fine dry still and sparkling wines, and some Pinot Grigio is also produced.

Veneto

The morning sun rising above the Adriatic gilds the peaks of the Dolomites in the north long before it touches the golden cupolas of San Marco in Venice. The land drops precipitously from rugged mountains. Cutting across southern Veneto, the Adige River passes through romantic Verona, where you can visit the houses of the Montagues and Capulets. There also stands majestically the Palazzo Scaglieri, where Cangrande toasted his guests with Vernaccia and where Dante Alighieri found refuge and protection.

Here along the eastern shores of Lake Garda, near Verona, are produced bright red Bardolino; Bianco di

Custoza, a flowery white; and again, dry white Lugana. The long narrow valley running north from Verona is where the Corvina, Rondinella, and other grape varieties are blended to produce one of Italy's fruitiest red table wines—Valpolicella. Valpolicella is a fine, ruby-colored wine of delicate bouquet and with a pleasant crisp finish. Both Bardolino and Valpolicella may be lightly cooled and consumed as a young, fresh wine.

A special Valpolicella produced in limited quantities is called Recioto della Valpolicella-Amarone. It used to be made entirely with the ripest grapes taken from the upper part of the bunch. To the imaginative person these grapes represent the "ears" of the bunch, ergo *Recioto*, which means "ears." Today, whole bunches that are the best of the vineyard are selected. The grapes are then dried on reed trays in a shed for three months and are vinified. The high sugar concentration ferments to a rich, dry wine with a high alcohol content. Amarone actually refers to this process or style of winemaking. *Amaro* is the Venetian equivalent of "slightly bitter," which has a pleasant connotation to it and signifies that the wine was vinified to complete dryness.

From the vineyards around the ancient walled city of Soave, the Garganega and ubiquitous Trebbiano grapes produce Soave. It is a really suave white wine, medium body, fairly dry, with a pleasant, subtle bouquet, and a bit of piquant bitter undertone.

Soave, Bardolino, and Valpolicella are available as Classico wines, with a more defined zone of production, and the best are Classico Superiore.

A wine made to the east of Soave, the Garganega di Gambellara, is produced as a dry white, a sweet white, and a sparkling wine.

Other excellent white wines, such as the Bianco, made from 85 percent Tocai grapes; the Pinot Grigio Superiore, made from Pinot Bianco and Pinot Grigio grapes; and the Vespaiolo, made from 100 percent Vespaiolo grapes, are found in the Breganze area in the province of Vicenza. Good red wines from this area are being made from such classic varieties as Merlot, Pinot Nero, and Cabernet.

Further east in the province of Treviso, are the communes of Conegliano and Valdobbiadene. Here the best known wine is vinified from the Prosecco grape, as a still, *frizzante*, or *spumante* wine. Other white wines from Treviso include Tocai di Lison, Verduzzo, Pinot Grigio, and Pinot Bianco. In addition to Raboso, a local red Cabernet and Merlot are also grown.

TRENTINO-ALTO ADIGE

Italy's northernmost region, bordering on Austria, is Trentino-Alto Adige. It produces many red and white wines using the traditional grapes grown in France and

Germany. Some varietal red wines are Trentino-Cabernet, Trentino-Merlot, and Trentino-Pinot Nero, which use 100 percent of the grapes named Among the white are Trentino-Riesling, Trentino-Pinot, and Trentino-Traminer Aromatico. These wines are similar to those made in the grapes' homelands. This area is known for its fine dry sparkling wines, thanks to advanced technology, and the availability of traditional sparkling wine grapes.

The province of Bolzano (Upper Adige) produces a wide variety of quality wines, but the best known are Santa Maddalena, Teroldego Rotaliano, and Caldaro—dry, red wines—and Lagrein—a dry, fresh rosé made from the Lagrein grape.

FRIULI-VENEZIA-GIULIA

Nestled between Veneto, Austria, and Yugoslavia is the individualistic region of Friuli-Venezia-Giulia. Some areas, such as Trieste, have been part of both Yugoslavia and Italy at different times and have developed cultures encompassing those of both countries. The wines come from three main areas: Colli Orientale del Friuli (Eastern Friuli Hills), Colli Grave del Friuli (Western Friuli Hills), and Colli Goriziano (Gorizia Hills). Three lesser areas are Isonzo, Aquileia, and Latisana. Some grapes used are the Pinot Nero, Cabernet, Merlot, and Refosco, which produce full, rich reds. Pinot Bianco, Pinot Grigio, Tocai, Sauvignon, Traminer, Riesling Renano, and Riesling Italico produce characteristic white wines. The Verduzzo grape, grown in the eastern and western hills, makes a full bodied and slightly tannic white wine called Verduzzo. Picolot, a rare grape grown in the Colli Orientali, makes a prized, delicate sweet wine.

While this area has its roots far back in history, much of it was destroyed during World War II. This has resulted in new plantings, coupled with modern equipment and advanced technology. Because of this, it can be considered a new wine area, producing high quality wines with world-wide acceptance.

Emilia-Romagna

We now come to the richest and most fertile region of the Po Valley. Surrounding the famed gastronomic center of Italy, which is Bologna, are the three main wine-producing areas. To the northwest are the Piacenza Hills, where Gutturnio, a dry, full-bodied red wine is made from Barbera and Bonarda grapes.

The central area around Modena and Parma, famous for Parma hams and Parmesan cheese, is the site of several different Lambrusco grape varieties. These grapes make the popular Lambrusco wine; lively, *frizzante*, semidry red wine that can be served chilled. (A dry version is also made, but it is consumed locally.) While this red wine has a D.O.C. classification, the same Lambrusco grapes are fermented off the skins to make both Bianco (white) and Rosato (rosé), with a similar flavor and effervescence to the red wine. Because of the difference in vinification, however, the Bianco and Rosato may not carry the D.O.C. on their labels. This has not affected their extreme popularity in the United States.

In the southeast corner of this region is the third wine-producing area, historically known as Romagna. It encompasses the provinces of Forli, Ravenna, and Bologna. The full red varietal Sangiovese di Romagna dominates premium wine production in Emilia-Romagna, and ranks third in volume behind Chianti and Soave among Italy's D.O.C. wines.

The white wines of this area are the dry, light Trebbiano di Romagna, and the Albana di Romagna, which varies from dry to semisweet, and from still to sparkling. Albana di Romagna is the first white wine to apply for D.O.C.G. classification.

TUSCANY

To the poets this region is Arcady—the home of Dante, Boccaccio, the Borgias, Saint Francis of Assisi, Saint Catherine of Siena. It bears the marks of the orgies and extravaganzas of its sinners and the pious virtues of its saints.

To most people Tuscany is the home of Italian wines, for it is the home of Chianti, the wine of the typical straw-covered flask (*fiasco*) originally used for breakage-free shipping. Of all containers for wine, it is the most picturesque, but difficult to fill, hard to stack, susceptible to mildew, and expensive to produce today.

The Chianti area is subdivided into seven districts, all of which lie on the beautiful rolling hillsides around and between Florence (Firenze) and Siena. Wines produced from the center of the Chianti zone may be called Chianti Classico.

The proud and independent Tuscans followed many historical winemaking traditions, whether or not they were the best viticultural and enological methods. To Barone Bettino Ricasoli must go the credit for having brought Piedmontese viticultural methods into Tuscany by the nineteenth century. The work of improvement in vinification as well has set an example that other vineyard owners have followed.

Chianti has been clearly defined and regulated by the D.O.C. laws, regarding area, grapes, and methods of production. Since many Chianti Classico producers have requested and received D.O.C.G. status, the regulations have changed somewhat.

Chianti is made from several different grape varieties. The principal grape is the Sangiovese, which accounts for from 50 to 80 percent of the must; the Canaiolo Nero from 10 to 30 percent of the must; and the white Trebbiano Tuscano and Malvasia del Chianti, which can also account for 10 to 30 percent of the must. Other local grapes can provide up to 5 percent of the blend. The actual proportions vary with the vintage year and the style of Chianti being made.

D.O.C.G. Chianti Classicos use less white grapes in the must, with only 8 to 10 percent permitted. In addition, the maximum yield per hectare has been decreased to ensure higher quality.

Three types of Chianti are generally produced: the wine for early consumption, light in color and body; a better quality, which comprises the largest quantity of all Chiantis produced and whose tannins soften after a year or so of aging; and the best quality, which requires longer aging to round out the increased alcohol, higher acids, and tannins.

For Chiantis meant to be drunk young, a process called governo is used in Tuscany. It consists of setting aside a small percentage of the harvest on mats to become raisins. These are added to the large vats of new Chianti. A slow, second fermentation takes place that softens the acids and makes the wine drinkable six months after this fermentation; it is lively, with a slight sparkle. This wine is called Chianti Governato, and it used to be shipped in the raffia-covered *fiaschi*. Since the *fiaschi* are expensive, as well as impractical, some producers are using the *Chiantiagiona* bottle or other exclusively designed bottles. The middle style of Chianti is found in either the *Chiantiagiona* or the claret-style bottle. The best quality Chianti is always found in the claret-style bottle, since the wine must develop in the bottle for a few years. Such Chianti will be a splendid, soft, rounded, and mellow wine of great character.

Young Chianti may be sold within a year of the harvest, but not before March 1. There is a two-year minimum-age Chianti called *Vecchio*, but it is not permitted in this country since U.S. laws do not permit words like *vecchio* ("old") on wine labels. Chianti Classico Riserva must be aged three years, and must also have an alcohol content of 12.5 percent, as opposed to 12 percent for Chianti Classico and 11.5 percent for Chianti.

Young Chianti is ideal to drink with rich, well-seasoned, oily foods because its tartness is just the thing to help digest these foods. Older aged Chiantis and Riservas have more elegance and can accompany more subtle dishes.

Southwest of Siena the hill town of Montalcino produces a noble red varietal wine called Brunello di Montalcino, made exclusively from a clone of the Sangiovese Grosso grape, locally called Brunello. This wine has attained international fame because of its limited production, high quality, ability to keep for a long time, and length of time before its initial release because of the high tannins and full body. Italy does not have the tradition of aging wine in most of its regions as it does here. D.O.C.

regulations state that Brunello must spend at least four years in oak casks, and if it is labeled Riserva, it must spend five years in wood. The law stipulates that the Bordeaux-shaped bottle be used.

Brunello was the first wine to be declared D.O.C.G. in November 1980. One reason for its having been declared a D.O.C.G. first, was that of all the red wines applying for D.O.C.G. at that time, Brunello required the longest aging before release. Other red wines have subsequently been approved in order of aging requirements, so that five D.O.C.G. red wines will all appear on the market in 1985.

We have already mentioned Barolo and Barbaresco from Piedmont, and Brunello and Chianti Classico from Tuscany. It now remains to discuss Vino Nobile di Montepulciano, the last of this initial group of red D.O.C.G. wines.

Traveling due east from Montalcino, we arrive at the town of Montepulciano, near Siena. This is where Vino

Nobile di Montepulciano is produced—so named because it was originally made by noblemen. The four major permitted grapes are the same as those permitted in Chianti, but the small amounts of local grapes vary, and are one reason that Vino Nobile di Montepulciano is different from Chianti. In making this wine, the *governo* method may not be used, and two years minimum time in oak is required. If the wine is labeled Riserva, aging is increased to three years. Riserva Speciale must be aged for four years before bottling.

A handful of independent producers are disqualifying themselves from D.O.C. classifications and are omitting white grapes altogether from their wines. Sometimes they are using Cabernet instead. Most notable examples are Antinori's Tignanello and Sassicaia.

White wine has always been made in Tuscany, since white grapes such as the Trebbiano and Malvasia are grown in abundance. It used to be shipped as White Chianti, but the D.O.C. laws defined Chianti as a red wine. Even though white wine is produced in the Chianti district, it now must be shipped as Vino Bianco Toscano ("White Tuscan Wine").

With percentages of white grapes to be used in Chianti being relaxed, producers are finding themselves with an excess of white grapes at a time when market pressures demand more white wines. They have created a wine with the fantasy name "Galestro," vinified with modern technology into a fresh, fruity, lower alcohol wine than the traditional Vino Bianco Tuscano. Galestro is in the category of Vino da Tavola, from the region of Tuscany.

On the southwestern border of the Chianti district, in the area surrounding the ancient hill town of San Gimignano, a full-bodied and complex wine is produced from the Vernaccia grape. It is called Vernaccia di San Gimignano. If aged for one year it may be called Riserva. It became Italy's first D.O.C. wine in 1966.

A traditional white wine that has added to Tuscany's fame is Vin (Vino) Santo, a rich, generous, sometimes sweet dessert wine with a Muscat flavor and high alcohol content. Practically all winemakers in the region produce some. The white Trebbiano and Malvasia grapes are gathered when fully ripened and the bunches are strung on poles that are suspended under the attic-roof of the house. There they remain to dry until late December, when they are pressed; the rich juice ferments very slowly during the cold winter months, and the wine remains in casks for some time before bottling.

The historic island of Elba off the coast of Tuscany provides clean, pleasant, dry white, red, and rosé wines. The Trebbiano is the most important vine but there is some Sangiovese as well. A trace of iron ore in the soil gives these wines distinction.

Marches and Umbria

The region of Marches on the Adriatic side of the peninsula is very hilly and exposed to the north wind. Several good wines are grown in this region. One in particular demands attention: the fine, light white wine Verdicchio dei Castelli di Jesi. It is one of Italy's distinguished white wines and the most crisply dry. It has a pale greenish cast, a delicate bouquet and flavor, a slightly tart aftertaste, and is customarily shipped in a green amphora-like bottle.

Another very similar wine, not as well known, is the Verdicchio di Matelica. The same grapes are used as for the first Verdicchio, but in different blending proportions. In general, the reds of Marches are good, ordinary wines. The best known are Rosso Piceno, Rosso Conero, and Sangiovese dei Colli Pesaresi.

Farther southwest is the region Umbria, where the beautiful cities of Assisi, Perugia, and Orvieto are located. It is a land of temperate climate and rolling hills through which flows the Tiber (Tevere) River. The well-drained soil is especially suited to growing grapes for fine white wines.

Traditionally, Orvieto wines have been bottled in a long-necked *fiasco* called *pulcinella*, but fortunately, the D.O.C. laws permit a more practically shaped bottle, which does not have the expensive straw wrappings.

The white wines of Orvieto are both *secco* ("dry") and *abboccato* ("semi-dry"). The grapes for *abboccato* are sometimes affected by "noble rot," called *muffa nobile* in Italy. Both are light straw-colored and have a fruity freshness, with a lingering aftertaste. The premium Orvieto wines are labeled Classico.

In the center of the region around the small town of Torgiano, the Lungarotti family holds court. Vineyard owners, winemakers, and museum curators, they produce about 85 percent of the region's wines. The reds are called Rubesco and Rubesco Riserva, the Riserva having no specified aging requirements, simply the winemaker's best. Grapes and blending proportions are similar to those in

Chianti, but without the white grapes. A fresh, drinkable white of the area is Torre di Giano.

Latium

Latium was the home of Horace, and his poetry tells of Tusculum (now called Frascati), of the vines that he grew, and of the trees that he loved.

The proud Romans left the shores of the Tiber for the pleasures of the countryside, and on the hills adjacent to Rome they built their villas. Hence the wines produced on these estates are called Vini dei Castelli Romani.

Chiefly white wines are made, as the conditions of soil and climate are more favorable for them, but some good reds are made also.

In Rome every restaurant offers the light white Frascati, the whites of Marino, and other Castelli Romani wines from the hills around Rome. These wines are most enjoyable when young and fresh.

A little farther north around the ancient town of Montefiascone on Lake Bolsena is produced a brilliant, straw-yellow dry wine with a fruity and fresh bouquet, poetically named Est! Est!! Est!!! While the wine is very good per se, the manner in which it got its name is most interesting.

As the story goes, a long time ago—perhaps four or five centuries—a German bishop named Johannes de Fuger was on his way to the Vatican to pay his respects to the Holy Father. Being a man of taste and discrimination, he sent his secretary-valet ahead to find suitable accommodations. Where the food, and especially the wine, was good, the valet was to write with chalk the word Est on the wall of the inn. When this good man tasted the wines at Montefiascone he could not describe them truthfully with just one "It is," so he chalked on the wall of the inn *Est! Est!! Est!!!* ("It is! It is!! It is!!!"). When the bishop arrived he agreed with his valet's judgment. In fact, he tarried so long and drank so freely that he finally died at Montefiascone, without ever reaching Rome.

We wished to verify this story, and on our last visit to Italy we made a special trip to Montefiascone to find the bishop's tomb. It is there, just within the entrance to the Basilica of Saint Flaviano. The inscription is almost illegible from the thousands of feet that have trod the marble slab through the centuries, but one can still make out the words: *Est, Est, Est et propter nimium est, Johannes de Fuger, dominus meus, mortuus est*, which means, "It is, it is, it is, and through too much it is, my master, Johannes de Fuger, dead is."

The sequel to the story is that the grateful winemakers of Montefiascone who produce Est! Est!! Est!!! commemorate the anniversary of Bishop de Fuger's demise by spilling a barrel of Est! Est!! Est!!! wine over his tomb.

In the same area the sweet Aleatico di Gradoli is produced from the Aleatico (Moscato Nero) grape; it achieves a high alcohol content.

Campania and Basilicata

Campania, dominated by Mount Vesuvius to the east of Naples, is one of the most unique spots on earth. The pumice of the volcano spreads over the land and enriches it. Hot springs and fissures evidence the volcanic nature of the soil. The climate is ideal and vegetation is luxuriant—three crops a year are rotated on farms. The vine is cultivated intensely, for the area is limited and the demand worldwide. Falernum, prized by the Romans, has fallen from popularity, and in its stead rules Lacryma Christi.

The still Lacryma Christi, made near Vesuvius, is a golden wine, not too dry, with a softness, delicacy, and somewhat aromatic bouquet that it gets from the hot volcanic soil. Some red and rosé Lacryma Christi is also made.

As does Umbria, this area has one predominant winemaking family that goes back for many generations. In Campania, it is the Mastroberardinos, who have added modern technology to the traditionally made wines of their forefathers. Grapes, such as Greco and Aglianico were introduced by the ancient Greeks. They achieve a special perfume in the mineral-rich volcanic soil.

In addition to the white Lacryma Christi, white wines include the dry Greco di Tufo and the almond-scented Fiano di Avellino. The red Taurasi, made from the historic Aglianico grape, benefits from wood aging and must be at least three years old before release; Taurasi Riserva must have four.

Off Campania's coast, surrounded by blue waters, lies Capri. Little original Capri wine is available, and most of it is used by the islanders themselves. More often than not, what we get is wine from the neighboring island of Ischia, where Ischia Rosso and Ischia Bianco are produced.

Basilicata is nestled in the arch of Italy's boot and offers just one D.O.C. wine from its meager resources. The Aglianico del Vulture is produced on the volcanic slopes of Monte Vulture, and when young is a pleasant, dry, red table wine. When aged, especially for the five years required to make it a *riserva*, it becomes deep, full, and can last for a decade or more.

APULIA AND ABRUZZI

One of the most prolific wine-growing regions is Apulia, or Puglia in Italian. Geographically it is the heel of Italy's boot, stretching from Molise and Campania in the north, along the Adriatic Sea, and dipping its peninsular heel in the Ionian Sea.

It produces generous, alcoholic wines because of the great amount of sunshine that bathes the land. This region is known as the wine cellar of Italy, for the wines are commonly shipped to northern Europe for blending with wines with lower alcohol content. As much wine is produced in Apulia as in Piedmont and Lombardy combined. Although there are eighteen D.O.C. wines from Apulia, these wines comprise only 2 percent of its total wine production.

The ever-present Aleatica grape makes wine throughout the region, labeled Aleatica di Puglia. The majority of the red wines are dark in color and high in alcohol, but they often lack acid. A few areas do produce better balanced wines, notably Castel del Monte and San Severo, which are available in red, white, and the particularly popular rosé. The Castel del Monte red and rosé are made from various blends of Uva di Troia, Bombino Nero, Montepulciano, and Sangiovese grapes, while the Bianco is made from mainly Pampanuto and Pampanino grapes with some Trebbiano varieties. San Severo red and rosé are mostly Montepulciano grapes, while the white is mainly Trebbiano Toscano. Locorotondo, a light, still or sparkling wine from the province of Taranto, blends local Verdeca and Bianco d'Alessano grapes for its dry delicate flavor.

Santo Stefano and Torre Quarto, made in the northern province of Foggia from a variety of grapes, are very big red wines that can take years of aging.

The Primitivo, believed to be the ancestor of the United States' Zinfandel, makes multistyled red wines called Primitivo di Manduria.

Experimentation is burgeoning now that Apulia is no longer just exporting nameless wine. Non-local grape varieties, such as Cabernet Franc, Pinot Nero, and Pinot Bianco, have added to Apulia's palette in developing new wines.

To the north of Apulia, the diverse region of Abruzzi follows the Adriatic coastline. Like its people, the wines of Abruzzi are uncomplicated, offering only two types: Montepulciano d'Abruzzo, which includes a big red of the same name and a cherry-colored Cerasuolo, and Trebbiano d'Abruzzo, a white wine well suited to fish. It should be noted that here, as well as in neighboring Apulia, "Montepulciano" is the name of a grape, while in Tuscany it is the name of a town.

Calabria

Here, in a wild country of bare, high mountains and fertile valleys, a country of contrasts, of chilly winds and tropical shores, the vine is cultivated extensively. It produces good local wines of rather high alcohol content. Much *vino da tavola* comes from this section, produced by growers' cooperatives.

The best wine of the region is the Cirò. The white is made from the Greco grape, and the red and rosé from the Gaglioppo grape. The red can be aged. The Gaglioppo grape can also be found in the red wines labeled Donnici and Lamezia.

SICILY

Homer speaks of Sicily as the land where "spontaneous wine from weighty clusters flows." "The Sicilians," said Plato, "build as if they were always to live, and sup as if they never were to sup again." The first to appreciate the enchanting beauty of the island were the English, who practically monopolized the output of Marsala, which produced Lord Nelson's favorite wine.

The most famous geographic feature of Sicily is the sometimes active Mount Etna in the east. Etna wines are produced in the province of Catania, on the slopes of the volcano. Etna Bianco is dry and straw-colored, with medium body. When it comes from the commune of Milo, it may be labeled *superiore* if it achieves a higher minimum alcohol. Etna Rosso is made from red Nerello varieties, and may have up to 10 percent white grapes added to the must. It is dry and full-bodied. Etna Rosato is a lighter, fresher version, a rosé made from the same grapes as Etna Rosso.

One of the famous wines of Italy is Corvo, which has spearheaded the acceptance of Sicilian table wines in the rest of the world. It comes from Casteldaccia, near Palermo in western Sicily. This wine is a development of Duca Salaparuta, whose desire to improve viticulture in Sicily has been achieved. Corvo is a fine dry wine, both red and white, with much character of the fire of Sicily.

From the province of Ragusa comes a full-bodied red, Cerasuolo di Vittorio. It is dry and has at least 13 percent alcohol.

Bianco d'Alcamo, produced in the northwest in the province of Trapani is a dry, fresh white wine.

New cooperatives in the major wine areas are enjoying modern technology in both viticulture and winemaking practices, and are producing many light, fresh table wines for contemporary tastes.

Sicily is famous for Marsala. Marsala is a fortified wine

obtained from the Catarrato, Grillo, and Inzolia grapes. It comes from the provinces of Trapani, Palermo, and Agrigento. Concentrates are used to vary the style, which can be dry, semidry, sweet, or very sweet. Volcanic soil gives Marsala an acid undertone that is similar to Madeira.

Many sweet dessert wines are made in the western part of the island from the Zibibbo, which is a variety of the Moscato di Allessandria grape.

The Moscato Passito di Pantelleria, produced on the island of Pantelleria, has an amber color, rich bouquet, and sweet flavor. The minimum alcohol is 15 percent, and the wine is usually served chilled.

SARDINIA

The cork, the olive, and the vine grow well on the island of Sardinia. The wines are mostly heady, liquorous, and strong. Like nearby Sicily, Sardinia is well known for dessert wines, but modernization of the industry is creating good table wines.

Cannonau di Sardegna, a hearty red wine, is produced throughout the island. It is available in dry, semisweet, and/or sweet, and a good rosé may also be made from the same grapes. Monica di Sardegna is a lighter red wine, made from grapes of the same name throughout the island.

Nuragus di Cagliari is a straw-colored table wine. Vernaccia di Oristano, from the same grape found in Tuscany, is also a straw-colored wine, but with a hint of almond in the bouquet.

Moscato di Cagliari and Malvasia di Bosa are two white dessert wines with the characteristic flavor of the grape varieties from which they are made, while the Cirò di Cagliari is a red dessert wine on the order of port.

WINES OF
AUSTRIA

Although Austria's history of winemaking goes back to Roman times, the history golden age of viniculture took place shortly after the Turks occupied neighboring Hungary in the 1500s, as Hungary ceased to produce wine during that period. Vine plantings increased greatly in Austria, and it is estimated that the total vineyards acreage was five to ten times what it is now.

One law, passed during Maria Theresa's (d. 1780) reign, led to a tradition that still prevails today. The winemaker was allowed to sell his own wine without having to pay any taxes on it. A hanging branch above his doorway signified to passersby that the owner had new wine to sell. This started the tradition of the *Heurige*, which occurs every year in the countryside around Vienna. Both local residents and tourists rush to purchase the new wine.

There are many wine regions in the eastern part of Austria, but the ones that are seen in this country are Wachau, Vienna, Südbahn, Burgenland, and Styria.

The vast Wachau region is northwest of Vienna, with vineyards along the Danube River, south of the Alpine ranges. This cool area, coupled with minerals in the soil, produces wines that are high in acid, crisp and elegant. The best resemble the Rieslings of Germany. Schluck is the important wine from the Sylvaner. The main towns are Krems, Dürnstein, Stein, and Loiben.

Vienna is the smallest wine growing region in Austria, producing mainly white wine, from the Grüner Veltliner and Neuberger grapes. The most famous wine producing suburbs are Grinzing, Nussdorf, and Klosterneuburg.

South of Vienna is the Südbahn region, where the famous Gumpoldskirchner vineyards lie. Baden and Vöslau are two other towns in this region, the latter producing a red table wine called Vöslau Rotwein.

Farther to the south and to the east is the Burgenland district, with extensive plantings around a large lake, the Neusiedler See. Some wines are produced from the

Furmint grape, which also grows in neighboring Hungary. The towns of Rust and Oggau produce red and white wines, with late-harvest wines a specialty of Rust. Since there is sandy soil that is not hospitable to *Phylloxera*, many of these wines are made from ungrafted vines.

Finally, the southern region of Styria, which borders Yugoslavia, is warm, and has a dry, clay soil. The wines are mostly white, and consumed locally.

Austrian grapes are a combination of native *vinifera* vines, the Furmint of Hungary, the Kadarka of the Balkan countries, and other, more famous, varieties that have taken Austrian names. Of the native varieties the Grüner Veltliner and Neuberger produce white wines, while the Rotgipfler is used for both white and red wines. Of the more familiar varieties, the Rheinriesling (Riesling), Traminer, Sylvaner, Müller-Thurgau, Wälschriesling, Ruländer (Pinot Gris), and Muskat-Ottonel are used to make the majority of white wines, which amount to 90 percent of the total production.

The Blauburgunder, or Spätburgunder (Pinot Noir), Blaufränkisch (Gamay), Blauer Portugieser, and Muskat Saint Laurent are the principal grapes used to make red wines.

Although Austria is a large producer of wine, averaging 80 million gallons annually, the per capita consumption is also very large, 9½ gallons, and Austria does not produce enough wine for its needs and must import large quantities, mostly red wines. Some of the more famous whites, however, are exported in small quantities. These include Gumpoldskirchner, Kremser, Klosterneuburger, and Ruster.

WINES OF HUNGARY

TOKAY

When we think of Hungary and wine, we think first of Tokay.* For generations only royalty could obtain the few bottles of Tokay produced each year, so it came to be known as a royal wine. The finest vineyards in the heart of the district belonged to the royal household, and Emperor Franz Joseph made the princely gesture of sending Queen Victoria a gift of Tokay every year on her birthday, a dozen bottles for each year of her age. Year by year, as the queen grew older, the present augmented in size, until on her eighty-first birthday, in 1900, the emperor sent 972 bottles of that rare wine, Tokaji Aszú, which Professor Saintsbury called "no more a wine but a prince of liqueurs."

*Tokay is the name of an American dessert wine. However, it has come to be the Americanized name of the wines from the Tokaj area in Hungary. Because the use of Tokay with regard to Hungarian wines has become so widespread, we bow to that common usage, and henceforth in this section the wines of Tokaj will be called Tokay.

The letter *i* affixed to the name of a town means "from." For example, an Aszú wine from Tokaj would be labeled Tokaji Aszú.

The wines commonly called Tokay derive their name from the small village of Tokaj in the Hegyalja country (northeastern Hungary) at the foot of the Carpathian Mountains. The delimited Tokaj district is a small plateau, less than half the size of New York City, around which rise the Carpathians. Although this district is fifteen hundred feet above sea level, the protecting mountains produce a special condition that makes possible extremes of weather highly beneficial to growing the grape. These climates vary from bitterly cold winters, accompanied by howling winds, to cool, dry weather in the spring, to very hot summer weather. The rains of early fall give way to a fine, dry Indian summer, important for the grapes, which are left hanging on the vine for extra maturing. The soil is rich in iron and contains some lime. It is of volcanic origin, and the dominant rock of the region is trachyte.

The most important grape in Tokay is the Furmint. Young Furmint grapes are quite thick skinned, but as they ripen the skin becomes thinner and more transparent. The sun penetrates it, evaporating most of the water in the juice, with a consequent concentration of the natural sugar. Sometimes the grapes that ripen earliest are so full of juice that the skin bursts and some of the juice runs out. Oddly enough, a new skin forms over the crack and the grapes do not rot, as would normally happen. The grapes are allowed to hang on the vine until they develop *pourriture noble*. They are called Trockenbeeren.

The combination of the grapes, which may also include Hárslevelü and the Muskotály, the minerals in the soil, the climatic conditions, and the special manner in which the grapes are treated is unique to the Hungarian Tokaj-Hegyalja. For this reason no other wine-producing region has been able to imitate Tokay. (Tokay grapes, said to have originated in Algeria, are no relation to the Furmint but are table grapes that are sometimes used to make a rather characterless wine that has no relation to the Tokay of Hungary.)

To make Tokay, the grapes are gathered in wooden vessels known as *puttonos*, which hold about 30 quarts. The universal measure in the Hegyalja is the *gönci hordó*, or "cask from Gönc," which holds 120 to 140 liters (about 30 to 35 gallons). It is the number of *puttonos* of overripe Furmint grapes per *gönc* cask that determines the quality and richness of the Tokay.

There are three main types of Tokay: Szamorodni, Aszú, and Eszencia.

Szamorodni. This wine is made in much the same way as any other white wine, in the lower sections of the plateau where the grapes do not shrivel and in those years when weather conditions have not been favorable for the Trockenbeeren. Szamorodni is an excellent dry wine, with a "fresh-bread-crust" flavor. It is a full-blown wine, with an alcoholic strength of 14 percent. In years when there are not enough Trockenbeeren to make a commercial quantity of Aszú, they are pressed with the other grapes and a sweet Szamorodni results.

Aszú. When one considers that the average yield of all the vines in the Tokaj-Hegyalja is only 2,650,000 gallons and that Aszú wine represents less than 1 percent, it is apparent that this wine is extremely rare.

In making Aszú (very rich Tokay), the Trockenbeeren are first kneaded into a pulp in a trough. Then the proper proportion of must, pressed from ordinarily ripened grapes, is poured over the pulp, and the mixture is stirred at intervals. The wine is racked after twelve to forty-eight hours of fermentation. In the gone cask, where the bung hole is not tightly closed, a slow fermentation-oxidation proceeds for several years in cool surroundings.

It is the number of *puttonos* of Trockenbeeren (overripe Furmint) that determines the quality of the wine. The wines are labeled three, four, or five *puttonos* in accordance with the number of *puttonos* of overripe Furmint grapes added to the must. Three Puttonos contains about 30 percent Trockenbeeren; Four Puttonos contains about 40 percent; and Five Puttonos, the richest and finest quality that we see in this country, contains about 50 percent Trockenbeeren. Aszú wines are not made every year, only when the vintage is moderately successful.

P. Morton Shand relates Robert Druitt as saying that "Tokay has a flavor of green tea, but an amalgam of the scents of meadow-sweet, acacia-blossom, and the lime-tree in flower, rendered perceptible to the palate . . . is possibly somewhere nearer the mark. No wine possesses such a tremendous force and volume of flavor."

It is the natural sweetness and natural high alcohol content, often exceeding 14 percent, that raise Tokaji Aszú wine so high in the estimation of wine lovers.

Eszencia, **Essenz**, or **Essence**. In exceptionally successful and plentiful years only Trockenbeeren are put in a cask. The juice that collects without any pressure other than the weight of the Trockenbeeren is allowed to ferment apart and is called Eszencia. This is a fabulous wine that takes years to develop and will live for centuries. There were Eszencias, notably in Poland, over 200 years old. A newspaper account of the marriage of the president of Poland in 1933 reported that toasts were made with 250-year-old wine: "The wine, if good, could only have been Essence of Tokay, and the centuries-old friendship between Poland and Hungary would seem to support this conclusion."

Very little Eszencia is ever made. It is rare and almost unprocurable, as what little is produced is used mostly for enriching the Aszús of poorer years.

How and When to Serve Tokay

Dry Szamorodni should be served well chilled. With its

full-bodied dryness it makes an excellent apéritif or all-around table wine.

Sweet Szamorodni may be served at room temperature or cooled. It can be used as any sweet white wine is, but it is more properly a dessert wine.

Aszús have a ripe, luscious quality and should be slightly cooled. They are "serf wines of the first order, but they are more often enjoyed by themselves. A small glass is often one of the most tonic and wholesome restoratives one can take.

Tokay wines spend three or four years in cask, and can develop even further in the bottle. They usually appear as vintage wines, with the number of *puttonos* stated on the label. While the traditional one-half-liter (500 ml, 17 ounce) long-necked bottle is used throughout the world, the U.S. laws now require the wine to be in a 750 ml bottle.

WINES OF CANADA

The vineyards of Canada can be considered extensions of the vineyards of the northern United States because the areas where grapes can be grown successfully in Canada are contiguous to American regions.

Canada is a very small producer, making about as much wine as the island of Cyprus, or about fifteen million gallons annually.

Canada's first vineyard and winery were established in 1811 by John Schiller in Ontario province. Generally, Canada's winemaking history parallels that of the United States, with a period of Prohibition for each country at about the same time. Both countries also planted experimental grapevines at about the same time.

In the eastern regions of Canada grapes are planted on the southwest shore of Lake Ontario and the northern shore of Lake Erie, in the Niagara Peninsula, which is in the province of Ontario. The mitigating effects of Lakes Erie and Ontario on the climate temper the winters and cool the summers. *Labruscana* grape varieties such as Concord, Niagara, Elvira, Agawam, Fredonia, and Catawba are planted, as are French hybrids such as De Chaunac, Maréchal Foch, and Baco Noir. Some *vinifera* grapes have been successful in small amounts; these include Chardonnay, Riesling, Gewürztraminer, Gamay Beaujolais, and Pinot Noir. Seventy-five percent of all Canadian wine is made in this area of the Great Lakes.

In the western part of the country the Okanagan Valley, in the province of British Columbia, produces the balance of Canada's wines. The seventy-five-mile-long Okanagan Lake lessens the effects of the low winter temperatures.

Even so, it is Concord and Thompson Seedless grapes that are planted in large quantities. Hardy Rieslings and other *vinifera* varieties are little more than experimental plantings. Much wine made in this region is blended with wine made from grapes that are harvested in California and trucked north for vinification.

Both eastern and western Canadian wineries produce table wines, baked and *flor* sherries, ports, and Tokays. Some wines are not vintage dated because of the need to blend for uniformity and quality.

Wine practices are controlled by individual provinces. The only way wines may be purchased anywhere in Canada is in a government-owned liquor store or in a restaurant. A small amount of wine is exported; most is consumed locally.

WINES OF ARGENTINA

Argentina is the largest producer of wine in the Western Hemisphere, ranking fifth among world producers. Only Italy, France, Spain, and the U.S.S.R.* outrank it. The country's vineyard acreage is over 750,000, about 15 percent more than that of California, but because the average yield per acre is almost double that of California, Argentina ranks much higher in total production, which is over 700 million gallons per year.

The earliest known vineyards in Argentina were planted in 1556 by the Jesuit Father Cedron in the Mendoza region. The variety planted was the Mission grape, called the *Criollo de vino* in Argentina. The later missionaries who brought the grape to South America belonged to the same religious order as those who brought the grape to California.

*Since production varies from year to year, there are some years when Argentina produces more wine than the U.S.S.R., and it then moves to fourth place in world production.

It was the Italian immigrants, arriving in Argentina during the latter part of the nineteenth century, who established the present wine-producing areas, methods, and grape varieties. Like their relatives who went to California, they worked hard, irrigated the land, and converted arid areas into magnificent grape- and fruit-producing regions. Finding that the grape had been cultivated with success since the establishment of the missions by the Spanish explorers, these settlers naturally paid attention to the expansion of vineyards and the production of wine. This activity, coupled with the Buenos Aires-Mendoza railway link, completed in 1884, turned wine-making into a viable industry.

The three principal wine regions of Argentina, all lying in the South Temperate Zone, are in the provinces of Mendoza, San Juan, and Rio Negro. Here spring is from October to December, summer is from January to March, fall is from April to June, and winter is from July to September.

Mendoza lies in the west, on the Chilean border, and is the "California Great Central Valley" of Argentina. It is only in the last hundred years that the province has been developed. Mendoza was a vast, arid, sandy desert, showing green patches only along the banks of the several rivers that cut through in draining off the melting Andean snows. Today Mendoza accounts for 70 percent of Argentina's total annual wine production and 90 percent of its table wine production.

The province of San Juan lies immediately north of Mendoza and has similar soil conditions, irrigation being always necessary. Because climatic conditions are on the whole somewhat hotter, the San Juan vineyards are the source of dessert wines, wines for vermouth production, and almost all the table or eating grapes, as well as the magnificent raisins that are available in such profusion in Argentina's public markets. San Juan also produces some very pleasant table wines that enjoy wide popularity. This province produces about 20 percent of Argentina's wine.

In the province of Rio Negro, south of Mendoza, the climate is comparable to the Champagne and German wine regions of Europe. Here are produced some of Argentina's best white table and sparkling wines. The quantities produced are small, from 3 to 5 percent of the country's total production. Very little, if any, irrigation is required in Rio Negro, and the soil is less sandy, being more argillaceous and containing sections that are quite chalky in character.

While some wine is produced in practically every province of Argentina, all that is produced outside the three principal provinces does not amount to more than 5 percent of the country's total annual production. In the mountainous Cordoba province there is a small region around Villa Dolores where interesting wine is produced. The quantity is small but both the red and the white are uniformly good—fruity, full bodied, and well balanced. They are wines of character.

Argentina's vineyards, like those of other wine regions, have suffered from and been subjected to attack from various diseases, such as downy mildew, *oïdium* ("powdery mildew"), and *Phylloxera*, which have ravaged vineyards, particularly in Mendoza and San Juan.

In Mendoza and San Juan the wines generally are made on a mass-production basis similar to the methods used in the large wineries of California. A dozen or so giants of the wine industry control about a quarter of the annual production. Some of the largest wineries and wine cellars in the world are found in Mendoza.

The viticultural and vinicultural experiment station that forms part of the University of Cuyo at Mendoza has made significant contributions to the advances and modernization of winemaking in Argentina.

The *vinifera* varieties are cultivated exclusively for

commercial wine production and are controlled by government regulation. Varieties permitted for red table wines are the Criolla, Malbec, Cabernet Sauvignon, Barbera, Petite Sirah, Pinot Noir, Tempranilla, Merlot, Sangiovese, and Lambrusco. For white table wines permitted grapes are the Criolla, Sauvignon Blanc, Sémillon, Chardonnay, Pinot Blanc, Riesling, and Trebbiano. Fortified and dessert wines are made from the Pedro Ximenez, Muscat of Alexandria, and Malvasia varieties.

The Criolla grape is the most widely planted grape in Argentina, and it is used for both red and white wines.

All classes and types of wines are produced in Argentina, and almost all of them are consumed there. The largest portion of the market is wines made from a blend of the wines of the Criolla, Malbec, and Barbera grapes.

Premium wines are emerging both for local consumption and for export. Labels indicating varietal wines, such as Cabernet Sauvignon, and labels indicating age, such as Gran Reserve or Viejo ("old"), are appearing on the market, with the definition of some of these terms being up to the producer. Aging often takes place in French oak casks.

A number of the leading wine houses also produce sparkling wines by all the methods known in the wine trade. Argentine Champagne may be made by the traditional bottle-fermented method; by the transfer process; by the Charmat, or bulk-fermentation, process; or by artificial carbonation. Sparkling rosé is also produced, generally by the Charmat method. Champagnes are labeled Brut, Extra Brut, Sec, Demi Sec, and Dulce, in ascending order of sweetness. The Argentines prefer the sweeter types. Pinot Noir, Chardonnay, Chenin Blanc, and Ugni Blanc are the most common varieties used to make the *cuvée*. Sherry and port wines of very satisfactory quality are offered, but the Muscatels of San Juan are of superior quality—comparable, in fact, to the Muscatel wines of the Mediterranean islands. These wines do not contain more than 16 percent alcohol.

Argentina is one of the largest consumers of vermouth, where one brand alone markets over 2 million cases a year of the 3½ million sold. Vermouth is consumed almost entirely as an apéritif, served on the rocks or with a dash of soda and a dash or two of Italian-style bitters.

Argentine table wines are well made, and most compare favorably with everyday drinking wines produced elsewhere. In Argentina wine is part of the diet. In every restaurant, whether it be the finest luxury establishment or a simple workers' eating place, there is wine on every table, while in the home it is always found on the host's table as well as the servants'. It is served as a matter of course, as coffee or soft drinks are served in the United States. The people of Argentina drink over twenty gallons of wine per capita each year.

There has been little Argentine wine for export, but

a few importers have begun to bring in the finer premium wines from Mendoza. The local preference has always been for soft, well-matured, nonacid wines; but the Argentine drive for greater acceptance in the world market has caused producers to modify their winemaking techniques and produce a bouquet and taste more similar to the fresher, drier wines preferred in Europe and America.

WINES OF AUSTRALIA

Grape cultivation in Australia began with Captain Arthur Phillip, who brought vine cuttings with his first fleet of eleven ships, when he arrived to found the penal colony of New South Wales in 1788. His cuttings came from Rio de Janeiro and the Cape of Good Hope, which had been stops along the way. Unfortunately his three acres of vineyards were attacked by fungus.

Three other pioneers made their mark on Australian winemaking during the nineteenth century. They were Gregory Blaxland, John MacArthur, and James Busby.

In 1816 Blaxland planted red-wine grapes, which he had obtained from the Cape of Good Hope, on his farm in Parramatta Valley.

John MacArthur and his two sons planted a commercially successful vineyard near Penrith in New South Wales and were producing twenty thousand gallons of wine annually by 1827.

James Busby, often called the father of Australian

viticulture, arrived in Australia in 1824 from his native Scotland. He was given a grant to teach viticulture and to organize an agricultural institute. His main contributions were writing two treatises on planting vines and on making wine and collecting and planting 678 varieties of vines from France, Luxembourg, England, and Spain.

Many other *vignerons* planted in the 1800s, with their growing areas widespread throughout southern Australia. The first development was in the Hunter Valley in New South Wales, closely followed by South Australia, and Victoria. From the late 1800s to the 1960s, most wines produced were fortified for home consumption and export to the United Kingdom. Table wine production was isolated, and it was mainly red wine.

During the last twenty years or so, there has been an era of growth and change unknown in Australia's earlier viticultural history. This was due to several factors. The first was the postwar migration of people from many

European countries, bringing with them a taste for table wine. As affluence increased in Australia, and travel abroad became more available, there was even more exposure to European lifestyles. This, coupled with increased technology that could produce fresher, lighter wines, created a new interest in wines, especially whites. Today, these are the clear-cut preference for the Australian public.

Australian States

Australian wine areas are spread across the southern part of the continent, for twenty-five hundred miles. These areas vary from warm districts that require irrigation to cooler, high altitude (1500´ to 2000´) regions. The warm areas are warmer and dryer than those of Europe. During the summer, dry conditions help to ensure disease-free crops.

South Australia

South Australia is the premier wine-producing state, providing 60 percent of all wines in the country. The Barossa Valley is the best known winemaking area in Australia. It was originally planted by German settlers, and still shows their influence. Connawarra, in the southeast part of the state, is especially known for its premium red wines.

The Riverland district provides much of the bulk wines of the country, and is one of the biggest wine-producing areas. Southern Vales and Clare-Watervale are historic areas that have made a significant contribution to the reputation of South Australia's wines.

New South Wales

New South Wales was the first state to produce grapes. The famous Hunter Valley actually produces only 1 percent of Australia's wines, but they are of premium varieties. The Murrumbidgee Irrigation Area (M.I.A.) or

"Riverina" supplies about 20 percent of Australia's total vintage. Mudgee is another region in this state, and it is benefiting from new technology. Cowra, still another region, is typical of the newly emerging districts, and is acquiring a reputation as one of Australia's premium Chardonnay areas.

Victoria

Victoria has recently enjoyed an influx of new winemakers and greatly increased production. The Yarra Valley has become known for many small, limited production wineries. North-east Victoria is well known for its fortified muscat and port wines, although good table wines are also produced there. The Goulburn Valley, with Tabilk at its center, has an excellent reputation for its table wines. The central Victorian district has also seen an increase in new wineries, primarily among the smaller winemaking operations. Great Western is the home of one of Australia's major sparkling wine producers, but is also renowned for its long-lived dry red wines. Mildura, in the northwest, produces a great volume of bulk wines.

Western Australia

The Swan Valley, around the city of Perth, has a long history of winemaking. This small enclave on the west coast of Australia, gets a great deal of sunshine, which helps to produce grapes that are rich in sugar and low in acid. Here, again, the area is benefiting from new technology, which has achieved significant refining of table wines. In the southwestern part, the areas around the Margaret River and Mount Barker have a cool climate that imparts strong varietal flavor. They are part of important new wine areas to emerge during the last decade.

Tasmania

In addition, Tasmania, off the coast of Australia, is south

enough of the equator to make its location comparable to fine wine areas of Europe. This area has begun to flourish, with a number of small wineries starting to produce some very fine Rhine Rieslings and Cabernet Sauvignons.

There is so much experimentation of both technology and planting of various grape varieties in different micro-climates, in this growing and expanding industry, that the producers are not ready yet for regulations on appellations. Many producers, in fact, buy grapes from different regions for their blends. The wine trade, at this point, is self-regulating. There are over three hundred wineries in Australia that produce 100 million gallons of wine annually for a 4 gallon per capita consumption.

For export, strict government and industry regulations ensure the highest possible quality. Wines and brandies are inspected by officers of the Department of Customs and Excise, as well as by inspectors appointed by the Australian Wine and Brandy Corporation.

Grape Varieties

There are many different grape varieties grown, all from *vinifera* stock. If a wine is varietally labeled, there must be a minimum of 80 percent of the named grape in the wine. The most prominent grapes are:

Shiraz. This grape is the most widely planted grape for the production of red table wines and fortified wines. In Australia there are over twenty thousand acres of Shiraz grown in virtually all districts. It is sometimes blended with other varieties, notably Cabernet Sauvignon.

Cabernet Sauvignon. As in Bordeaux and California, this is Australia's most sought-after grape. Its acreage has increased dramatically, and there are now over 10,000 acres under cultivation. The Cabernets from Connawarra have been traditionally highly regarded, but there is competition from newly emerging areas.

Merlot and Pinot Noir. These French grapes are not yet planted in large amounts, but they will increase in importance as winemakers learn more about growing and vinifying them.

Grenache. This grape is used in the commercial, bulk wines, but is diminishing in importance. Still second to Shiraz, it has now decreased to 13,000 acres.

Sémillon. This premium variety is widely planted, with over 8,000 acres. It is usually vinified as a full, dry wine, and is sometimes known as the "poor man's Chardonnay."

Rhine Riesling. The Rhine Riesling is the true Riesling of Germany or California. It makes a fruity wine with good acidity in the cooler regions, and a smoother wine with more glycerine in the warmer areas. In some years and areas, it is late picked, sometimes affected by *Botrytis*. It then produces in tensely flavored sweet wines.

Chardonnay. This variety has emerged in the last fifteen years as a premium varietal. It is vinified in either a full, rich style, often aged in oak, or a lighter, fruitier style that is ready to drink sooner.

Sultana and Muscat Gordo Blanco. The Sultana is the Thompson Seedless of California (a table grape) with 45,000 acres planted. It is used for commercial table wines, fortified wines, and for distillation. The Muscat Gordo Blanco is the Muscat of Alexandria. It is used a great deal for cream sherry, but can be fermented dry for table wines. It is grown in over 10,000 acres, and is also used as a table and raisin grape.

Traminer (Gewürztraminer), **Sauvignon Blanc**, and **Chenin Blanc**. These grapes round out Australia's white table wine production, and will most likely emerge as important varietals.

Doradillo, Palomino, and Pedro Ximenez. These grapes used to be important in fortified wine production, but with consumption patterns changing towards lighter, table wines, they are much less useful than before, and acreage is decreasing.

All classes and types of wines are produced in Australia. The wine industry shows great diversity with its fine table and sparkling wines, as well as its impressive fortified wines. The constant experimentation on the part of new winemakers is producing many wine styles.

High technology, combined with low taxes on alcoholic beverages, is creating affordable wines of good quality. Labeling is clear and explicit, and the implication of the various wine districts is becoming clearer to the public.

While many wineries used to use predominantly generic names, such as claret, Burgundy, Chablis, sherry, Sauternes, port, Moselle, etc., now many wines are marketed under district names, such as Barossa, Hunter Valley, Coonawarra—as well as varietal names, such as Cabernet Sauvignon, Shiraz, Pinot Noir, Rhine Riesling, and Chardonnay.

The patterns of production and consumption have been surprisingly similar to those of the United States, and there is a similar "pioneer" spirit as well, in the exploration and development of new wine regions.

WINES OF NEW ZEALAND

The wine industry in New Zealand can be traced directly to Australia in the 1800s, with European influences not appearing until the early 1900s. New Zealand's first winemaker was James Busby, British Resident to Waitangi in 1838. Before that appointment, Busby had already established vineyards in Australia.

Romeo Bragatto, a graduate of Italy's school of viticulture in Conegliano, became New Zealand's first official head of viticulture in the Department of Agriculture in 1902. He urged research on the proper choice of vines for the different regions, and struggled against *Phylloxera*, disease, and mildew. At the same time, Yugoslavian immigrants from Dalmatia entered the wine business. In fact, New Zealand's largest winery, Montana, means "mountain" in Yugoslavian.

Efforts to use resistant varieties led to the changing of *vinifera* varieties to *labruscana* and hybrid varieties, with a consequent reduction in wine quality. This, coupled with new efforts by prohibitionists caused New Zealand's wine industry to dwindle to a few small wineries and home winemakers.

After World War II grape acreage and wine production began to increase, and in 1957 restaurateurs and retailers were licensed to sell single bottles of wine rather than two-gallon lots. From a mere 600 acres in 1940, acreage now stands at 12,000, and 10 million gallons of wine are produced annually. Table wines account for 72 percent, and by 1980 *vinifera* varieties had climbed back up to 85 percent, and hybrids accounted for only 15 percent.

New Zealand is made up of two large islands, North and South. Winemaking in New Zealand began in the warmer north, but the search for good microclimates for various grape varieties has led to large plantings in the cooler south. The newest wine-growing area, Marlborough, is, in fact, at the north end of South Island.

The value of this area for grapes was determined after a thorough survey of the islands in the early 1970s. The Wairau Valley in Marlborough has the highest sunshine hours, low rainfall, temperate climate, and good soil types. These conditions are especially good for crisp, white wines.

On North Island, the most important areas are Poverty Bay in Gisborne and Hawkes Bay, both on the east coast. Auckland, which used to be the largest growing area, has dropped in importance because of high humidity and urban development. Waikato, south of Auckland, is last in acreage.

In an effort to combat *Phylloxera* and continue growing *vinifera* varieties, wines are increasingly being grafted onto resistant rootstock.

White grape varieties account for more than 80 percent of the total plantings. The Riesling-Sylvaner (Müller-Thurgau) accounts for about 30 percent of this. Chardonnay, Gewürztraminer, Sauvignon Blanc, Rhine

(Johannisberg) Riesling, Dr. Hogg Muscat, and some Siebel hybrids complete the list.

Red varieties include Cabernet Sauvignon, Pinot Noir, and Pinotage (a cross between Pinot Noir and Cinsaut), and Shiraz.

Fortified wines have declined to 28 percent, and the thrust is for premium varietals.

WINES OF CHINA

The first vines in China came from the Arabs in Turkestan in the late second century B.C. By the seventh century A.D. vines were widespread. One major setback came in 1322, when vines were uprooted by order of the emperor so that cereals and grains could be planted. Even though some vines were replanted, to this day more beer and rice wine is produced and consumed than grape wine. Recently, however, some agricultural experimental stations have been studying the vine, and cooperative vineyards are becoming more important.

Grapes are grown in the region around old Turkestan, called Turfan. They are also grown north of the Yangtze River and south of the Great Wall. Five provinces along the Yellow River—Shantung, Honan, Kiangsu, Hopeh, and Shansi—are growing grapes successfully. Some vines are also planted around Beijing (Peking).

The grapes that grow in China include some native Asian stock, such as the early ripening Kashikar and the late ripening Koumiss, and some *labruscanas*. *Vinifera* varieties include Muscat, the Dimiat of Bulgaria, Riesling, and Sylvaner. Grapes are used for wine, table grapes and raisins, and medicine.

White, rosé, and red wines (*p'u t'ao chiu*) that go up to 16 percent alcohol are produced. A sweet wine called Chefoo is available in red and white. A dry wine called Tsingtao is also available in red and white from the Shantung province in northern China. Sparkling wines (*ba-xiangpin-chiu*) are also made. In addition to grapes, sweet wines are made from plums and litchis. Shaohsing and Hua Tian are dry rice wines.

WINES OF JAPAN

The wine industry is small in Japan, with production averaging 6 million gallons a year. Native varieties of grapes, the Koshu and Jaraku, have been planted since the twelfth century. They are believed to have European origins that go very far back. In the nineteenth century Americans and Europeans brought in *labruscana* grapes, such as Concord, Delaware, Campbell Early, and Baily A, a Muscat hybrid. Some *vinifera* grapes were also introduced, including Sémillon, Chardonnay, Riesling, Cabernet Sauvignon, and Merlot.

The main island of Honshu contains the two most important wine-growing regions, although grapes are grown to the north and to the south. The main regions are the Kōfu Valley and the Osaka Valley, and the acreage equals more than half of Japan's total acreage under vine. Japan is generally quite humid, but on Honshu Island the humidity is lower and the grapes have a better chance against fungus, *oïdium*, and mildew.

Other wines are produced on the island of Hokkaido in the north and at Katsunuma in Yamanashi province west of Tokyo.

As in China, wines are made from native, *labruscana*, and *vinifera* grapes. Problems with humidity and with acid soil, however, produce wines that are astringent and unbalanced. Torrential rains around harvest time point up the need for early-ripening varieties. Sugaring wines is quite common, and many more sweet and fortified wines are produced than table wines.

Because the most popular imported wines are French reds and German whites, the finest Japanese *vinifera* wines have French or German labels. Phrases such as *Vin Blanc*, *Vin Rouge*, or *Mise au Château* are not uncommon.

PINEAPPLE WINE

Pineapple wine is made in Hawaii and Puerto Rico. In

Hawaii the wine is made from juice obtained from pineapple processing plants. It is then fermented at the winery and, when completed, does not have a strong pineapple taste. Some sparkling pineapple wine is also made.

A very fruity pineapple wine is made in Puerto Rico from the red Spanish pineapple. It is fortified with pineapple brandy and has a beautiful golden color and tart pineapple character.

Saké

The word *saké* means "the essence of the spirit of rice." Saké, made from rice, is a specialized form of beer. Saké is produced in Japan, and a small amount is made in Hawaii and California. It is not a spirit; it is not a wine.* Because of its high alcohol content, and because it looks like wine,

*The U.S. Government, in the Standards of Identity for Wine, lists saké in Class 6, wine from other agricultural products.

many people call it Japanese rice wine. Unlike beer, as we know it, saké is almost colorless and quite still. It has none of the carbon dioxide that is in creamy beers.

The preparation of saké is unique to brewing. Polished rice is soaked in water for about twelve hours, and then steamed in a *koshiki*, a rice-steaming tub. Some steamed rice is treated with a culture of a special spore, *Aspergillus oryzae*, which produces an enzyme that converts the starch in the rice to sugar. This step takes about thirty-five hours and produces a culture called *koji* that is rich in this enzyme.

In order to develop the fermenting yeast culture, some *koji* is added to a thin paste of steamed rice and water, with a small amount of yeast starter. The yeast begins to multiply slowly, feeding on the sugar produced by the *koji*. After two to three weeks, the mash becomes a fully ripened *moto*. Finally, the *moto*, more *koji*, and water are slowly added to freshly steamed rice, and alcoholic fermentation begins. The quality of finished saké, by the way, is determined by the amount that the rice has been polished down in size, getting closer to the heart of the kernel. The finest saké is made from rice that has been polished down to 50 percent of its original size. Most sakés are made from 70 percent rice. A combined process of two conversions, starch-to-sugar and sugar-to-alcohol, now occurs in a single vat. Sakés are generally fermented at 60 degrees Fahrenheit for about three weeks. The best sakés are fermented for about four weeks, at 50 degrees Fahrenheit. When fermentation is complete, the liquor, now saké, is drawn off, filtered, allowed to settle, and then run into casks to mature for a short period. Finally the saké is pasteurized before being bottled or casked. While sakés are graded as Special, First-, and Second-Grade, this grade does not appear on export labels.

Saké is quite strong for a brewed beverage, usually having 14 to 18 percent alcohol by volume. It has a slightly sweet first taste and a dry aftertaste. Traditionally, saké is served warm because heating releases its heady bouquet.

To warm saké, place the opened bottle in a pot of boiling water. Remove it when the saké is about 100 to 105 degrees Fahrenheit. To serve saké in the Japanese manner, decant the warm saké into small ceramic bottles, called *tokkuri*, and then pour it into tiny porcelain bowls, called *sakazaki* which hold a little more than an ounce. Saké should be sipped from these bowls.

Saké may also be drunk at room temperature, chilled, or on the rocks, with assorted mixers. It can be used to replace the vermouth in Martinis.

Rum is a potable spirit, suitably aged in wood, obtained from the distillation of a fermented mash of sugarcane juice or molasses. Examples are Jamaican rum, Demeraran rum, Barbados rum, Martinique rhum, Cuban ron, Puerto Rican ron, Haitian rhum, Philippine ron, Batavia arak, and others.

BRANDIES

Brandy is a potable spirit, suitably aged in wood, that is obtained from the distillation of wine or a fermented mash of fruit. An alcoholic beverage answering this description may be produced in any part of the world.

BRANDIES OF FRANCE

The art of distillation, although known to the ancients, was not applied to wine commercially until the sixteenth century, when the brandy trade began. Supposedly, a brisk trade in wine existed between the port of La Rochelle, on the Charente River in France, and Holland. All of this trade was carried on by sea, and the perils of war placed a premium on shipping.

Casks of wine take up quite a lot of space, particularly on small sailing vessels. The story is told of one very bright Dutch shipmaster who hit upon the idea of concentrating the wine—eliminating the water—and transporting the spirit, or the "soul," of the wine to Holland, where the water could be put back. In his thrifty mind he figured that he could save an enormous amount on the freight charges.

When this enterprising man arrived in Holland, however, with his "concentrated wine," his Dutch friends tasted it and liked it as it was. It would be a waste of water, they decided, to try to make it wine again. And thus the brandy trade had its inception. The Dutch called the new product *brandewijn* ("burned wine"), presumably because fire, or heat, is used in the process of distillation. In time this term was Anglicized to the present-day word—*brandy*.

Cognac

When we say brandy, we usually mean the delightful "soul" of wine. There is one brandy that the world has accepted and recognized as superior to all others: Cognac. It is important to understand that all Cognac is brandy, but all brandies are not Cognac. Cognac is a brandy distilled from wines made of grapes grown within the legal limits of the Charente and Charente-Maritime departments of France.

The ancient city of Cognac, on the Charente River, is in the heart of the district that produces the brandies that have carried its fame throughout the world. In fact, they have done the job so well that *Cognac* is one of the best-known French words in the world.

The quality that makes Cognac superior to all other brandies is not only the special process of distillation that has been used in this district for centuries, but also the combination of ideal soil, climate, and other conditions. While it might be possible for another section to reproduce one or two of these essentials, the combination of all the factors cannot be achieved elsewhere.

The Charentais, or Cognac district, has seven subdivisions, or *crus*, but the last two are often combined. This explains why some references list only six.

Subdivision	Rank	Acres Under Cultivation
Grande Champagne (Grande Fine Champagne)	1st *Cru*	32,250
Petite Champagne (Petite Fine Champagne)	2nd *Cru*	40,310
Borderies	3rd *Cru*	10,200
Fins Bois	4th *Cru*	94,230
Bons Bois	5th *Cru*	44,630
Bois Ordinaires }	6th *Cru*	7,380
Bois Communs }		

The entire Cognac region was delimited by law in 1909; the seven subdivisions, in 1936. The Grande Champagne is a small district that is the kernel of the region. In it lies the town of Cognac, around which everything centers: the territory, the commerce, and the fame of the product. Almost completely surrounding it is the Petite Champagne. To the north, and situated at about the point where the encirclement of the Grande Champagne is incomplete, is the smallest district, the Borderies. Completely surrounding these first three districts are the Fins Bois. Around all these are the Bons Bois, and advancing from the Bons Bois to the Atlantic Ocean in the west are the Bois Ordinaires and the Bois Communs or "Bois Communs dit a Terroir."

Actually, in 1918 two maps were drawn to define the region. One map was done by local geologists, and the other by a committee of tasters. Both maps came out the same, confirming the significance of the soil.

In Cognac the small farmer may have his own still. Big shippers very often own a vineyard or two but they cannot possibly own the amount of vineyard land they would need to take care of the worldwide demand for their brands.

It is the custom in Cognac, therefore, for all shippers to buy the brandy from the farmer. Each farmer has his little vineyard, gathers his grapes, makes his wine, and distills it as soon as it falls bright or has it distilled for him by one of the regional distillers. Distillation of brandy in France, and especially in Cognac, is supervised by government inspectors. At vintage time the inspectors visit each farm, measure the wine, and thereafter control the amount of brandy that each farmer may distill.

The subsoil in Cognac is chalky, and the more chalk, the more suitable are the wines produced for making Cognac. The two Champagne heartland regions have the highest amounts of chalk. Outside the Champagne area the chalky layer becomes shallower, while the earthy top layer becomes deeper. The Bois are so named because they used to be covered with woods, whose life cycle added to the soil layer. The Atlantic Ocean and the Gironde River modify the variations in temperature and help maintain humidity levels favorable to the production of Cognac.

In 1936 French law decreed that wines that produce Cognac should be made from Folle Blanche, Saint-Émilion, and Colombard grapes, with up to 10 percent permitted to be made from other white grapes. Since then,

Saint-Émilion, also known as Ugni Blanc, has emerged as the predominant variety because of its high yield of wines that are low in alcohol, about 8 percent, and high in acid. It is this type of wine, thin and unpleasant to drink, that produces the best Cognac. Cognac, by law, may be produced only from white grapes.

The grapes are picked, pressed, and allowed to ferment; skins, pips, and all are necessary to give the full character to the brandy.

The wine is brought to the distilleries in modern tankers. This wine often contains the lees of fermentation. Some producers allow the wine to settle before it enters the still to remove the lees; others prefer to leave a small amount of lees for extra flavor. The stills are old-fashioned, copper pot stills, or alembics. Copper is used because it is resistant to the lengthy contact with acid wine. There are no patent stills permitted in Cognac.

Distillation begins in a simple boiler, heated directly

by a coal or wood fire. On top of the boiler is a metal hood to collect the vapors produced from an initial batch of wine put into the boiler. These vapors travel through a thin, curved tube, which leads them to a preheating chamber, known as the *chauffe-vin*. Remaining in the tube, the hot vapors preheat the wine, placed in the *chauffe-vin*, which is to be distilled. From the *chauffe-vin* this warmed wine now enters the boiler. The vapors, having given up some of their heat in the *chauffe-vin*, give up the rest of their heat in a condensing coil, which is surrounded by cold water. The vapors have now become a liquid, and it trickles out into a receiving pan. All of the metal used in a still of this type is pure copper.

The conversion of the wine into *eau-de-vie de Charente* is accomplished in two operations, the *première chauffe* and the *bonne chauffe*, which are ingeniously connected. In the *première chauffe* the first vapors that are distilled from the boiling wine are the heads, and they are collected separately, to be added back to a subsequent *première chauffe*. The middle distillate, or *brouillis*, is collected for use in the second distillation, known as the *bonne chauffe*. The alcohol content of the *brouillis* is 24 to 32 percent. What remains in the boiler, and what comes off with little alcohol, is called the tails. This, like the heads, is put back into the next *première chauffe* with a new lot of wine.

When enough *brouillis* have been collected, the *bonne chauffe* distillation begins. As before, the first vapors to come off, the heads, are collected separately and added back to the *première chauffe*. The middle-range vapors, or heart, will become Cognac. These vapors are condensed at an average of 70 percent alcohol. The next distillate, now called seconds, varies in alcoholic strength from 50 percent to around 5 percent. This is put back in the *bonne chauffe* with additional *brouillis* for further distillation. The last part, from 5 percent to no alcohol at all, is again known as tails, and goes back into a *première chauffe*. Hand regulation of all steps is the key to traditional Cognac production. Most important are uniform procedures, evenness of heating, and precise control of the separation of distillates and the quantities produced. The alembics work continuously, twenty-four hours a day, seven days a week, during the distilling season, which starts in November and lasts from three to five months—perhaps six months if there is a large harvest. All distilling must be completed by April 30.

With so many different people carrying out this process of distillation, it stands to reason that some sell directly to various shippers, who examine and taste the new brandy. Others are part of a large cooperative that buys either grapes or wine from the farmers, and then distills and matures it.

Right out of the still, the distillate is colorless and has a sharp, but fruity, coppery bouquet and taste. The coppery character, *gout de cuivre*, passes after the brandy has been in wood for a year.

Cognac is aged in casks made of Limousin oak obtained from the forest near Limoges. After the first year the brandy is transferred from new casks to old ones to prevent the brandy from absorbing too much tannin from the wood. The cooperage must stand up for forty to fifty years. The casks are laid away in many cellars or warehouses to guard against fire loss.

In the cask the Cognac changes by action of the wood and by contact with the oxygen in the air that enters through the pores of the wood. In the same way that the air enters, the brandy evaporates.

There is a continual yearly loss in volume that amounts to 15 percent of the world's annual consumption. As the alcohol evaporates more rapidly than the water and other constituents of the brandy in the humid atmosphere around Cognac, there is a corresponding diminution of strength. It is rapid during the first few years and becomes more gradual after that, the average being about 2 percent a year. This loss of proof is considered essential to the proper development of Cognac. During this time the brandy gradually changes from a colorless state, taking on a beautiful amber tone, and the taste and perfume are changed, so that what finally results is a finished Cognac, a delicate mellow essence with a natural bouquet of grapes.

Today the demand is for a standard of quality that remains the same year in and year out. This requires large stocks being held by the brandy merchant as well as judicious and exact blending.

This *coupage*, or blending, is done many months before bottling. The various brandies are put into tremendous oak vats and are brought down to shipping strength—40 to 43 percent alcohol as required—by the addition of distilled water or diluted brandy. Coloring matter (caramel) is added to ensure uniform color in every bottle.

Inside these vats wooden propellerlike paddles rotate from time to time, mixing the brandies. After several months the blend thoroughly "married," is put in bottles, cased, and is ready for market.

The French government has passed laws to protect the public as to what is and is not Cognac. Every consignment travels with a certificate, called an *Acquit Régional Jaune d'Or*, which guarantees that the product comes from Cognac; it has nothing to do with age.

The various qualities of Cognacs are often indicated by stars: one, two, or three, in ascending quality. Wine people are superstitious. One of their firmest beliefs is that comet years produce fine wines. The legend is that in the comet year of 1811, when a superb brandy was produced, one of the shippers decided to designate the brandy of that year with a star. An equally excellent brandy was produced in the following year and this he designated by two stars. By this time he had acquired the habit, but fortunately he stopped when he reached five stars. The firm of Hennessy claims to have originated the system. Each house blends its brandies for uniformity of quality, which is maintained year in and year out. The standards represented by the stars vary with the different houses, but since 1975 French law has decreed that a three-star Cognac, the youngest blend on the market, must have spent at least two and a half years in wood. Most Cognacs average three to five years. In order to enter the United States, Cognac must be at least two and one-half years old. No age statements are permitted on the labels of Cognacs brought into the United States, so beware of so-called vintage Cognacs you may see in your foreign travels.

Better-quality brandies are sometimes identified by letters to indicate quality. The letters, oddly enough, represent not French words but English, because of the traditional importance of the English market. They represent the following:

C means Cognac

E means Extra or Especial

F means Fine

O means Old

P means Pale

S means Superior

V means Very

X means Extra

These words used to appear on the label at the discretion of the producer. Since 1955 certain combinations of letters have had age significance. For instance the letters VO or VSOP not only mean Very Old or Very Superior Old Pale, respectively, but they also mean, as does the word *Réserve*, that the Cognac has been aged in wood at least four and a half years. In reality, VSOP Cognacs are usually aged seven to ten years.

Since Cognac by and large is a business of brands,

many houses have abandoned the stars and letters and identify their various qualities either by proprietary names or by the district of origin.

Some other words producers use to describe their best Cognacs are now also regulated by French law. Extra, Napoleon, and Vieille Réserve require that the Cognac has been in cask for a minimum of 6½ years. The romantic nonsense about the 80- and 104-year-old so-called Napoleon brandies is nothing but a ploy for the unknowing buyer.

Cognac improves in wood for roughly fifty to fifty-five years. The cost of aging the brandy for this length of time is very high, as the losses through evaporation and the risk of aging too long are considerable and make the ultimate selling prices excessive. Once the Cognac is bottled, it neither varies nor improves. A Cognac bottled in 1900 will taste exactly the same today as it did the day it was placed in the glass. Yet the question naturally arises: What is the best age for Cognac? It is at its best between the ages of twenty-five and forty.

From the consumer's point of view there are several other questions that are frequently asked.

What is Fine Champagne? This means that the brandies have been made from grapes grown in either the Grande or Petite Champagne, with at least 50 percent of the grapes coming from the Grande Champagne region. Consequently, a Fine Champagne Cognac should be very good.

What is *Fine*? Legally, a *Fine* is a Cognac. In France, however, every restaurant includes among its list of brandies a *Fine de la Maison*, which is bar brandy. More than likely, if you just order a *Fine* (pronounced *feen*), you will get a good French brandy, even though you should be getting a Cognac. It is wiser to ask for Fine Champagne Cognac, if that is what you want.

Cognacs should be examined with the nose before

actually being tasted. The best way is to put one's nose on the rim of the glass, and not too deeply into the glass. The alcohol is quite strong for the nose. For this reason, many prefer small chimney glasses or tulips to large snifters. The glass should never be larger than one is capable of holding and warming in one hand, but the one-ounce pony or cordial glass should be avoided. When evaluating Cognacs, a few drops on the tongue is all that is necessary. Good Cognacs should be light.

Since distilled spirits do not change once they are bottled, old bottles mean nothing. Large magnum bottles should be avoided, since once the Cognac is started, it may remain partly full for a long time. Then, both evaporation and oxidation will make the Cognac deteriorate. While a bottle of cognac need not be consumed at one sitting, ideally, it should not be left open for more than six months.

A good test of a fine Cognac is to smell a glass that has had some Cognac poured into it. Hours after it has been consumed, the glass should retain its delicious aroma. A good long drink, by the way, is Cognac with ginger ale.

Armagnac

Second only to Cognac is the Armagnac brandy produced predominantly in the Department of Gers, southeast of Bordeaux in the heart of Gascony. The center of the trade is the city of Condom. There are three subregions: Bas-Armagnac, the most westerly growing area, Tenareze in the center, and Haut-Armagnac to the east. These areas were defined by the *Appellation Contrôlée* authorities in 1936. Brandies from any of these subregions are so named on the label. Armagnac by itself on a label means that the liquid is a blend of brandies from two or three subregions.

Only white grapes are permitted in making the wines for distillation into Armagnac. The predominant grape is the Saint-Émilion (Ugni Blanc), which, as in Cognac, is replacing the Folle Blanche in importance. Other varieties permitted are the Colombard, Meslier, Jurançon, and a few others. The hybrid Baco 22A has been planted in the sandier areas of the Bas-Armagnac. Armagnac has chalk in the soil, but less chalk than in Cognac.

A major difference in the systems of distilling Armagnac and Cognac is that in Armagnac the original and redistillation operations are continuous, whereas in Cognac they are two separate batch operations. Another difference lies in the fact that the Armagnac aging casks are made of black oak from the Monlezun Forest, instead of the Limousin oak used in Cognac.

Armagnac is regulated and labeled similarly to Cognac, with the same age requirements for three-star, VSOP, and so on. Age statements may appear on the label, and must be the age of the youngest component of the blend. Armagnac is often seen at ten years old, and *Hors d'Age* is more than ten years old.

Armagnac has a pungent bouquet, but a dry and surprisingly smooth taste.

Marc

Brandies distilled from the grape pomace of the wine press are called *eaux-de-vie de* Marc (pronounced *mar*) and are obtained in various parts of France, but notably in Burgundy. They have a strawlike, woody taste and rustic character appreciated by some devotees.

Other French Brandies

Substantial quantities of good brandy, not necessarily made from pomace, are distilled in various parts of France, outside the delimited Cognac and Armagnac regions. They are, generally speaking, good, clean, pleasant brandies that do not pretend to have the character or quality of Cognac. Their production is less restricted, and they are less costly.

Brandies of Other Lands

California Brandy

"California Brandy" is a controlled appellation applied only to beverage brandy distilled entirely from California grapes. Production is at almost nineteen million gallons, and California brandy comprises 75 percent of all brandy consumed in the United States. In addition, about thirty-five million gallons of high-proof brandy is produced for use in fortified wines and cordials.

California brandy is produced mainly from Thompson Seedless and Flame Tokay grapes, with some Colombard, Ugni Blanc, and Folle Blanche used at times. Most grapes are grown in the San Joachin Valley, from Lodi to Fresno.

The continuous still (also known as patent and Coffey) is preferred in California because it yields an extremely clean distillate and at the same time retains the highly desired congeners of the wine, when distillation is performed at appropriate proof. It is very efficient and produces a uniform product.

The pot still is used in 20 percent of California's distilleries. Some of this product is used to enhance blends. Other producers are developing stocks to produce only pot still brandies. A major Cognac company has even joined one Napa Valley producer to make California brandy in the French tradition.

Fifty-gallon white oak barrels from Tennessee and Arkansas are used for storage and aging, during which time the wood imparts the characteristic oak flavor and golden color. Some producers use previously aged whisky barrels that are charred inside and routed. By law, California brandy must be aged two years in oak, although it usually is not released until four years. Some eight-year-old brandies are available both as straights and blends.

Ample stocks of sound, mature American brandy—

forty-five million tax gallons—have now been accumulated, despite the fact that the industry was compelled to restart from scratch in 1933, when Prohibition ended.

Typical California brandies are light and mellow, with a pronounced grape flavor. They vary widely in degree of dryness to sweetness.

Germany Brandy

From Germany comes a soft grape brandy with characteristic mellow taste and fine aroma and bouquet. It is blended from especially selected distillates of wines from Germany, as well as from other countries, and is matured in oak. It has a great deal of finesse.

Greek Brandy

A great deal of brandy is distilled in Greece and much of it is exported. Greek brandy is becoming more popular. It usually has a clean flavor, with a touch of sweetness from the caramel used to give it color. The most popular Greek brandy in the United States, Metaxa, is technically a liqueur since it has been sweetened to the minimum level of a liqueur to give it wider appeal.

Cyprus is an independent country today, but it cannot separate itself from its Greek heritage. Cypriot brandies are good and very similar to those of Greece.

Israeli Brandy

Good, sound, clean grape and other fruit brandies have been distilled in the Holy Land for many years, but it is only since the State of Israel came into being that any serious efforts have been made to export them. Israeli brandy is always kosher.

Italian Brandy

Italy produces an excellent, clean grape brandy whose foreign market popularity increases every year. It is a good, all-purpose brandy that has a touch of sweetness. Grappa brandy, like Marc, is distilled from grape pomace. Grappa is usually unaged and sharp in taste, and it has its devoted following.

Mexican Brandy

Brandy was not produced in Mexico in any quantity before 1950, but in the past twenty-five years it has become the national drink, surpassing rum and Tequila. Many brandies are made in the Spanish style, following the Spanish methods of *solera* blending and aging in white oak barrels, after local wines have been distilled. Some brandies are produced in pot stills and may have Limousin oak aging, in the French style.

Peruvian Brandy

The brandy of Peru is Pisco, which takes its name from the port in southern Peru whence it is shipped. This brandy is distilled from Muscat wines produced in the Ica Valley, near Pisco. Pisco is matured in clay jars and is consumed in Peru quite young.

Pisco Punch, which is really a sour, is the most popular cocktail in Peru and also in Chile. It is a delightfully pleasant drink.

Muscat brandies are also produced in both Chile and Argentina.

Spanish Brandy

Very little Spanish brandy is distilled from sherry wine. Spanish brandies are distilled from wines of other wine regions of Spain, mostly from Valdepeñas. They are developed, aged, and marketed by many sherry shippers. In fact, there is slightly more brandy shipped from Jerez than sherry. Spanish brandy has a distinctive aroma and flavor and is different from Cognac or Armagnac. It is a sweeter brandy with an earthy character.

This list would not be complete without mentioning that brandy is made in Portugal, Yugoslavia, South Africa, Australia, and all other wine-producing countries in both hemispheres.

FRUIT BRANDIES

The fermented mash of fruits other than grapes is the source of a wide variety of unique brandies. They form three broad categories: brandies made with apples and pears; brandies made with stone fruits, such as cherries, plums, and apricots; and brandies made from berries, such as raspberries, strawberries, blackberries, and elderberries. These brandies come from Switzerland, France, Germany, Hungary, Israel, Yugoslavia, and the United States. Some of these fruits and the brandies they produce are as follows:

Fruit	Brandy
Apple	Apple brandy Applejack or apple jack Calvados
Apricot	Apricot brandy Barack Palinka
Blackberry	Blackberry brandy
Cherry	Kirsch Kirschwasser
Elderberry	Elderberry brandy
Pear	Pear brandy Eau-de-vie de poire
Pineapple	Pineapple brandy
Plum	Slivovitz Mirabelle Quetsch Prunelle Pflümli
Raspberry	Framboise
Strawberry	Fraise

Apple Brandy

The two principal sources of apple brandy are the United States and France. In the United States it is commonly called applejack, while in France the most famous is called Calvados, from the Department of Calvados in Normandy, center of apple and cider production in France. In France Calvados is also made in other parts of Normandy and in Brittany and Maine.

The production of Calvados begins with the juice of only sound, ripe cider apples. The juice is allowed to ferment for at least a month until no sugar remains, and it is then distilled. The best Calvados, with the appellation Calvados du Pays d'Auge, is distilled only in pot stills. Pot or continuous stills are used to produce brandies with the appellation Reglementees Calvados. Ordinary French apple brandy is called *eaux-de-vie-de-cidre de Normandie*, . . . *de Bretagne*, or . . . *du Maine*. The

Calvados du Pays d'Auge is double distilled, similar to the way Cognac is made. The first, or low, wines are redistilled to obtain the high wines, or brandy. These spirits are drawn off at around 140 proof and then aged in Limousin oak barrels, where they pick up color as they mature. Calvados may be aged up to forty years, when it can acquire the finesse of Cognac. Aged Calvados has a very pronounced apple flavor, and its bouquet combines wood and fruit. It is bottled at 80 to 84 proof. Age phrases are similar to Cognac and Armagnac.

Applejack is made in a manner similar to Calvados. The legal U.S. minimum age for applejack is two years in wood, but most is aged longer. Applejack is bottled as a straight brandy at 100 proof, aged brandy at 80 proof, or it may be blended with neutral spirits and bottled at 80 proof as a blended applejack. *Applejack* and *apple brandy* are synonymous terms.

Pear Brandy

Pear brandy, or *eau-de-vie de poire*, is made in both France and Switzerland. It is distilled from the Williams pear, which is the Bartlett pear of the United States. Pear brandy is unaged and colorless, with a distinct aroma. The production is similar to other colorless fruit brandies.

Other Fruit Brandies

After apple brandy the most widely produced fruit brandies are distilled from cherries and plums. All are produced in a similar fashion, except that only some are aged.

Those that are aged in wood and have a golden brown color are the plum brandies of central Europe (Hungary, Romania, Yugoslavia), known as Slivovitz; the apricot brandy of Hungary, called Barack Palinka; and some blackberry brandy, whose color is enhanced by the addition of some dark-colored juice to the matured spirit.

The brandies that are unaged are always colorless and are generally referred to as white alcohols. They include those distilled from a fermented mash of cherries, from varieties of plums, from raspberries, from strawberries, as well as from Williams pears.

The source of the finest Kirschwasser (cherry brandy) is the small black wild cherry from the valley of the Rhine. Because of geopolitics, however, the three best sources are in three different countries: Switzerland, where the Rhine starts on its way to the sea; Alsace, on the French side of the Rhine; and the Black Forest, on the opposite side of the Rhine in Germany. One can always find those who will claim that the Kirschwasser of one of these three sources is superior to the others, but they are all excellent.

Fruit brandies are made in the following manner. The fully ripened fruit is gathered and thoroughly mixed or mashed with wooden paddles in a wooden tub, where it is allowed to ferment—stones and all. After six weeks, when fermentation is complete, the entire contents of the tub are placed in a pot still and distilled twice. A small amount of oil from the stones is distilled over with the spirit. This oil imparts the characteristic bitter almond flavor usually found in good Kirschwasser or Slivovitz.

All of these white brandies are distilled off at a fairly low proof, usually around 100 proof or slightly less. In this way the maximum fruit aroma and flavor are retained. Since this is their most attractive and desired characteristic, they are bottled promptly, without any further reduction, so they will not lose any of their fragrance, or else they are stored in either glass-lined casks or earthenware containers. If aged in plain oak they would take on color, which is not desirable. Slivovitz, however, is preferred with color, so it is matured in wood.

So much fruit is required to obtain these essences that white alcohols are very expensive and luxurious.

How and When to Serve Brandies

Aside from their medicinal uses, which are well established, all brandies, those obtained from wine in particular, find their primary use as after-dinner drinks. They are most attractive when served neat, although brandy and soda is a pleasant drink after dinner or at any time when a refreshing and relaxing long drink is desired. Since brandy was considered a sort of wine concentrate, it has traditionally been drunk with water also, either mixed into the brandy or on the side. Brandy is also excellent in coffee.

Brandies have many uses in the kitchen. They may be flamed, which leaves a concentration of flavor after the alcohol burns off.

Kirsch, or one of the other white alcohols, is a delightful addition to any fresh fruit cup and as one of the flavorings in the delicious French dish Crepes au Kirsch. The intensity of the white alcohols makes it possible to impart flavor with very small amounts. They are especially good as flavorings in desserts, puddings, cakes, and ice creams. Unlike other brandies, the white alcohols are most enjoyable when served ice cold.

All brandies, both aged and unaged, may be used in making mixed drinks of all kinds.

When a palate cleanser is called for around the middle of a formal dinner, a small glass of Calvados may be served. This is known as a *Trou Normand* and is said to aid digestion.

WHISKIES

After the process of distillation was discovered, it was inevitable that man should use the product closest at hand, easiest to obtain, and least expensive for distillation. As a result, where there is an abundance of grain, whisky is distilled.

The word *whisky* comes from the Celtic *uisgebeatha* or *uisgebaugh* (pronounced *whis-geh-BAW*), the Scottish and Irish words, respectively, for "water of life." Whether it was the Scots or the Irish who first used the word or first distilled whisky is a source of never-ending argument between them.

The English found the Celtic word too difficult and too long, so they shortened and Anglicized it to *whisky*. The Canadians and the Scottish use the same spelling, without the *e*, the Irish keep the *e*. The United States used to use the *e*, but it now omits it in the Standards of Identity but permits its use in a traditional context.

Scotch Whisky

In the beginning every Highland laird had his own still, and the spirits he obtained were rough and harsh, with a smoky pungency appreciated only by the Caledonians. The whiskies were distilled freely and their distillers paid no taxes. In 1814 distillation from all stills of less than five hundred gallons' capacity was prohibited in Scotland, and the law almost caused a revolution. The British government continued to tax whisky throughout the 1800's, and illicit distillation and smuggling were prevalent right up to 1823. A similar situation prevailed in Ireland at the same time.

Four regions of Scotland produce malt whisky: the Highlands, the Lowlands, Campbeltown, and Islay (pronounced *I-lay*). Each produces a whisky with an individual character.

Scotch whisky is obtained primarily from barley from

East Anglia, England, since Scotland cannot produce enough barley for its distilling purposes.

There are five main stages in making Scotch: malting, mashing, fermenting, distilling, and maturing and blending.

On arrival at the distillery the barley goes into the barley-receiving room, where it is dressed, that is, sieved, or passed over screens so that small and inferior grain will be eliminated, after which the best grain is stored. When required for use, it is placed in tanks, called steeps, where it is soaked in water until thoroughly softened. It then used to be spread out on the floor of the malting house for about three weeks. Today this is rarely done. This traditional method has been replaced by mechanical drum maltings. The barley is fumed regularly to control temperature and rate of germination, or sprouting. This is done by hand using wooden shovels, known as shields.

When the sprouts are about three-quarters of an inch

long, the grain is known as green malt. It is already malt, for malt is germinated grain. During this germination process a chemical change occurs in the grain that is important in its future function of producing whisky. The enzyme amylase, traditionally called diastase in the beverage industry, is produced and has the property of converting the starch into sugars—maltose and dextrin—which are fermentable, whereas the starch in its original state is not.

The green malt is transferred to a kiln, where it rests on a screen directly above a peat fire.* Like green wood, peat gives off a much more acrid and oilier smoke than soft coal. This swirls around the grain, which becomes impregnated with the aroma of the smoke. Drying is then completed by burning coke or anthracite. The length of time that the peat is burned determines the smokiness

*Peat is coal in its primary stage and consists of partially carbonized vegetable material, usually heather, found in bogs. Pressed and dried peat is used for fuel.

of the malt and, eventually, of the whisky.

The kilning, or drying, process is very important, as it is here that the malt acquires a good part of its character, and a variation occurs here in the various regions. The malt in the Lowlands is kilned less than that in the Highlands, whereas the Campbeltown and Islay grains are more heavily roasted.

The kilned malt is now screened to remove the culm, or dried sprouts, after which it goes to the mill room, where it is ground into meal, or grist.

The next step is mashing. The ground malt is thoroughly mixed with warm water in a mash tun, also referred to as a mash tub, where it soaks until the water has liquefied all of the starches and the diastase has converted them into sugar. When the water has absorbed all of the goodness from the grain, it is drawn off, cooled, and is known as wort.

The wort now passes into the fermenting vats, where

a small quantity of carefully cultivated pure yeast is added and fermentation takes place. The yeast acts upon the sugars in the wort in the same manner as the natural yeasts act upon the sugars in grape juice, producing alcohol and carbon dioxide gas. When fermentation is completed, the liquid is known as beer, or wash. To this point the process is identical with that of brewing ales and beers, except for the omission of hops.

The beer now goes into a pot still, which is known as the wash still. The result of the first distillation is a distillate of low alcoholic strength, which is known as low wines. The low wines pass into the spirit pot still where they are redistilled. The first part of the distillation, "foreshots," and the last part, "feints," are gathered separately from the middle portion, which is the useful part of the distillation. At the beginning and at the end of the distillation operation too high a percentage of impurities is carried over with the spirit, which, if used, would impair the flavor of the spirit when matured. The feints, however, contain a substantial quantity of useful alcohol and are returned to the spirit still with the next charge of low wines, and the alcohol is distilled out. The impurities are disposed of with the residual slop from the spirit still operation, that is, the waste material that is thrown out.

The useful spirit, distilled off at between 140 and 142 proof, flows into a spirit vat from where it is put into casks. It is now called "plain British spirits," but after three years of aging, it may be called "whisky." These casks, generally made of American white oak, vary in size from the 34-gallon quarter cask to the 132-gallon butt. The different sizes are used for convenience. They may be new or old, and very often they are casks that have previously been used for maturing whisky, or in which sherry has been shipped. The choice of cask affects the flavor, and whiskies matured in sherry casks are sweeter and fuller.

At the time of barreling the whisky is reduced in proof to 124 to 126.8 by the addition of water. According to Dr. P. Schidrowitz, whose notes are quoted by Peter Valaer in his excellent paper on Scotch whisky, "It is held that the best water is that which has its origin as a spring served with water which has passed through a red granite formation, and which, after rising from its source, passes through peaty country. Such waters are generally very soft and possess certain qualities which are apparently due to the peaty soil or heather-clad moor through or over which the water passes on its way to the distillery."

Until 1853 Scotch whiskies were either straight malt or straight grain whiskies, but at that time the firm of Andrew Usher & Company, and later other companies, began the practice of blending malt whiskies with grain whiskies. These grain whiskies, produced primarily from corn with a small amount of barley malt, came from distilleries in lower Scotland and were distilled in the patent still. Grain whisky in Scotland is *whisky* and not neutral spirits, as some people believe. The Scotch grain whiskies are distilled out at slightly over 180 proof. They are reduced to 124 proof when barreled in seasoned sherry or Bourbon casks for aging.

Before this time the taste for Scotch had been confined to Scotland, but after blending became a general practice, Scotch whisky became popular in England and throughout the rest of the world. Blending grain whiskies with malt whiskies produced a drink that people generally liked.

The blending is done after the whiskies are three to four years old. A master blender examines them and indicates the exact proportions of Highland, Lowland, Campbeltown, and Islay malts of various ages and of grain whisky that are to be married. This is accomplished by placing the whiskies in a large vat where they are thoroughly mixed both by rotating paddles and by compressed air blown up from the bottom. The whisky is then returned to the sherry or Bourbon casks for a further period of maturing (marrying) before bottling or shipping in bulk.

The usual Scotch blend contains 20 to 50 percent malt whisky, the balance being grain whisky. The original object of using grain whiskies, which are always distilled in patent stills, was to reduce the cost, but in doing so a lighter whisky was produced that appealed much more to the other peoples of the world than had the fuller, smokier Scotch whiskies previously made.

The essential difference between blends is the proportions used of different single malts. Of these, the Highland malts are considered the finest and are always the most costly. They are fairly light in body and flavor and do not have too much smoke. The finest Highland section is Banffshire, and within it the Glen Livet and Speyside regions are considered the best. Next in importance is

Moray. Lowland malts are also light in body, but not as smoky in flavor. Almost all of the grain whisky distilleries are in the Lowlands. Campbeltown malts are very full in body and quite smoky. The Islay malts are also very full, smoky, and pungent. In each category, however, malts can vary tremendously, some being much heavier than others.

In the last analysis, the reasons for blending are to obtain a smoother, more balanced product than any of the blend's single components and to ensure uniform continuity of a given brand. In this way the consumer can expect the same character, flavor, taste, and quality year in and year out. A Scotch whisky blend can very easily be the result of a marriage of as many as thirty or forty malt whiskies, together with five or more grain whiskies.

The ages of the individual whiskies at the time of blending may vary widely, since no single whisky is employed before it has reached its proper maturity. The number of years required for this is governed by the character of the whisky itself and the climatic conditions under which it is matured. The fuller-bodied malts of Islay and Campbeltown take much longer, sometimes ten to twelve years, while the Highland and Lowland malts may be ready in six to eight years, and the grain whiskies may require only four years. The greater the climatic dampness, the slower the aging process.

The secret of fine Scotch whisky, therefore, lies in the art of the blender. On his unique ability depend the polish, smoothness, and uniformity of the whisky. There are 130 distilleries in Scotland (95 Highland malt, 11 Lowland malt, 8 Islay malt, 2 Campbeltown malt, and 14 grain whisky distilleries) producing about 150 internationally marketed blends and single malts, and about 1,000 more private label and lesser brands. As we have already indicated, there are many reasons why Scotch whisky from one area differs from Scotches of other areas. Local conditions, such as water, peat, and climate, and traditional distilling practices of individual distilleries are all contributing factors. But to understand fully the Scotch picture, it is important to remember that there are many distilleries, each one turning out a whisky that has its own individual characteristics. By combining the full-flavored malt whiskies with gentler grain whiskies, the blenders obtain the individuality of character and quality that distinguishes their brands. Blends may also be tailored to producers' interpretations of consumer preferences, even to having different blends produced for various countries under the same label. The United States consumes about one-third of all the Scotch whisky sold each year. Thus, the Scotch whisky blender tries to supply what appeals most to the important American customer.

There has been an unquestioned trend in the United States toward lightness of flavor and body in most of the beverages Americans consume. An indication is the continuing, enormous increase of the share of the market in the United States held by "white goods" (gin, vodka, rum, and Tequila).

Those brands of Scotch whisky that have been blended for lightness by judicious selection of light-bodied, lighter-flavored malts are among the largest-selling brands in the United States. The American public has come to associate paleness or lack of color with lightness and dryness. This is nonsense, since the depth of color in a Scotch whisky as shipped is governed by the amount of caramel (burned sugar) used in all blends to ensure color uniformity.

Even though more than 99 percent of the Scotch whisky consumed outside Scotland is blended whisky, there are also marketed in small quantities straight, unblended Highland malt whiskies, as well as blends of only malt whiskies, known as vatted malts, in which no grain whisky has been used. Such whiskies are much fuller bodied and usually are of very fine quality.

A liqueur Scotch whisky is one that, through proper aging and blending, has acquired a mellow softness both in the bouquet and on the palate. The word *liqueur*, when used with Scotch whisky, applies to older, finer whiskies, particularly the premium or deluxe brands, and should not be confused with a sweetened cordial or liqueur. These whiskies are rare and expensive.

The high regard for age statements in the United States may frequently lead us astray. A Scotch whisky with a ten-year-old age statement on the label is not necessarily a better whisky than one with no age statement at all. Naturally aging is important in making a Scotch (or any other whisky) mellow and more palatable, but the quality of the whisky and the skill of the blender's hand must be there first. Some fully aged Scotch is laid away in casks, after it has been blended, for marrying for periods of up to one year. The law stipulates an aging period of at least three years for Scotch whisky, and none can enter the

United States under four years of age. Practically all Scotch malts remain in their casks for a minimum of five years. Blends with higher percentages of malt whiskies are usually aged longer than those with more grain whiskies. Thus, when a brand is marketed with different age statements, it is not simply the same whisky aged for different lengths of time. The whisky indicating the oldest age was fuller to begin with, and always required more time in cask to mellow.

Before 1979 the duty and Internal Revenue tax on imported distilled spirits was assessed on total gallonage, at 100 proof, even if a case of Scotch whisky, for example, was only 86 proof. It was economical, therefore, to import Scotch in bulk at 100 proof, and to reduce it to 86 proof with distilled or deionized water after it arrived in the United States, for a 14 percent duty and tax saving. Since 1979 both domestic and foreign producers are taxed on proof-gallons, based on the amount of alcohol rather than the volume of liquid. The price advantage of Scotch whisky imported in bulk over bottled-in-Scotland whisky now comes solely from savings in freight and handling.

There is no difference in flavor between the two, since distilled or deionized water is used universally to bring whisky down to bottling proof. In 1982 bulk imports accounted for 41 percent of all Scotch imports.

Irish Whiskey

There is a common belief that Irish whiskey is a potato whiskey. This is not true at all. No doubt the misconception stems from the fact that the Irish refer to illicitly distilled whiskey as *poteen*, a term derived from the pot still in which it has traditionally been distilled.

Whiskey in Ireland is distilled from a fermented mash of grains, namely, malted barley, unmelted barley, corn, rye, wheat, and oats, similar to the mash used in Scotland.

The barley malt is dried in a kiln that has a solid floor. Even when peat was used as a fuel the smoke could not come in contact with the malt. Now peat has been replaced by smokeless anthracite, and the malt is not smoke cured, as is the case in Scotland.

Much Irish whiskey is distilled in the pot still. There are three distinct distilling operations. The wash is first distilled in a large wash still, yielding the low wines. These low wines are then distilled in a smaller pot still, producing strong and weak feints, which are collected separately. Thus far the process is similar to the distillation of Scotch malt whisky. The distillation of Irish whiskey differs from Scotch whisky, however, in that a third pot still is used to obtain the final whiskey from the distillation of the strongest feints. That is why Irish whiskey is said to be triple distilled.

Some houses distill grain whiskey in column, or patent, stills. These are blended with pot-still whiskies to produce lighter-bodied and lighter-flavored whiskies, mostly for export.

Irish whiskies must be aged in seasoned cooperage for at least four years, but usually they are aged seven to eight years before being shipped.

Irish is a particularly smooth whiskey, with medium body and a clean, unique flavor. It is consumed in the same manner as Scotch whisky and also is popularly used in Irish Coffee.

American Whisky

Early American settlers brought spirituous liquors with them, as they were considered essential in with-standing the hardships of an ocean voyage and a medicine in cases of illness in the new, savage land. For a long time spirits had to be imported from Europe.

The first commercially distilled spirit in what is the

present-day United States was New England rum. Distilling whisky on a commercial scale began over a century later.

There is a record of distilling on Staten Island in New York in 1640, but it was not until the early eighteenth century that whisky distilling began to develop. The grains used along the eastern seaboard were rye and barley. As the settlements began extending westward, however, it became apparent that transporting newly grown grain back to the populous seaboard cities was difficult for the settlers, particularly those in western Pennsylvania. They found it was simpler to distill their grain, both rye and corn, into whisky. It not only kept longer, but it was easier to transport to the cities. Whisky and furs, indeed, became the best means of exchange, particularly during the Revolutionary War, when Continental currency was worth less than five cents on the dollar.

Whisky played a prominent part in early U.S. history, in determining the right and ability to be a self-governed nation. Whisky had always been distilled in small, family-owned distilleries without legal interference from any government. In 1791, money being a crying need for the new nation and an excise tax was levied on whisky.

The independent Pennsylvania distillers resented the tax on their product, and the tax collectors in some cases were even tarred and feathered. There were riots and stormy scenes in these "western" communities, and President Washington, in great haste, sent a force of militia to quell the insurrection. It was done without bloodshed and accomplished its object. While in itself the insurrection was of minor importance, it was of tremendous significance to the future of the federal government and is still known as the Whiskey Rebellion.

Many of the disgruntled Dutch, Scottish, and Irish farmer-distillers decided to move out of reach of the tax collector, which meant going farther west into Indian territory. They found the proper water for distilling in southern Indiana and Kentucky.

The first whisky distilled in Kentucky is generally attributed to the Reverend Elijah Craig at Georgetown, in Bourbon County. The grain he employed was corn (maize), as it was more plentiful than rye. His product became known as Bourbon County whisky, and the name Bourbon has remained as the designation of whiskies distilled from a corn mash.

The important whisky-distilling areas in the United States are not located where they are by pure chance but because of the most important factor in making whisky—the quality of the water. It comes from springs that pass up through layer on layer of limestone rock. The limestone mantle runs along western Pennsylvania and cuts across southern Indiana over into Kentucky. There is another isolated limestone region in Maryland around Baltimore.

With the advancement of science and the development of inexpensive water technology the distiller has been freed from the necessity of locating his production at or near these limestone mantle outcroppings. Today he can and does distill whisky in many other parts of the United States.

The early distillers used very crude and primitive equipment. Fermentation was carried on in open mash tubs, the yeast being the wild varieties the air afforded. Since that day tremendous changes have taken place.

Briefly the steps in making whisky are as follows:

1. Upon arrival at the distillery the grain is carefully inspected and cleaned of all dust.
2. It is ground in the gristmill to a meal.
3. The meal is first cooked to release starch from its tough cellular coating, then malt is added to convert the starches.
4. Pure cultured yeast is propagated in increasingly large containers—a flask in the laboratory, a done tub in the yeast room, the yeast tub in the distillery.

5. The cooled wort is yeasted with the propagated yeast and goes to the fermenting vats to become beer.
6. The beer goes into a patent, or double-column, still. The result is whisky, which is distilled out at below 160 proof. It is then reduced in proof to 105 to 110 by adding deionized (demineralized) water.

All *new* whisky (except corn whisky and light whisky) is placed in new charred white oak barrels to mature in bonded warehouses, under the custody of the distiller. Taxes are paid, based on proof, at the time that the whisky is shipped.

Spirits are generally matured in porous containers so the air can seep in to oxidize and mellow the alcohol. The most common container is made of wood (generally oak). Wood is a porous substance, and when liquid is stored in a wooden barrel, even though it be tightly closed, some of it seeps through, that is, evaporates or escapes through the pores of the wood.

Aged spirits, such as brandy, rum, and Scotch whisky, are barreled for aging at proofs varying from 124 to 150 proof. These spirits lose some alcoholic strength as they mature because they are stored under humid conditions.

American whiskies, on the other hand, are barreled at 105 to 110 proof (52½ to 55 percent alcohol), and as they mature their alcoholic strength increases because of the warm, dry conditions under which they are stored.

To illustrate this point, after four years of aging, a fifty-gallon barrel of new whisky at a hypothetical 100 proof (twenty-five gallons of alcohol and twenty-five gallons of water) has lost ten gallons of liquid, but the alcoholic strength is 110 proof. This means that 55 percent of the forty gallons remaining is alcohol (twenty-two gallons) and the remaining eighteen gallons are water.

No one knows exactly how the advantage of charring barrels was learned One legend is that as a result of a fire in a warehouse in Jamaica some barrels of rum were heavily charred. After some time it was learned that the rum in the charred barrels had acquired both color and quality it had lacked before.

Another explanation is that in order to bend the barrel staves into the proper shape for the barrel, the early Kentuckians heated them before an open fire, and often they became charred. Discovering that the more charred the staves the more palatable the whisky, charring became an accepted practice. Kentuckians were also said to have burned out the inside of used barrels so that the whisky would not pick up off-flavors. It is likely that none of these stories is true, as it is probable that the virtues of charring the barrels in which whisky was to be stored were stumbled upon quite by accident. Staves average one inch in thickness, and one-eighth-inch depth of char is most common.

There are two yeasting processes used in America—the sweet-mash, or yeast-mash process, and the sour-mash, or yeasting-back process. The sour-mash process is used primarily in making Bourbon whisky.

A sweet mash is produced by adding all or almost all freshly developed yeast to the mash, that is, no stillage (liquid recovered after the alcohols have been distilled off) from a previous distillation is mixed with the fresh mash to adjust the acidity. It is allowed to ferment from thirty-six to fifty hours and the fermenter can be, and usually is, refilled almost immediately when empty.

Sour mash means that at least one-quarter of the fermenting mash must be stillage, or spent beer, from a previous distillation, along with the fresh mash. The mash is allowed to ferment from seventy-two to ninety-six hours. Fermentation generally takes place in open fermenting vats at low temperatures. When emptied, the fermenters are sterilized, aerated, and allowed to "sweeten" for twenty-four hours before being used again.

Sour mash offers a favorable pH for yeast growth and

inhibits bacterial contamination. Sweet mash is more difficult to control and must be done above 80 degrees Fahrenheit to end quickly and avoid contamination.

There are three main categories of whiskies produced in America: straights, blends, and light whiskies. Each one has several subcategories. Because these products are often blended together, a whisky may appear in more than one category.

A straight whisky, under federal regulations, is one that has been distilled off at a proof not exceeding 160, aged in new, charred white oak barrels for at least two years, and reduced by the addition of water at the time of bottling to no lower than 80 proof, from a minimum of 51 percent of a grain. Nothing may be added other than the water. Straights include Bourbon, Tennessee, rye, corn, and wheat whiskies.

The higher the proof at which a spirit is distilled out, the lighter it will be in character, flavor, and body. This is because more and more of the congeners (flavor and body components) are eliminated as the proof of the spirit is increased.

Under U.S. regulations the theoretical critical point is reached at 190 proof (95 percent alcohol). Any spirit distilled out at 190 proof or higher is called a neutral spirit and should not possess any noticeable aroma, flavor, or character. Conversely, the lower the proof of distillation the greater the amount of congeners that will be distilled over and become a part of the distillate to give character, aroma, flavor, and body. Since straight whisky by regulation cannot be distilled out at a strength exceeding 160 proof, it possesses very definite aroma, flavor, and body characteristics when suitably aged in wood.

The predominant grain used in the mash formula determines the final designation under which the whisky is labeled and marketed. If 51 percent or more of the grain is corn, it is straight Bourbon; 51 percent or more rye grain makes it a straight rye; 51 percent wheat, straight wheat whisky; 51 percent barley malt or rye malt, straight malt whisky or straight rye malt whisky; 80 percent or more corn, aged in uncharred oak barrels or reused charred oak barrels, is designated straight corn whisky.

Tennessee whisky is a straight whisky that must be distilled in Tennessee from a fermented mash containing 51 percent or more of *any* grain. Even though there is no grain criteria, corn is usually used. This is a Bourbon-type whisky, but it is very full-bodied since it is treated with maple wood charcoal to remove the lighter flavors.

Straight whiskies may be mixed, provided the mixture is made up of whiskies of the same distilling period and from the same distillery. Such whiskies do not lose their straight whisky designation.

Straight whiskies of different distilling periods and from different distilleries may also be mixed or blended, but they must be labeled blended Bourbon whisky, blended rye whisky, and so on. When straight whiskies that are homogeneous are mixed, the mixture carries the age of the youngest whisky it contains. Most straight whiskies on the market greatly exceed the minimum age requirement because each distiller attempts to age his product until he feels his whisky has reached the ripeness or maturity that is ideal for that particular whisky. Most authorities agree that the average Bourbon attains this stage in about six years, but this varies with the flavor intensity of the initial distillate.

Two-thirds of the American-distilled whisky consumed in the United States is straight whisky or blends of straight whiskies.

The term *bottled in bond* is generally misunderstood not only by the public but too often by people in the retail liquor trade itself. The term is *not* a guarantee of quality; it refers only to the Internal Revenue tax. Only straight whiskies are bottled in bond.

The Bottled in Bond Act of 1894 permitted distillers to bottle whisky (or other distilled spirits) without paying the excise taxes, provided the whisky was at least four years old, distilled at one plant by the same proprietor, and bottled at 100 proof, under the supervision of the U.S. Treasury Department. After bottling, the whisky remained in the bonded warehouse until the distiller was ready to sell it, at which time the tax was to be paid or determined, before withdrawing the whisky from bond.

In 1980 the All-In-Bond system was put into use. This created an atmosphere of joint custody between the proprietor and the U.S. government. The proprietor now has full custody of spirits whose production must be fully documented. So long as there are complete records, it is no longer necessary for a government inspector to be in the plant every day, and no strip stamps are required on the bottles. No taxes have to be paid until the whiskies are shipped.

Bottled in bond spirits still have the same meaning

as before, which is that they have been distilled out below 160 proof, are straight, are four or more years old, and are bottled at 100 proof. In addition to whiskies, other products may include rum and grape and apple brandies.

Bottled in bond is not a guarantee of purity or quality of spirits, and the government assumes no responsibility with respect to claims by dealers when advertising these spirits in this connection.

Nearly half of the American-produced whisky consumed in the United States is blended whisky. The blender devotes his art to mixing carefully selected, full-bodied, straight whiskies with grain spirits and/or light whiskies to produce a lighter, more harmoniously balanced whole and to duplicate, day in and day out, an identical, uniform product. The straight whiskies contribute aroma, flavor, and body, while the grain spirits and/or light whiskies give the final product lightness and smoothness without sacrificing character.

To be a blended whisky, at least 20 percent of the blend must be straight whisky. The balance may be grain neutral spirits, grain spirits, and/or light whiskies. Grain neutral spirits are spirits that are distilled out at over 190 proof and have no recognizable aroma or flavor. Grain spirits are neutral spirits that have been aged in reused oak barrels to give them a delicate flavor and soft mellowness. It is important that the barrel be compatible with the flavor intensity of the grain neutral spirits, since the woody character of a new barrel would overwhelm the light flavor of the grain neutral spirits. Light whiskies, the newest category, have become an important component for the blender.

Regulations also permit the use of certain blending materials in blended whiskies, up to 2½ percent by volume. Those most often employed are sherry wine and prune or peach juice.

There is an unending discussion as to the merits and

demerits of blended whisky in comparison to straight whisky. Both usually are fine, very drinkable products. The one you enjoy more—the one that pleases your palate—is the one you should choose. It is absurd to consider one inferior to the other; they are simply different. The straight whisky is full bodied and full flavored, while the blended whisky is comparatively light bodied and light in flavor.

Curiously, many people in the northeastern states refer to blended whisky as rye. It is not. While this is probably the result of the long tradition of using a great deal of rye in making whisky in that area, true rye whisky contains at least 51 percent of that grain and has a pronounced rye flavor. If someone unknowingly gets a true rye whisky, the strong flavor and full body may shock his palate.

Light whisky is whisky that has been distilled in the United States at more than 160 proof and less than 190 proof and stored in seasoned, charred oak containers. This whisky is permitted to be entered for storage at proofs higher than 125. The Standard of Identity for light whisky became effective in 1972.

The primary purpose for this category was to permit the production of light distillates that could be aged in seasoned oak casks—that is, reused cooperage—which are more compatible in developing the lower flavor intensities found in this type of whisky.

In general, the techniques used in the production of straight whisky and grain neutral spirits are followed in making light whisky. The proportions and types of cereal grains used in the formula are left entirely to the discretion of the distiller, but most distillers use corn (up to 90 percent) as the major portion of their formula. The main emphasis in this process is on distillation techniques. The higher proof requirements permit the use of more sophisticated distillation systems, such as those used in distilling grain spirits. The distiller also has a wide range of proofs in which to work. At 161 proof the whisky is still flavorful; at

189 proof it is extremely light in flavor and character. At almost every level of proof in between, a changing relative amount of flavor components is left in the distillate to affect the body, flavor, and character of the whisky. The distiller can distill his light whisky out at any of these proofs and achieve different weights of flavor. He can mix different batches of different proofs for his final product.

The age of light whisky as it is withdrawn for bottling affects its final character. As with America's straight whiskies and imported whiskies, a major factor in the character of the light whisky brands is their maturity.

It had been hoped that this category would be enjoyed by the segment of the population that enjoys "white goods," but this has failed to materialize. The biggest use for light whiskies has been in blends, as a replacement for grain neutral spirits, which even if they were aged, could not show an age statement. Light whisky is available in three ways:

1. As light whisky, in the bottle as distilled and reduced in proof, and including mixtures of these distillates.
2. As blended light whisky, a mixture of less than 20 percent straight whisky at 100 proof with light whisky.
3. In the traditional blended whisky, with the light whisky portion unidentified in a mixture with 20 percent or more straight whisky at 100 proof.

Canadian Whisky

According to U.S. federal regulations, "Canadian whisky is a distinctive product of Canada, manufactured in Canada in compliance with laws of the Dominion of Canada . . . containing no distilled spirits less than three years old . . . such whisky is blended Canadian whisky. Canadian whisky shall not be designated as straight."

According to Canadian law, Canadian whisky must be produced from cereal grain only. While the Canadian

Excise Tax Bureau exercises the customary controls to ensure proper collection of the tax, the government sets no other limitation as to grain formulas, distilling proofs, or special type of aging cooperage. It believes the distillers are better judges than the government of what the public, both at home and abroad, wants in a Canadian whisky.

Many people believe that Canadian whisky is a rye whisky, which it is not. Corn, rye, wheat, and barley malt are the grains generally used, and none can be more than 50 percent. The proportions of grains used are the trade secrets of the individual distillers.

The methods of production are similar but the procedures of maturing differ somewhat from U.S. standards and practices. For example, any loss from evaporation may be made up by adding new whisky to replace the amount lost.

The distillers have developed a whisky with a delicate flavor and light body. They obtain these characteristics with mash formulas designed to produce lightness and delicacy and by distilling out at varying strengths, ranging from 140 to 180 proof. Practically all Canadian whisky is six years old or older when marketed. If it is less than four years old (it may be bottled when it is three years old), its age must be listed on the label.

More than half of the Canadian whisky coming to the United States is in bulk.

Japanese Whisky

The Japanese wine and spirits industry is an old one, going back into antiquity. However, until relatively recent times (about 1870) it was in large part devoted to such traditional beverages as saké, Umeshu (a Japanese plum wine made by infusion), and Umechu (a Japanese medicinal wine). With the advent of Westernizing influences in Japan, distillation was also introduced. Since then products such as Japanese whisky, liqueurs, brandies, and

Sochu (a neutral spirit made from grain or sweet potatoes) have become part of the Japanese culture.

Although historically much of the technique of distillation was learned from the West, especially Scotland and France, the Japanese adapted the methods to their own economy. For example, their whisky is primarily a blended whisky made up of varying percentages of fuller-bodied whiskies produced in pot stills and lighter-bodied whiskies produced by continuous distillation using column stills, many of which were adapted from French designs. While the original Japanese whiskies were an attempt to duplicate Scotch whisky, the grains employed in these whiskies were different from those used in Scotland. Japan now produces a whisky different from any currently made in the United States and from any of the other imported whiskies entering the United States.

Many of the fuller-bodied whiskies are made from malted barley, some small portion of which is cured over peat. Most of the whisky used in blended Japanese whisky is made from millet, corn, Indian corn, some small quantities of rice, and other grains in varying proportions in their mash bill (formula). Wheat and rye are seldom used. The milling and fermentation procedure is similar to that of the Western methods. The saccharification method differs, however, in that most of the lighter whisky uses the Japanese *koji* enzyme, an enzyme similar to that used in making saké to convert the starch to sugar.

The proofs of the whiskies, when removed from the stills, vary from about 130 proof for the fuller-bodied whiskies to about 180 proof for the lighter-bodied whiskies. The whiskies are aged separately in used charred oak barrels before blending. Blending, the subsequent marrying period, and further aging last from months to years, depending on the quality of the whisky. The laws of Japan define various classes of whisky primarily for Japanese tax purposes and regulate the aging and handling of whisky.

Other Whiskies

Whisky types are also produced in Holland, Germany, Denmark, and Australia. In Australia the Scotch method—first producing malt whisky and then a blend of malts and grains—is followed. Although made on the Scotch pattern, Australian whisky has a distinctive character.

Taste of Whiskies

The principal taste distinction of Scotch whisky is its smoky peat flavor, whereas Irish whiskey has a similar barley-malt whisky character without the smoky flavor. Both are somewhat lighter in body than American straight whiskies because high proof, very light-bodied grain whiskies are used for blending. Also, because Scotch and Irish whiskies are matured in old, previously used cooperage they require a longer aging period. This is usually seven to eight years, and up to twelve for the heavier distillates, which require more time to smooth out.

Rye and Bourbon whiskies have the distinctive tastes and characters of the rye and corn grains used respectively. Because of the different methods of mashing and the lower proofs at which they are distilled out, which give them a higher congeneric content, they are both sweeter and fuller bodied than Scotch or Irish. Furthermore, aging in new charred oak cooperage makes it possible for the American whiskies to reach maturity sooner.

With the trend towards lightness in American taste, American blended whisky and Canadian whisky are quite popular.

How and When to Serve Whiskies

Aside from their most common use as a straight drink

or on the rocks, whiskies may be used in innumerable cocktails, punches, and other mixed drinks. They are also very popular in long drinks, such as highballs and coolers.

VODKAS

When this book first appeared in 1940, only half a page was devoted to vodka. In the short space of four decades this most neutral of spirits has risen from its "also ran" listing among the "other spirits" to a degree of popularity that has made it the largest-selling individual type of spirits in the United States, replacing Bourbon and blended whisky. It was not until 1950 that vodka was separately reported in trade statistics. In 1955 it represented only 3.4 percent of the total distilled spirits market, and by 1982 it had risen to 22 percent.

The word *vodka* is a diminutive of the Russian word for "water," *voda*, and it was the Russians who originated this particular "water of life." In Russia, Finland, Czechoslovakia, Poland, and elsewhere in northern and eastern Europe, spirits have long been distilled to a very high proof, resulting in a minimum of flavor.

According to many historians vodka was first produced in Russia in the fourteenth century. The vast

Smirnoff distilleries in Moscow, dating from 1818, passed out of the family's control with the 1917 revolution. The formula was brought to America in the 1930s via Paris, and Smirnoff was the first and only American-made vodka for many years. It alone can be given credit for generating a new fashion of drinking in the United States.

Vodka has always been distilled from the most plentiful and least expensive materials available to the distiller, wherever he might be. Vodka is made from potatoes and various grains, principally corn, with some wheat added. The best export vodkas, and all those produced in the United States, are made from grain.

Vodka, like whisky, is an alcoholic distillate from a fermented mash.

Whisky, however, is distilled at low proof to retain flavor. Vodka is distilled at high proof and then processed still further, if required, to extract all congeners.

In a sense vodka is like gin, but with one big difference. Both are made from neutral spirits; neither has to be aged. But in making American gin, the neutral spirits are delicately flavored with juniper and aromatics. In making vodka nothing is added to the neutral spirits; instead all character is absent, leaving the spirits colorless and without distinctive odor or taste.

Vodka is made neutral by either of two processes. In the first, neutral spirits flow continuously through tanks containing no less than one and a half pounds of vegetable charcoal for each gallon of spirits, so that the spirits are in intimate contact with the charcoal for a minimum of eight hours. At least 10 percent of the charcoal is replaced after each forty hours of operation. In the second method spirits are agitated for a minimum of eight hours in contact with no less than six pounds of new vegetable charcoal for every one hundred gallons of spirits. Vodka can also be made by purifying or refining the spirits by any other method that the government finds will result in a product without distinctive character, aroma, or taste. American vodka is bottled at proofs ranging from 80 to 100, the majority of sales being at the lower figure.

IMPORTED VODKAS

The most significant and prestigious imported vodkas are those from the original Russian, Finnish, and Polish sources. With vodka's increasing popularity, however, an increased flow has come from England, France, Holland, Czechoslovakia, Turkey, and China. There is a kosher vodka from Israel.

FLAVORED VODKAS

Flavored varieties of vodka are popular, particularly in Poland and Russia, where infusions and mixtures with herbs, grasses, leaves, spices, and seeds are involved. Some of these vodkas are colored and, as vodka-based liqueurs, are sweetened and fruit flavored. The most common of the flavored vodkas, which range from 70 proof up, are:

Zubrowka. Flavored with a type of grass found only in the forests of eastern Poland. These grasslands are the breeding grounds for a particular species of bison indigenous to Poland, and the zubrowka ("bison grass vodka") has a slightly yellowish tinge and an aromatic bouquet. The FDA, however, has questioned the effects of bison grass on the human body.

Stárka ("old"). Vodka ages for about ten years in special oak casks previously used for fine-quality wines. This maturing imparts an amber color and flavor to Stárka, which is a vodka for brandy lovers.

Yubilevneya Osobaya (jubilee vodka). Contains brandy, honey, and other ingredients.

Pertsovka. A dark brown Russian pepper vodka with a pleasant aroma and burning taste. It is prepared from an infusion of capsicum, cayenne, and cubeb. History records that Czar Peter the Great seasoned his vodka with pepper, and numerous Russians apparently continue to enjoy its sharp bite.

Okhotnichya ("hunter's vodka"). A spirit flavored with many herbs; has a scent that suggests heather honey.

Russian vodka makers produce about thirty other vodkas with a wide range of flavors, some of which are available in the United States.

Fruit-flavored vodka is made in the United States. There are orange, lemon, cherry, and other flavors that must be stated on the label. U.S. flavored vodka is a product of rectification, and pays the $.30-per-gallon rectification tax.

How and When to Serve vodka

In the middle of the twentieth century general consumption of vodka was confined almost entirely to Russia, Poland, and the Baltic states. Vodka has been produced in the United States since 1933, but until 1948 it was an exotic specialty consumed by a few people of eastern European origin. It was drunk straight, ice cold, in a small, one-ounce glass, at one gulp, and almost always with a sharp-tasting appetizer. Drinking vodka in this way, however, did not have much appeal for Americans, and it would have remained little known except for an accident of chance—an accident that had nothing to do with vodka.

After World War II a Hollywood restaurant owner found himself with a large and unsalable stock of ginger beer. Realizing that he had to find a new use for it or take a heavy loss, he tried mixing it with any number of products without success, until he used vodka. He added half a lime, served it in a copper mug, and named it the Moscow Mule. The Mule caught on, and other distillers made vodka and created new drinks. From Hollywood the vodka fashion swept across the country.

Because it has no flavor of its own, vodka was quickly recognized as the most versatile of all mixers. It combines exceedingly well with fruit juices and flavors of all types. This fact, perhaps more than any other, accounts for the remarkable growth of vodka's popularity. The Screwdriver (vodka and orange juice) was one of the earliest drinks specially created. The most significant vodka drink, which has become part of the American scene, is the Bloody Mary (vodka and tomato juice). Vodka and Tonic is also enormously popular, and vodka is substituted freely for gin in the Martini and other drinks.

America has also begun to enjoy vodka straight—chilled in the refrigerator or freezer—particularly with spicy appetizers, smoked salmon, and caviar. Vodka is often served on the rocks.

GINS

Gin is one of the few liquors in whose production man plays a more important part than nature. In the wines and spirits studied so far, we have seen that natural forces age and develop the liquor. But here man has manufactured the whole product. Gin did not happen by chance; it was created quite intentionally for a specific purpose. Credit for this belongs to Franciscus de la Boe (1614–1672), also known as Doctor Sylvius, a seventeenth-century physician and professor of medicine at Holland's famed University of Leyden.

Doctor Sylvius was not thinking of a beverage spirit, much less a Dry Martini. His objective was medicinal in the purest sense. Knowing the diuretic properties of the oil of the juniper berry (*Juniperus communis*), he felt that by redistilling a pure alcohol with the juniper berry he could obtain its therapeutic oil in a form that would provide an inexpensive medicine. And he succeeded. Within a few years all Holland found itself suffering from ills that could be cured only by Dr. Sylvius's medicine. He named it Genièvre, the French name for the juniper berry. The Dutch called it Genever, which they still do, and today it is also known in the Netherlands as Hollands and Schiedam (a gin-distilling center near Rotterdam). The English shortened and Anglicized it to gin.

The popularity of gin in England came about as the result of a demand for distilled spirits that were palatable and also inexpensive. During the reign of Queen Anne (1702–1714) the only way distillers knew how to satisfy this demand was to take the lees of wine or beer and distill out the alcohol. Such seventeenth-century spirits did not possess a very pleasant flavor, and something had to be done about it. The solution was found in gin.

English soldiers returning from the seventeenth-century wars on the Continent brought back a taste for "Dutch Courage," as they dubbed the beverage. In no time at all gin became the national drink of England, as it has remained ever since. (Contrary to the general belief, the popularity of Scotch whisky among the English is quite recent, only a little more than a century old.)

Queen Anne helped matters along by raising the duties and taxes on French wines and brandies and at the same time lowering the excise tax on English distilled spirits. Naturally the production of this new, inexpensive beverage flourished. In fact, gin was so cheap for a time in England that one innkeeper put up a sign that read:

Drunk for a penny,
Dead drunk for twopence,
Clean straw for nothing!

This gives a mild idea of the kind of gin that was made, although it is unlikely it was much worse than the kind many people drank in America during the bathtub gin era of the twenties.

During the course of the years tremendous improvements have been made in production methods. Today making gin is a highly refined science, with very precise quality controls to ensure continuous uniformity. This does not mean that all gins are identical. Each distiller has his own closely guarded secret formula and method of making gin.

There are only two basic styles or types of gin: Dutch—Hollands, Genever, or Schiedam gin; and Dry—English or American gin, often called London Dry.

Dutch gins are very full flavored and full bodied and possess a complex, malty aroma and taste.

English and American gins are quite light in flavor and body by comparison. They are more aromatic and flavorful.

Hollands Gin

In the Netherlands gin is generally made in the following manner:

1. A grain formula of approximately equal parts of barley malt, corn, and rye is mashed, cooked, and fermented into a beer.
2. The resulting beer is distilled in a pot still and the distillate may be redistilled once or twice. The final spirits, known as malt wine, are distilled off higher than the first distillates, but still at a very low proof, between 100 and 110.
3. The malt wine is then redistilled, together with juniper berries, in another pot still. The first gin is distilled off at between 94 and 98 proof. (Other botanicals are included with the juniper berries, but not in the quantity or variety employed in England and the United States.)

Because of the low proof at which it is distilled, Hollands, Genever, or Schiedam is a very full-bodied gin with a clean but pronounced malty aroma and flavor.

Dutch gin cannot be mixed with other ingredients to make cocktails because its own definite taste will predominate and overshadow whatever other wine or spirit it is mixed with, but a dash of bitters is pleasant.

Dry Gin—English

Originally the term *London Dry Gin* signified gin produced in or near London, where most English gin has always been distilled, but today the term has been adopted by American gin distillers as well as gin producers in other countries. Therefore it has lost its geographical significance. The term *dry* does not have much meaning either, since all English, American, and Dutch gins are equally dry.

English and American gins are very different in character from Dutch gins. This is the result of the different production methods used.

In England making gin begins with a grain formula made up of 75 percent corn, 15 percent barley malt, and 10 percent other grains. This is mashed, cooked, and fermented, much the same as the mash is handled for the production of whisky. After fermentation is completed, the wort, or beer, is distilled and rectified in a column still to obtain a rather pure spirit above 190 proof. This is reduced to 120 proof by the addition of distilled water. The reduced spirit is placed in a gin still, which is usually a pot still, and redistilled in the presence of the flavoring agents, primarily juniper berries. However, other flavoring materials, known as botanicals, are used in rather small quantities to add flavor nuances to the gin. Among those generally used are dried lemon and orange peel, cardamom and coriander seeds, bitter almonds, angelica and orris root, as well as anise, caraway, fennel, licorice, and so on. The precise formula is always a secret. There is also a variation in the method of distilling. Some producers mix the botanicals with the spirit and distill the entire mash, while others place the botanicals on wire mesh trays that are suspended above the spirit in the still, so that the alcohol vapors, upon rising, will pass through and around the botanicals, thus becoming impregnated with the aromatic flavoring oils they contain.

The resulting spirit comes off the gin still at 150 to 170 proof and is recovered as gin. Character can be influenced by adjusting the cutoff in the run, since the aromatics are extracted in varying amounts during the process. Only the heart of the run is used, and it is reduced in proof to bottling strength—80 to 97 proof—and is ready to be marketed. If it is not to be bottled at once, it is stored in glass-lined or stainless steel tanks, since gin is generally not aged.

There is a difference in character between English and American gin, primarily because of the slightly lower proof of the spirits employed by English distillers. These spirits retain some character.

While virtually the whole trade in gin in the British Isles is concerned with London Dry, there are some other varieties. The most important of these is Plymouth Gin. It is a heavier, more strongly flavored gin than the London Dry type.

A few English gin distillers still produce in small amounts a sweetened gin labeled Old Tom Gin. It is rarely sold today.

Dry Gin—American

American gin is either distilled or compounded. Distilled gin can be made by adding the flavor ingredients as part of a continuous process, during which the alcohol is first distilled from the mash, or by redistilling distilled spirits.

In some cases the botanicals are suspended above the liquid so that the flavor is removed by the alcohol vapor. In other cases, when redistillation occurs, the ingredients may be put directly into the alcohol to be redistilled.

Compound gin is made by combining distilled spirits with essential oils or extracts of the botanicals. The main characteristic flavor must be from juniper berries, although many other ingredients are used, each according to the formula of the maker.

Gin produced by original distillation or redistillation may be designated distilled. Compound gin needs no special designation. In every case the type of spirits used must be mentioned on the label.

To make a quality gin the producer must start with neutral spirits that are clean and free of any foreign flavor. The juniper berries and other botanicals must also be of the best grades. Because botanicals vary in flavor content each season, the distiller must continually adjust the proportions to maintain his brand's consistency.

As stated earlier, virtually all gins on the market use the word *dry* as descriptive of the brand. The label may read Dry Gin, Extra Dry Gin, Very Dry Gin, London Dry Gin, or English Dry Gin, but all express the same meaning—lacking in sweetness.

Dry gin is also produced in Germany, Italy, Israel, Norway, the Balkans, and Africa.

FRUIT-FLAVORED GINS

In all gin-producing countries there are people who enjoy a gin with a special flavor: orange, lemon, pineapple, mint, and so forth. These are gins to which the specific flavoring has been added and the name of the flavor put on the label. In the United States these are considered the product of rectification and pay the $0.30-per-gallon rectification tax.

For a product to be a gin the one requirement *sine qua non* is that its principal flavoring agent be juniper berries. There is one exception, however: sloe gin. Sloe gin is a gin in name only since it is a cordial.

Aging Gin

U.S. regulations do not permit any age claims to be made for gin. In fact, gin does not require aging to be smooth, palatable, and drinkable. It is ready for consumption when it comes off the gin still and has been reduced to potable strength. Some producers in the United States do age their gin in wood for short periods of time, which gives the gin a light golden color. This product is often called "Golden" gin, but the producers cannot advertise or make any age claims on the label.

There is a general misconception about Dutch gins being aged. In the Netherlands aging is not recognized by law, although it would still not be illegal to practice it. Whether labeled Hollands, Genever, or Schiedam, the gin is not aged. As it comes from the still it is stored for bottling, either in large, glazed earthenware vats or more often in glass-linked tanks. Any slight yellowish or golden color to be found in Dutch gin is the product of a slight amount of caramel coloring that has been added.

How and When to Serve Gin

Hollands gin should be drunk straight; in the East Indies, however, it is drunk with bitters. Take a regular whisky glass and add two dashes of bitters, roll the glass around until the inside of the glass is covered with the bitters, then throw out the rest. Fill with Hollands gin. It is a quick drink and a good apéritif.

The most popular dry gin cocktail by far is the Dry Martini, but it is only one of hundreds of gin cocktails, such as the Alexander, Negroni, Gibson, and Gimlet. Dry gin is also widely used in long drinks, such as the Gin and Tonic, Tom Collins, Gin Rickey, and Gin and Bitter Lemon, all especially refreshing in warm weather.

Because of the strong juniper flavor, gin may be used in cooking where recipes, such as those for game dishes, call for juniper berries.

RUMS

Rum*, the name of that multifaceted alcoholic beverage, conjures up pictures of Sir Henry Morgan, the Spanish explorers in the New World, and the smugglers, or rum runners, of Prohibition. Its career has been romantic, colorful, and replete with legends, some of which are doubtless apocryphal.

Rum has been in and out of fashion in the United States, but recently its popularity has soared. In fact, one single brand of rum has become the largest selling brand of *any* spirit in the United States. Rum, as a category, doubled from 1975 to 1982, and rum now has 7 percent of the spirits market.

Rum comes from a grass whose botanical name is *Saccharum officinarum*, but it is more commonly known as sugarcane. The earliest mention we have of sugarcane dates back to 327 B.C., when Alexander the Great returned from his expedition to India. Whether sugar-

**Ron* (Spanish); *rhum* (French).

cane originated in the northeastern valleys of India or in the islands of the South Pacific we may never know, but it was finally brought to Europe by the Arabs after A.D. 636. Still, crystallized sugar was a costly rarity until Columbus took cane cuttings from the Canary Islands to the West Indies. It prospered so well there that sugar made from cane became inexpensive and could be enjoyed by everyone.

Almost at once, distillation of rum sprang up as a by-product of the sugar factory. Today it is made in all parts of the world, wherever sugarcane grows.

Rum is any alcoholic distillate or a mixture of distillates from the fermented juice of sugarcane, sugarcane molasses, or other sugarcane by-products distilled at less than 190 proof (whether or not such proof is further reduced before bottling to not less than 80 proof). The distillate must possess the taste, aroma, and characteristics generally attributed to rum.

The early Spanish settlers of the West Indies noted that the residual molasses of their primitive sugar factories fermented easily, so it was natural that they experimented with distilling. The result was a pleasant-tasting alcoholic beverage. The freebooters of the period took the product back to Europe, where it found ready acceptance.

How rum got its name is a matter of conjecture. Its origin is lost among the legends of sixteenth-century swashbuckling pirates. Purists believe it is a shortened form of the Latin *saccharum*, which means "sugar." Another idea is that the wild lads of the Spanish Main first called the product *rumbullion* or *rumbustion*. Still others credit the name to the English Navy. In 1745 Admiral Vernon discovered that his men were suffering from scurvy. Not knowing what to do about it, he cut the daily ration of beer from their diet and replaced it with the strange, new West Indian beverage, which conquered the scurvy problem and won him the lasting regard of his men, who referred to him affectionately as Old Rummy and in his honor called the new drink rum. (In eighteenth-century England the word *rum* was a slang expression used to describe people, things, or events that were very good, the very best. Thus, when the British sailors named the beverage rum it was the highest accolade they could bestow upon it.)

For over three hundred years rum has been made in the West Indies, but it is also produced in other sugarcane-growing sections of the world. It was made in New England, which imported molasses from the West Indies for this purpose. Many New England shipping families engaged in an infamous cycle of trade in the production of New England rum.

Rum, distilled in New England, was carried to Africa, perhaps with stops at Madeira, the Azores, or the Canaries, where some of it was sold. The remainder was exchanged for African blacks, who were brought back to the West

Indies to become slaves, in exchange for molasses that was brought back to New England to be distilled into rum so that the cycle could begin all over again.

The production of rum begins with harvesting the cane. The freshly cut cane is brought to the sugar mills, where it is passed through enormous, very heavy crushing rollers that express the juice. The juice is boiled to concentrate the sugar and evaporate the water. Then it is clarified. The result is a heavy, thick syrup.

The syrup is pumped into high-speed centrifugal machines, whirling at over twenty-two hundred revolutions per minute, where the sugar in the syrup is crystallized and separated from the other solids. After the sugar is removed, what remains is molasses. Sometimes this still retains up to 5 percent sugar. The only economical way to recover, or not to lose, the residue of sugar is to ferment this molasses and distill it into rum.

There are four main classifications of rum: the first is

the very dry, light-bodied rums, generally produced in the Spanish-speaking countries, of which Puerto Rican rum is today's outstanding example; the second is the medium-bodied rums; the third is the rich, full-bodied, pungent rums usually produced in the English-speaking islands and countries, the best example of which is Jamaican rum; and the fourth is the light-bodied but pungently aromatic East Indian Batavia arak rum from Java.

The rums of the various islands of the West Indies, as well as those from elsewhere, all have their own individual character. So we have Jamaican rum, Puerto Rican rum, and so forth. The B.A.T.F. declares that the word type cannot be used in identifying a rum, as is done in the case of many wines; rather a rum must carry the name of the locality from which it comes. Therefore there cannot be a Jamaica-type rum made in some other place.

Rums are mainly produced in the region of the Caribbean Sea, including the West Indies and the northern countries of South America. Light-bodied rums are produced in Puerto Rico, the Virgin Islands, the Bahamas, the Dominican Republic, Brazil, Colombia, Venezuela, Mexico, Spain, and Canada. Medium-bodied rums, which are more in the style of the light rums, include those from Haiti, Barbados, Trinidad, and Guyana (known as Demeraran rums). The full-bodied, pungent rums come primarily from Jamaica and Martinique. This does not mean that Puerto Rico produces only light-bodied and Jamaica only full-bodied rums. Both countries can produce both types, but they are better known for their own traditional type.

PUERTO RICAN RUM

The molasses is placed in large vats holding thousands of gallons. Water is added, together with a substantial proportion of mash from a previous distillation. Special yeast strains are added to a small amount of molasses in a test tube. Fermentation begins, and the mixture is transferred to successively larger containers until it reaches the fermenting tanks. Fermentation lasts two to four days.

After fermentation is completed, the fermented mash, containing about 7 percent alcohol, is pumped into a column still, where the spirit is distilled off at 160 proof or higher. Distilling at a high proof produces a spirit low in congeners, light in body, and fairly neutral in flavor.

Only the middle rum (middle part of the distillation), the *madilla*, also called *aguardiente* in the trade, is used for rum. It is aged in seasoned oak barrels, some charred and some uncharred, when color is not desired.

When the rum has matured—after a minimum of one year under Puerto Rican law to more than six years for some special aged rums—it is passed through a filtering and leaching vat. At this point rums are clear with a very light taste and lightness of body. These clear, more neutral rums are designated as White or Silver.

Deeper-colored and more flavored rums, designated as Amber or Gold, are aged a minimum of three years and have caramel added to give a deeper, more uniform color. In the case of rum, caramel does not affect the flavor because rum is a sugar-based product. Most of these rums are marketed at 80 proof.

The characteristic taste of the White and Gold Label rums is dry, with a very slight molasses flavor, the Gold Label being slightly mellower and having a more pronounced taste. A spiced and flavored Puerto Rican rum is available.

The older "liqueur" rums are usually shipped under brand names. While these rums are generally quite dry, they have a fine, mellow, rummy bouquet and flavor. Because of their dryness they can be likened to a fine old brandy. Puerto Rican producers now offer full-bodied rums in addition to the light. These may be labeled either Red Label or Heavy Dark, for Planter's Punch.

Virgin Islands Rum

The Virgin Islands have always been known for three things: rum (the kind you drink), bay rum (the kind you put on your hair), and as pirate hangouts during the days of the Spanish Main.

Purchased by the United States in 1917, the Virgin Islands were subject to our Prohibition laws and had to confine their efforts to bay rum until 1933. The islands were in bad financial straits, and our Department of Insular Affairs decided to assist the islands by reestablishing the Virgin Islands rum industry. Eventually the first shipments of the new rum arrived amid the greatest fanfare of free publicity any liquor ever had. Virgin Islands rum is of the light-bodied type. The best rums are from the island of Saint Croix.

Since the Virgin Islands are part of the United States, much local rum, as well as other spirits, are brought back to the mainland duty-free by visiting American tourists.

Other Light-bodied Rums

While Puerto Rico, the Virgin Islands, and Cuba are the principal areas that produce light-bodied rums, this type is also distilled in the Dominican Republic, Venezuela, Mexico, Brazil, Argentina, Peru, Paraguay, and more recently in Jamaica, Bermuda, and Guyana. Light-bodied rum is also made in Hawaii, the Philippines, and the continental United States.

Medium Rums

Among others in this group are rums from Haiti and Martinique that are made from sugarcane juice, rather than from the more usual molasses. They are made in pot stills, in the French brandy-making tradition, and develop a fine mellow bouquet.

Demeraran Rum

Demeraran rum is distilled from sugarcane molasses grown along the Demerara River in Guyana (formerly British Guiana), South America. The chief difference between Demeraran rum and fuller-bodied rum is the result of the variations in character of the sugarcane and the soil and the fact that Demeraran rum is distilled in column stills. Demeraran rum is much darker and not nearly as pungent as Jamaican rum.

Demeraran rum is obtainable in this market at 80, 86, and 151 proofs. The overproof rum is used in northern lumber camps, by the Grand Banks fishermen, and in Alaska. After exposure to intense cold, these outdoorsmen need a very strong bracer to thaw them out. The rum is generally consumed in the form of grog, that is, mixed half and half with very hot water, as well as in many fancy rum drinks.

When the Zombie became a popular drink, the 151-proof Demeraran rum found a new outlet.

JAMAICAN RUM

The typical Jamaican rum is a full-bodied rum, and its manufacture differs considerably from that of light-bodied rum.

To the molasses in the fermentation vats are added the skimmings from previous distillations—the dunder, known also as burned ale. The natural yeast spores in the air promptly settle on the surface of the liquid mass, multiply rapidly, and cause fermentation to begin.

Some call this wild fermentation and others spontaneous fermentation. The correct term is *natural* fermentation. In addition to the dunder, usually a certain amount of the residue from a previous fermentation is added. This natural free method of fermentation is slower, taking anywhere from five to twenty days, depending on the abundance of free yeast spores and climatic or temperature conditions at the time.

This also permits a larger amount of congeners to develop, which in turn are carried over in the distillation.

The fermented liquor is pumped into a pot still, where it is distilled, producing a low wine. This is then redistilled in another pot still. Only the middle rum, taken off after the heads and before the tails begin to come over, is used.

The new rum is taken off between 140 and 160 proof, sometimes lower. The result is a very full-bodied, very pungent rummy spirit.

The new rum, like all distillates, is colorless, but with time in oak puncheons (casks) it takes on a golden hue. The depth of color of Jamaican rum, however, is governed by the amount of caramel added. Jamaican rums are always blended, and being full bodied and rich in congeners they require more aging than lighter-bodied rums, anywhere from five to seven years and more. Some "liqueur" rums of Jamaica are aged fifteen years before bottling.

Dark mahogany-colored rums have become very popular because they give greater color to the drinks made with them. These darker rums are generally labeled "for Planter's Punch," as this is the drink in which they are used most often. The intense color is produced by adding caramel.

Jamaica's best market is Great Britain, where much of the rum is shipped for aging and blending. The damp climate is excellent for maturing rum. (Jamaican rums are usually shipped to Britain at their original high proof. They are reduced to potable strength at the time of bottling by adding only water.) Such rums, when they are stored and blended in bonded warehouses at the London docks, are known in the trade as London Dock rums.

Jamaican rums are usually marketed at 86 to 97 proof and occasionally at 151 proof. Traditional Jamaican rum is the most pungent of all alcoholic beverages. It has a unique, buttery molasses aroma and flavor. Recently some producers have installed column stills and are making light rums.

Batavia Arak

Arak is a rum produced from molasses that comes from the sugar factories near Batavia (the former name of Djakarta), on the island of Java, in the Republic of Indonesia (formerly Dutch East Indies). Because of the special treatment given the molasses and the special quality of the river water used in fermentation, a dry, highly aromatic rum results. The quality of arak owes much, too, to the wild, uncultured yeast *Saccharomyces vordermanni* and to the little cakes of specially cooked and dried red Javanese rice that are placed in the fermenting tubs of molasses.

The arak is aged for three or four years in Java, after which it is shipped to Holland, where it is aged for another four to six years, blended, and then bottled.

Arak is a brandylike rum of great pungency and rumminess and is used as is any other rum. In Sweden, however, its greatest use is for making Swedish Punsch.

New England Rum

New England rum is now obsolete and was eliminated from the U.S. Standards of Identity in 1968. It was straight rum, distilled at less than 160 proof, with considerable body and pungency.

How and When to Serve Rum

In rum-producing countries rum is drunk straight, rather than in mixtures, and this is the best way to appreciate the qualities of a fine rum. In the United States the most popular ways of drinking rum are with cola, in Daiquiris (see page 403 for recipe), on the rocks, with water and other mixers, such as 7-Up, tonic, and orange juice, and as a substitute for gin in Martinis.

There has been a great change in the market in the last few years, and exotic drinks made with rum, while still consumed, particularly in Polynesian restaurants, have been overtaken by the more contemporary drinks, which are simpler to prepare.

Rums are used extensively in the kitchen for making sauces, for desserts, and in ice creams and candies.

Finally, rum, when it has been denatured to make it unsuitable for beverage purposes, and thus not subject to high consumption taxes, is one of the most widely used flavors in the tobacco industry.

OTHER SPIRITS

In all countries where spirits are produced, man has always used the most available and least costly basic material. Thus we find brandies where grapes and fruits are grown, whiskies where corn and barley are grown, and rum where sugarcane is grown.

This chapter will discuss some of the more interesting and popular spirits produced from, and occasionally flavored by, local products.

ANISE/LICORICE-FLAVORED SPIRITS

No alcoholic beverage has been less understood than absinthe, poetically described as "the water of the Star Wormwood—the Green Muse." It was supposed to be wicked, to drive the drinker insane, and to have killed many. In France its sale was prohibited before World War I because of the belief that it would cause a decrease in the birthrate. Possibly it could have done all these terrible things, as it was one of the most potent of all alcoholic beverages. It was not, however, because of the wormwood that it was so dangerous, but rather because of its alcoholic strength. Absinthe was generally shipped at a proof of 136 (68 percent alcohol). The sale of absinthe is prohibited in Switzerland, where it was invented, as well as in France, the United States, and most other countries.

Just what was this absinthe of which we heard so much and of which we know so little? The "elixir" absinthe was composed of aromatic plants, *Artemisia mayoris* and *vulgaris*, balm-mint, hyssop, fennel, star-anise, and a high-proof spirit. It was invented toward the end of the eighteenth century by a physician and pharmacist, Dr. Ordinaire, a French exile living in Couvet, Switzerland. In 1797 Henri-Louis Pernod acquired the recipe, and since that time the Pernod name has been so closely associated with absinthe that they have become synonymous.

The classic absinthe drink was the Absinthe Drip,

which required a special two-piece glass. A jigger of absinthe was poured into the glass, then a cube of sugar placed over the drip hole of the upper section, which was then packed with cracked ice. Cold water was added to fill the dripper. When all of the water had dripped through, the drink was ready. Some people preferred a slightly sweeter drink, which was made by using one ounce of absinthe and one ounce of anisette. This drink was an excellent restorative in cases of seasickness, airsickness, and nausea. One was enough.

Since absinthe is prohibited in the United States and other countries, the Pernod firm produces, in France, an anise-flavored spirit of 90 proof that is reminiscent in flavor and character of absinthe. It has a light yellow-green color and a sharp, pronounced aroma, in which the dominant note is licorice. When it is mixed with water (as it always should be), it changes color, becoming streaked, then milky, and finally a cloudy opalescent color.

The highly concentrated natural essential oils that give the flavor to these products are more soluble in alcohol than in water. Therefore when water is added the oils precipitate, making the mixture cloudy. If a great deal of water is added, they become clear again. Since anise has a strong flavor, up to five parts water are added to these spirits for general consumption.

There are other anise products produced throughout the world. They vary one from another, but none is absinthe, since the formulas do not contain wormwood. They are popular drinks of the countries bordering the Mediterranean. The product is known in each country by its local name—thus in Spain it is Ojen; in France it is Pastis, the best-known brand of which is Ricard; in Italy it is Anesone; in Greece it is Ouzo and Mastikha; in Israel it is Arak; in Turkey it is Raki; and in the U.S. it is Herbsaint. They are rarely ever drunk neat but usually mixed with water, similarly to Pernod, producing a long opalescent cooler. They are served both as apéritifs and as refreshers.

Aquavit (Akvavit)

Aquavit literally means "water of life," since it has been considered a cure for various ailments since the 1500's. It is the national beverage of the Scandinavian countries.

The method of producing Aquavit is similar in Denmark (where it is called Akvavit), Norway, Sweden, and Iceland, although there are some variations, mainly in the proportions of flavorings.

Aquavit may be made from a fermented mash of either barley malt and grain or potatoes, depending on the time of the year. The potatoes have an especially high starch content, grown for this purpose. The principal flavoring is the caraway seed. Aquavit is first distilled as a neutral spirit at 190 proof, reduced with demineralized water to 120 proof, and then redistilled with flavorings, similar to the production of gin. In addition to caraway, other botanicals may be used, such as coriander, fennel, cinnamon, anise, cardamom, and other botanicals originally selected for their medicinal properties.

Aquavit is matured for about a year before bottling. It is colorless, with an alcoholic strength of 80 proof. There is also an Aquavit that is amber-colored, and 90 proof. This has a strong yellow-dill flavor in addition to the caraway.

Some compare Aquavit to the liqueur Kümmel, because they both have a pronounced caraway flavor. Kümmel, however, is sweetened with syrup, and is only 70 to 80 proof. Aquavit, of course, is quite dry.

Aquavit is always served ice cold. While it may substitute for the gin or vodka in cocktails, it is usually taken neat with food—appetizers, small open sandwiches in the Scandinavian style, caviar, and smoked fish—often with a beer chaser. The usual portion of Aquavit is one ounce, not sipped, but taken at one swallow. It is traditionally drunk to this Scandinavian toast:

Skaal! Min skaal—din skaal,
Alla vackra flickornas skaal!
Health! My health—your health,
All the pretty girls' health!

Bitters

Bitters consist of bitter and aromatic essences and flavors incorporated into an alcohol base. The flavors come from fruits, plants, seeds, flowers, leaves, bark, roots, and stems. Most bitters are made from closely guarded formulas, proprietary secrets handed down from generation to generation. These products are the result of infusion and distillation processes and their one common characteristic is bitterness.

Bitters are classified into two categories: fit for use as

beverages and not fit for use as beverages. Those fit for beverages are subject to the Internal Revenue tax of $10.50 per tax gallon plus $0.50 per tax gallon duty if imported. Bitters not fit for beverage use made in the United States have a $1.00 per tax gallon Internal Revenue tax. If bitters are imported and are not fit for beverages, there is no Internal Revenue tax and the applicable duty is $0.94 per tax gallon.

Bitters not fit for beverages contain components of such nature or in such amounts that only small quantities of the bitters can be used as flavoring agents in cocktails and general cuisine. The best known of this type is Angostura Bitters, which is made in Trinidad. Other such bitters are Peychaud's from New Orleans, Underberg from Germany, and various orange bitters.

Bitters fit for beverages include stomachics or aids to digestion such as Fernet Branca and Unicum from Italy. Campari is a beverage bitter from Italy, where its consumption is so pervasive that premixed and bottled Campari and soda is sold everywhere.

Okolehao

Hawaii has made several contributions to our way of life, but the most exotic offering is Okolehao, or Oke, as it is known on the islands.

According to the producer of Okolehao, it is distilled solely from fermented mash of the roots of the sacred ti plant of Hawaii (*Cordyline australis*). Okolehao was first made by an Australian, William Stevenson, about 1790. He cooked the ti roots, which are rich in levulose (fructose), and allowed the mash to ferment in the bottom of a canoe. He then distilled the fermented mash in a still constructed from a ship's cooking pot, with an inverted calabash for a lid and a water-cooled gun barrel for a coil.

Today, of course, Okolehao is distilled in a modern

distillery employing column stills and all the most advanced scientific mashing and distilling control techniques.

Okolehao is not aged. After distillation it is filtered through charcoal. Both a Crystal Clear and a Golden Oke are produced. It has an unusual and subtle flavor. Okolehao is marketed at 80 proof. It is drunk straight, on the rocks, in tall drinks, and in highballs, and it is employed in the preparation of a number of intriguingly named cocktails, such as Mahalo, which means "thank you" in Hawaiian, Ti A'A Sour, Scratch Me Lani, Okole-Wow, No-Mo-Pain, Aloha, and Coke and Oke.

Pimm's Cup

Pimm's Cup is a drink that dates back more than a century. The story is that a bartender in a Pimm's restaurant in the London financial district invented the original gin sling many years ago, and the patrons liked it so much they used to ask that it be prepared for them in quantity so they could take it up to the country when they went on holiday. From the numerous requests of this nature, it was natural that the drink be prepared commercially. Today it is produced in England as Pimm's No. 1, at 67 proof. It is sweetened, and flavored with herbs, spices, and fruits. Pimm's is served over ice with soda and a twist of lemon or lime, for a satisfying, cooling thirst quencher.

Tequila and Pulque

Tequila is a descendant of the first alcoholic beverage produced in North America, the origins of which are interwoven with Aztec history. Before the Spaniards brought the art of distillation to Mexico in the early 1500s, the Aztecs were drinking a winelike liquid called pulque. Pulque is the fermented product of the mezcal plant, which belongs to the genus *agave* (which the Spanish referred to as *maguey*). Pulque has a rather heavy flavor resembling sour milk, but it is much appreciated by the Mexicans because of its cooling, wholesome, and nutritional properties. Pulque is always consumed freshly made and is not readily available very far from its source.

When pulque is distilled it makes a *maguey* brandy, known as *vino mezcal*. The best *vino mezcal* is Tequila, which comes from the upland valleys surrounding the town of Tequila, northwest of Guadalajara, in the state of Jalisco, Mexico.

The Mexican government has decreed that only the superior *vino mezcal* from a carefully delineated section of Jalisco may be called Tequila, just as the French, for example, earlier declared that only brandies from the province of Charente could be called Cognac. There are about twenty-six Tequila distillers in the town of Tequila.

The best species of mezcal plant, grown near Tequila,

is the *Agave tequileana* Weber, blue variety. There are hundreds of varieties of the proliferous mezcal *agave* plant, and their differences are marked enough that one makes a good Tequila and another does not. The blue *agave* is cultivated for Tequila production. Many people believe that the mezcal plant is a type of cactus, but technically it belongs to the amaryllis family (*Amarillydaceae*). The mezcal plant takes ten to twelve years to reach proper maturity, at which time the sap flows to the base. When the plant reaches maturity, the outer leaves are removed and the base, resembling a pineapple but larger and heavier, weighing 75 to 150 pounds, is cut from the plant, leaving a stump.

These "pineapples," or heads of the plant, are heavy with sweet sap called *aguamiel* ("honey water"). When the matured agave heads arrive at the distillery, they are split open and placed in an oven, where they are steamed for nine to twenty-four hours at 200 degrees Fahrenheit.

This causes a considerable amount of *aguamiel* to run off freely. The heads are then shredded and the remaining juice is expressed by mechanical means. The juices are placed in large vats to ferment, creating *madre pulque* ("mother pulque").

Because the mezcal plant takes ten to twelve years to mature fully, while consumption of Tequila has increased dramatically, the Mexican government now permits the addition of up to 49 percent of other sources of fermentable sugars to the must. Premium Tequilas may still be made from 100 percent blue agave. To start fermentation and to ensure uniform character, a small amount of must from a previous fermentation is added to each new batch. Fermentation takes about two and a half days. The fermented product is distilled in copper pot stills, first to 28 proof, and then redistilled at 104 to 106 proof.

The Tequila shipped to this country as White is unaged. It is reduced in proof with demineralized water when it leaves the still, and bottled at 80 proof, although some Tequila is shipped to the United States in bulk and is bottled here. A few producers ship a Gold Tequila, which is purported to be aged in oak vats. Gold Tequila has no official government recognition and is aged and colored before bottling at the discretion of the producer. *Anejo* ("aged") Tequila, which has been aged for at least one year in seasoned oak, is recognized officially. *Anejo* Tequilas are often shipped at from 92 to 101 proof.

Tequila has a distinctive flavor, quite different from other spirits. Its flavor is assertive and reveals its herbaceous origins. Tequila has a natural affinity to lime juice and salt. The traditional method of drinking Tequila in Mexico is a ceremony in itself. The imbiber takes a wedge of lime or lemon, puts a pinch of salt on his thumbnail or on the back of his hand, and pours a chilled jigger of Tequila. He then bites the lime, licks the salt, and gulps down the Tequila.

Another way Mexicans enjoy Tequila is with Sangrita, a spicy tomato and citrus juice mixture that is held in one hand while the Tequila is held in the other. They are sipped alternately.

The Margarita, a Tequila cocktail developed in Los Angeles, was the springboard to Tequila consumption in this country. Since 1969, when Tequila imports were 770,000 gallons, or 0.2 percent of the total distilled spirits market, consumption has jumped to 8 million gallons in 1982, or 1.8 percent of the market. This is a remarkable increase of over 1,000 percent.

Tia Maria from Jamaica is claimed to be the original coffee-flavored liqueur. It is made on a rum base with local Blue Mountain coffee. 63 proof.

COCKTAILS AND OTHER MIXED DRINKS

The cocktail is a purely American institution, and there are almost as many versions of the origin of its name as there are legends about the beds George Washington is said to have slept in. Actually, the first cocktail was made by the first person who mixed his wine with a bit of honey or an herb or two to give it zest.

One story is that Betsy Flanagan, a spirited Irish lass who had a tavern near Yorktown, New York, was responsible for naming the cocktail. In 1779 Betsy's Tavern was a meeting place for the American and French officers of Washington's army. Here they came to relax and to fortify themselves for the rigors of the campaign with a concoction called a bracer. The officers used to tease Betsy about the fine chickens owned by a Tory neighbor, until one day she threatened to make them eat their words.

No true patriot would buy anything from a Tory, but Betsy arranged for the patrons of her tavern to have a Tory chicken feast, and when it was over they repaired to the bar to continue the celebration with bracers. To their amusement, they found each bottle of bracer decorated with a cock's tail from the Tory farmer's roost. A toast was called for, and one of the Frenchmen exclaimed: "*vive le cock tail.*" Thenceforth Betsy's concoctions were known as cocktails, a name that has prevailed to this day.

A cocktail is a fairly short drink made by mixing liquor and/or wine with fruit juices, eggs, and/or bitters, by either stirring or shaking in a bar glass. A mixed drink is liquor with a mixer, usually served in a tall glass over ice.

Cocktails made from liquor and wine are always stirred, except in a few private clubs, where traditionally they are shaken. Cocktails that include sugar or eggs are always shaken. Mixing in an electric blender gives the same effect as shaking.

The object of a cocktail is to mix two or more ingredients so that the result is a pleasant, palatable drink. No single ingredient should overshadow the rest. An unbalanced mixture produces an unsatisfying drink. Because cocktails are always mixed with ice, their strength varies with the length of time they remain in contact with the ice, which dilutes the liquor as it melts.

If you want to be sure that your cocktails are always the same, use a measure for the ingredients and always use exactly the same quantities. While experienced bartenders usually measure by eye, their drinks vary. This does not necessarily mean that they produce a good cocktail and then a bad one, but simply that at a large bar, where there are several bartenders, no two will make identical cocktails unless they all use a measuring jigger. Here are some important measurements:

A jigger is 1½ liquid ounces
A pony is 1 liquid ounce
A liquid ounce is 2 tablespoons
A dash is ⅙ teaspoon, or about 10 drops
A teaspoon is ⅙ ounce
A wineglass is 4 ounces

Sometimes recipes are given in parts, as cocktail glasses vary greatly in size. Melting ice adds from ½ to ¾ ounce liquid to a cocktail if it is shaken for ten seconds, and proportionately more if shaken longer.

There are a few fundamentals that if followed with care will contribute to making pleasant, palatable mixed drinks.

1. Accuracy in the formula ensures uniformity. Follow recipes carefully.
2. Measure ingredients. Use a measuring jigger.
3. Mixed drinks are only as good as the ingredients used. Always use the best, whether it be liquor, fruit juice, or mixer.
4. Always use fresh, clean ice. Never rinse or reuse ice even for making a new batch of the same cocktail. Use ice cubes for long drinks and cocktails that are stirred. Use cracked ice for cocktails that are shaken. Shaved ice is too fine in a hand-shaken cocktail; it will melt

and dilute before chilling the drink properly. When making drinks in a blender, however, shaved ice is the most practical to use.

5. To remove the snowy look on ice cubes, sprinkle them with lukewarm water.
6. Use only perfect, fresh fruit. Do not slice oranges or lemons too thinly; they will curl and appear to droop. Cover the sliced fruit with a damp napkin to keep it fresh and prevent it from drying out. When preparing orange or lemon peel for garnish, remove the white pithy underlining, as it is bitter. A twist is a small strip of peel that is twisted over the glass to release its aromatic oils. It is then dropped into the drink.
7. Lemons and oranges give more juice if you first soak them in warm water.
8. Use only the best mixer, be it soda water,* tonic (or

*Wherever soda water is mentioned, it is used as a generic term that includes sparkling water, charged water, mineral water, seltzer, and club soda.

quinine water), ginger ale, or whatever. A mediocre or poor mixer will spoil the finest liquor.

9. For aromatic bitters* or other ingredients where the recipe usually specifies only a dash, use a special dasher stopper. Thus will ensure the proper dash, which is 1/6 teaspoon.
10. Whenever granulated sugar is called for, use superfine sugar, as it will dissolve more easily than the standard granulated sugar.
11. Use white of egg only for foaming cocktails.
12. When mixing the ingredients for a cocktail, always add the liquor last. For a mixed drink, put the liquor in first.
13. Stir briskly cocktails that should be stirred. These are generally mixtures of liquor and wine. Stir long enough to mix—approximately seven stirs.
14. Shake firmly (do not rock) cocktails that are shaken.

*Wherever aromatic bitters are mentioned, use Angostura or Peychaud's brand.

These are usually cocktails that contain sugar, fruit juices, cordials, or cream.

15. To muddle ingredients, use a wooden muddler or the back of a spoon to crush solid pieces so they may be mixed with the liquid.
16. Glassware should sparkle.
17. Always strain cocktails before serving them.
18. Do not leave ice in the "dividend" remaining in the cocktail shaker. It will dilute the remains and produce a watery second round.
19. Serving a cocktail in a prechilled glass will keep it cold longer than serving it in a warm glass. If you wish to frost the rim of the cocktail glass, moisten the rim lightly and dip it in powdered sugar.

Sometimes recipes call for a syrup, three of which are described below.

These may be either made or purchased.

Sugar Syrup may be prepared in advance and stored in the refrigerator. To make sugar syrup, dissolve 2 cups sugar in 1 cup water in a saucepan. Simmer for 5 to 10 minutes. Pour into a bottle or jar, cool, and cover. Larger amounts may be prepared for punches. Use wherever recipes call for sugar syrup or simple syrup.

Grenadine is sweet and has a deep red color and the flavor of pomegranates. In fact, the French word for pomegranate is *grenadier*. Grenadine is available without alcohol or with very little alcohol, about 5 proof. It is an ingredient in certain mixed drinks, but it may also be used as a general sweetening agent.

Falernum is a pleasant flavoring syrup, with a small amount of alcohol (6 percent), made up of simple syrup, lime, almond, ginger, cloves, and other spices and flavorings. It is milky colored.

Falernum was invented over two hundred years ago in Barbados, British West Indies, and was named after the ancient Falernian wine of Roman times. Aside from this, Falernum has no connection with wine or Italy, for it is made in the West Indies and the United States. Its principal use is as a flavoring and sweetening ingredient in rum drinks.

Orgeat is a sweet, white, nonalcoholic, almond-flavored syrup.

TYPES OF MIXED DRINKS

Mixed drinks have a very special nomenclature. The following list should be helpful in identifying the type of mixed drink, the glass in which it is served, and the ingredients of which it is made.

Drink	Glass	Ingredients	Ice
Apéritif	Wine or cocktail Old-fashioned	Straight and mixed	Chill Cubes
Cobbler	Stemmed goblet	Whisky, sherry, or port; sugar; fruit	Cracked or shaved
Cocktail	Cocktail Old-fashioned	According to recipe	Cracked—in shaker only Cubes
Collins	Collins	Liquor, lemon juice, sugar, soda water, fruit	Cracked
Cooler	Collins	Liquor, lemon juice, ginger ale or soda water, grenadine or sugar, bitters, fruit if desired	Cracked
Crusta	Wine	Liquor, orange slice, lemon juice, maraschino, aromatic bitters (sugar rim of glass)	Cracked—in shaker only
Cup	Stem glass or cup (serve in pitcher or bowl)	Liquor, Curaçao, cucumber rind, brandy, fruit, mint	Cubes or block
Daisy	Highball or metal stein	Liquor, grenadine, lemon juice, soda water, fruit	Shaved
Eggnog	Cup or old-fashioned	Liquor, egg, milk, sugar, nutmeg	Cracked—in shaker only
Fix	Highball	Liquor, lemon juice, sugar, water, fruit	Shaved
Fizz	Highball	Liquor, lemon juice, sugar, soda water	Cubes
Flip	Cocktail	Liquor, sugar, egg, nutmeg	Cracked—in shaker only
Frappe	Cocktail or saucer	Liqueur	Shaved

Drink	Glass	Ingredients	Ice
Highball	Highball	Liquor, ginger ale or soda water	Cubes
Hot Buttered Rum	Mug	Rum, sugar, hard butter, cinnamon, cloves, nutmeg	Boiling water
Julep	Tankard or Collins	Liquor, sugar, mint	Shaved
Puff	Collins	Brandy, fresh milk, tonic	Cubes
Punch	Cup, Collins, or tankard	According to recipe	Cubes or block (serve in bowl)
Rickey	Highball	Liquor, lime, soda water	Cubes
Sangaree	Highball	Liquor, sweetening, nutmeg	Cracked
Sling	Collins	Liquor, fruit juice, liqueurs, soda water, fruit	Cubes
Smash	Old-fashioned	Liquor, lump sugar, mint	Cubes
Sour	Sour	Liquor, lemon juice, sugar, fruit	Cracked—in shaker only
	Old-fashioned		Cubes
Swizzle	Highball	Liquor, sweetening, soda water	Cubes
Toddy	Toddy (hot) Old-fashioned (cold)	Liquor, lemon, sugar, cloves, cinnamon	Boiling water Cubes

MARTINI

There is no standard recipe on which all professionals agree. Tastes change with time. The best example of this is the manner in which the fashion has changed for the Martini.

The Martini has always been the most popular cocktail. It is a dry, sharp, appetite-whetting drink, and it is simple to make, requiring less fuss and bother than many other mixtures. Consequently it is made more often in the home.

Those who make this cocktail at home develop a taste for it and naturally order it when they go to a bar.

There is some question as to the origin of the Martini and how it got its name. The earliest recipe we have been able to find is for the Martinez Cocktail, which appeared in Professor Jerry Thomas's *Bon Vivant's Companion* or *How to Mix Drinks*, originally published in 1862. His recipe is a far cry from today's.

Through the years the cocktail became progressively drier. By the time it was referred to as a Martini it had become a mixture of equal parts gin and dry vermouth. Before World War I the accepted standard was two parts gin to one part dry vermouth, stirred briskly with large pieces of ice and strained into a cocktail glass. For twenty years after Repeal the standard recipe was four parts gin to one part dry vermouth. The ratio gradually crept up to fifteen to one, and eventually to the foolishness of chilled gin being called a Martini because it was served in a cocktail glass. When one of the basic ingredients of a recipe is totally eliminated, it is time to give the recipe a new name.

To give you a clearer picture of the development of the Dry Martini recipe, note the changes that have taken place over the past century.

Martinez Cocktail

(Professor Jerry Thomas's original recipe)

1 dash bitters

2 dashes maraschino liqueur

1 pony Old Tom gin

1 wineglass vermouth

2 small lumps of ice

Shake up thoroughly and strain into a large cocktail glass. Put a quarter of a slice of lemon in the glass and serve. If the guest prefers it very sweet, add two dashes of gum syrup.

Martini Cocktail

(Mauve Decade recipe)

1 part gin

1 part dry vermouth

Dry Martini Cocktail

(pre-Prohibition)

2 parts gin

1 part dry vermouth

1 dash orange bitters

Very Dry Martini Cocktail

(pre-World War II)

4 parts gin

1 part dry vermouth

1 dash orange bitters or twist of lemon

Martini

(post-World War II)

15 parts gin

1 part dry vermouth

garnishes

Naked Martini

gin on the rocks

garnishes

There appears to be a reversal taking place in Martini fashion. Some devotees who enjoy a not-so-dry Martini have reverted to the pre-World War II recipe of a four-to-one Martini. These ingredients are stirred in a mixing glass with ice, and in most bars a piece of lemon peel is twisted over the cocktail after it is strained into the glass to give the added zip of the oil from the peel. A Martini can also be served on the rocks and should be garnished with a small olive. If garnished with one or more pearl onions, the drink becomes a Gibson. Some variations that have captured popular fancy are:

Vodka or Aquavit Martini

7 parts vodka or aquavit

1 part dry vermouth

Saké Martini (Sakini)

3 parts gin

1 part saké

olive

COCKTAILS

The following are standard recipes for the most popular cocktails and long drinks. In addition to these, new cocktails are continuously being developed. Some are successful and endure, while others last only a short time.

Alexander

½ ounce créme de cacao

½ ounce gin

½ ounce heavy cream

Shake well with cracked ice and strain into cocktail glass.

Variation: For a Brandy Alexander, substitute brandy for the gin.

Americano

1½ ounces Campari

1½ ounces sweet vermouth

Pour over cracked ice in old-fashioned glass and stir. Add twist of lemon.

Bacardi

juice of ½ large or 1 small lime

½ teaspoon sugar

1 dash grenadine

1½ ounces Bacardi White Label rum

Shake lime juice, sugar, and grenadine with cracked ice until cold. Put in rum and shake until shaker frosts. Strain into cocktail glass.

Banshee

1 ounce cream

½ ounce simple syrup

¾ ounce white créme de cacao

¾ ounce créme de bananes (1½ ounces chocolate banana liqueur may be substituted for the créme de cacao and créme de bananes.)

Blend with shaved ice and strain into cocktail glass.

Between The Sheets

juice of ¼ lemon

½ ounce brandy

½ ounce Triple Sec or Cointreau

½ ounce light rum

Shake well with cracked ice and strain into cocktail glass.

Black Russian

1 ounce vodka

½ ounce Kahlua

Pour over ice cubes in old-fashioned glass and stir.

Variation: For a White Russian, add ½ ounce cream.

Brandy Crusta

Moisten the edge of a cocktail glass with lemon juice and dip in sugar. Cut the rind of half a lemon into a spiral and place in glass. To a bar glass add:

1 teaspoon lemon juice

1 teaspoon maraschino

¾ ounce Triple Sec

1½ ounces brandy

1 dash aromatic bitters

Shake well with cracked ice and strain into cocktail glass. Add slice of orange.

Brave Bull

1½ ounces Tequila

1 ounce Kahlua

Pour over ice cubes in old-fashioned glass and stir. Add twist of lemon.

Bronx

In a mixing glass muddle several pieces of sliced orange that have a bit of the rind on them to give flavor. To this add:

½ ounce sweet vermouth

½ ounce dry vermouth

1 ounce gin

Shake well with cracked ice and strain into cocktail glass.

Champagne Cocktail

Place 1 cube of sugar saturated with 1 dash of aromatic bitters in cocktail glass. Add cube of ice. Fill glass with chilled Champagne and add twist of lemon.

Clover Club

¾ ounce lemon juice

white of 1 egg

1½ ounces gin

1 teaspoon grenadine

Shake well with cracked ice and strain into cocktail glass.

Daiquiri

This is the most popular cocktail made with light rum. The origin of the recipe is unknown, but the drink got its name shortly after the Spanish-American War of 1898, when a group of American engineers was invited to Santiago, Cuba, to help develop the Daiquiri iron mines. The job was hard, the climate was hot, and at the end of a long day's work the men needed a refreshing relaxer. It was made from the ingredients most readily available—rum, limes, ice, and sugar to balance the acidity of the lime juice. On weekends the engineers' headquarters in Santiago was the bar of the Venus Hotel, where the bartender would make this cocktail for them. On one such occasion, early in 1900, Jennings S. Cox, the chief engineer, suggested that the cocktail be named the Daiquiri after the mines, and so it has remained ever since.

Perhaps the biggest Daiquiri ever made was mixed right at the mines in honor of Charles M. Schwab, president of Bethlehem Steel Company, on one of his inspection trips. According to accounts, the hosts used half an oak barrel into which they emptied two big pails of ice, the juice of a hundred limes, a pound of sugar, and ten bottles of Bacardi Carta Blanca rum. This was stirred briskly with a wooden paddle and ladled out to Schwab and his entourage when they emerged from the mine pits.

If it is properly made, a Daiquiri is a most delightful and refreshing cocktail. It must never be made with lemon juice; only freshly squeezed lime juice will make a proper Daiquiri. You can also use the frozen Daiquiri mix, which contains lime juice. For the Daiquiri as it was prepared in the Floradida Bar in Havana, Cuba, add ¼ ounce maraschino.

Daiquiri

juice of ½ lime, freshly squeezed

1 teaspoon sugar

1½ ounces light rum

Shake the lime juice and sugar with cracked ice until it gets cold. Add rum and shake until the shaker frosts. Strain into cocktail glass.

Important: A Daiquiri should be drunk immediately because the rum, lime, and sugar tend to separate if the drink is allowed to stand.

Frozen Daiquiri

For a Frozen Daiquiri, use the basic Daiquiri ingredients, with shaved ice instead of cracked ice, and mixed in a blender. Add ⅓ Cup sliced strawberries to blender for a Frozen Strawberry Daiquiri.

Dubonnet Cocktail

½ ounce gin

1 ounce red Dubonnet

Stir well with cracked ice and strain into cocktail glass.

Frappé

Pour 1½ ounces of any liqueur into a cocktail or saucer glass filled with finely shaved ice. Serve with a straw.

Gimlet

½ ounce Rose's Lime Juice

1½ ounces gin

Stir with an ice cube and strain into cocktail glass or serve over ice cubes in old-fashioned glass. Garnish with a slice of lime.

Variation: For a Vodka Gimlet, substitute vodka for the gin, or white rum for a Rum & Rose's.

Godfather

1½ ounces Scotch whisky

1½ ounces amaretto

Pour over ice cubes in old-fashioned glass and stir.

Godmother

1½ ounces vodka

1½ ounces amaretto

Pour over ice cubes in old-fashioned glass and stir. Some cream may be added.

Golden Cadillac

2 ounces light cream

¾ ounce Galliano liqueur

¾ ounce white créme de cacao

Shake well with cracked ice and strain into cocktail glass.

Grasshopper

¾ ounce light cream

¾ ounce green créme de menthe

¾ ounce white créme de cacao

Shake well with cracked ice until very cold. Strain into cocktail glass.

Half & Half

2 ounces sweet vermouth

2 ounces dry vermouth

Pour over ice cubes in old-fashioned glass and stir. Add twist of lemon.

Jack Rose

juice of ½ lime

1 teaspoon grenadine

1½ ounces applejack

Shake well with cracked ice and strain into cocktail glass.

Mai Tai

½ teaspoon sugar

½ ounce lime juice

1 ounce light rum

1 ounce dark rum

½ ounce Curaçao

½ ounce Orgeat

1 ounce grenadine

Shake well with cracked ice and strain into cocktail glass or serve over ice cubes in old-fashioned glass. Decorate with fresh pineapple and cocktail cherry.

Manhattan

This was named after the Manhattan Club, which first mixed this drink in 1870.

1½ ounces rye or blended whisky

½ ounce sweet vermouth

1 dash aromatic bitters

or Dry Manhattan

1½ ounces blended whisky

½ ounce dry vermouth

1 dash aromatic bitters

Stir well with cracked ice and strain into cocktail glass.

Decorate with cocktail cherry or twist of lemon.

Margarita

juice of ½ lime or lemon

1½ ounces Tequila

½ ounce Triple Sec

Shake well with cracked ice and strain into cocktail glass rimmed with salt.

Navy Grog

½ ounce lime juice

½ ounce orange juice

½ ounce pineapple juice

½ ounce Falernum

2 ounces dark rum

1 ounce light rum

½ cup finely cracked ice

Blend all ingredients and pour into large old-fashioned glass half filled with shaved ice.

Negroni

1 ounce Campari

1 ounce sweet vermouth

1 ounce gin

Shake well with cracked ice and strain into cocktail glass.

Variation: For a tall drink pour over ice cubes in highball glass and fill with soda water.

Old Fashioned

Place in an old-fashioned glass:

1 cube sugar muddled with ½ jigger water

1½ ounces whisky

3 dashes aromatic bitters

Add ice cubes and stir. Garnish with slice of orange and cocktail cherry. Add twist of lemon and serve with cocktail pick.

Orange Blossom

1 ounce orange juice

1 teaspoon sugar, optional

1½ ounces gin

Shake well with cracked ice and strain into cocktail glass.

Pink Lady

1 egg white

juice of ½ lemon

1½ ounces gin

1½ ounces applejack

½ ounce grenadine

Shake well with cracked ice and strain into cocktail glass.

Pink Squirrel

1 ounce light cream

1 ounce créme de noyaux (almond) or cherry liqueur

½ ounce white créme de cacao

Shake well with cracked ice and strain into cocktail glass.

Presidente

1½ ounces light rum

¾ ounce dry vermouth

2 dashes Curaçao

1 dash grenadine

Shake well with cracked ice and strain into cocktail glass.

Rob Roy

1½ ounce Scotch whisky

½ ounce sweet vermouth

2 dashed aromatic bitters

or Dry Rob Roy

1½ ounce Scotch whisky

½ ounce dry vermouth

2 dashes aromatic bitters

Shake well with cracked ice and strain into cocktail glass.

Rusty Nail

½ ounce Drambuie

1½ ounces Scotch whisky

Pour over ice cubes in old-fashioned glass and stir.

Salty Dog

3 ounces grapefruit juice

1½ ounces gin

dash salt

Pour over ice cubes in old-fashioned glass and stir.

Variation: Substitute Tequila for the gin.

Sazerec

1 cube sugar

1 teaspoon water

½ ounce Pernod, Ricard, or Herbsaint

1 dash aromatic bitters

1 dash Peychaud Bitters

2 ounces Bourbon whisky

Coat the inside of a chilled glass with the Pernod, Ricard, or Herbsaint. Discard any excess. Muddle the cube of sugar with the teaspoon of water and the 2 dashes of bitters. Add ice cubes. Pour in Bourbon and top with twist of lemon. If Peychaud Bitters are not available, use an extra dash of aromatic bitters.

Scarlett O'Hara

2 ounces orange juice

1 ounce grenadine

¾ ounce Southern Comfort

Pour over ice cubes in old-fashioned glass and stir.

Scotch Mist

Pour 1½ ounces Scotch whisky into old-fashioned glass filled with shaved ice. Add twist of lemon.

Variation: For a Whisky Mist, substitute any whisky for the Scotch.

Sherry Flip

1 egg

1 teaspoon sugar

1½ ounces sweet sherry

Shake well and pour over ice cubes in old-fashioned glass. Sprinkle a little nutmeg on top.

Variations: Brandy, port, rum, or whisky may be substituted for the sherry.

Side Car

½ ounce lemon juice

½ ounce Triple Sec

½ ounce brandy

Shake well with cracked ice and strain into cocktail glass.

Stinger

¾ ounce brandy

¾ ounce white créme de menthe

Shake well with cracked ice and strain into cocktail glass. Add twist of lemon.

Tequila Sunrise

4 ounces orange juice

1½ ounces Tequila

½ to ¾ ounce grenadine

Pour orange juice and Tequila over ice cubes in old-fashioned glass and stir. Add grenadine and let it settle to the bottom. Stir very gently and watch the "sunrise."

Whisky Smash

1 cube sugar

1 ounce water

mint sprigs

1½ ounces whisky

Muddle sugar with water and a few sprigs of mint in old-fashioned glass. Add ice cubes. Pour in whisky and stir. Decorate with four or five sprigs of mint. Serve with soda water on the side.

Whisky Sour

¾ ounce lemon or lime juice

1 teaspoon sugar

1½ ounces Bourbon or blended whisky

Shake well with cracked ice and strain into sour glass. When served over ice cubes, use old-fashioned glass. Add cocktail cherry and slice of orange.

Variations: Scotch, gin, brandy, rum, Tequila, or vodka may be substituted for the whisky. For an Apricot Sour, substitute apricot-flavored brandy for the whisky.

LONG DRINKS

Apricot Cooler

juice of ½ lemon or 1 lime

1½ ounces apricot-flavored brandy

2 dashes grenadine

soda water

Shake lemon or lime juice, apricot-flavored brandy, and grenadine well and pour over cracked ice in highball glass. Fill with soda water.

Bloody Mary

3 ounces tomato juice

juice of ½ lemon

1½ ounces vodka

2 dashes Worcestershire sauce

dash of salt and pepper

Shake well (shaking produces a superb drink) and pour over ice cubes in highball glass. This recipe makes an excellent Bloody Mary, particularly when Sacramento or another thick tomato juice is used. Some people use more Worcestershire sauce, some add a dash of Tabasco sauce, and some substitute gin for the vodka.

Bull Shot

1½ ounces vodka

4 ounces beef bouillon

dash of salt and pepper

Pour over ice cubes in highball glass and stir.

Coffee Royale

5 ounces very hot black coffee

1 sugar cube

1½ ounces brandy

Pour coffee into a cup. Place spoon across cup and pour some brandy into spoon with sugar cube. Pour balance of brandy into the coffee. Place before guest and ignite brandy in spoon. Stir when flame subsides and add twist of lemon.

Cuba Libre

1½ ounces light or dark rum

6 ounces cola

Pour over ice cubes in highball glass and stir. Some people squeeze and insert a wedge of a fresh lime.

French 75

juice of 1 lemon

1 teaspoon sugar

1½ ounces brandy

Champagne

Shake lemon juice, sugar, and brandy well and pour over ice cubes in highball glass. Fill with chilled Champagne.

Gin and Bitter Lemon

1½ ounces gin

6 ounces bitter lemon

Pour over ice cubes in highball glass and stir. Add twist of lemon.

Gin Daisy

juice of ½ lemon

½ teaspoon sugar

1 teaspoon grenadine

1½ ounces gin soda water

Shake lemon juice, sugar, grenadine, and gin well and pour over shaved ice in highball glass or metal stein. Add soda water as desired. Garnish with fruit.

Variations: Brandy, rum, vodka, or whisky may be substituted for the gin.

Gin Fix

juice of ¼ lemon

1 tablespoon sugar

1 ounce water

1½ ounces gin

Shake well and pour into highball glass filled with shaved ice. Garnish with lemon slice and other fruit.

Variations: Brandy, rum, or whisky may be substituted for the gin.

Gin Fizz

juice of ½ lemon

1 teaspoon sugar

1½ ounces gin soda water

Shake lemon juice, sugar, and gin well and pour over ice cubes in highball glass. Fill with soda water and add twist of lemon.

Variation: For a Silver Fizz, make as above but shake with 1 egg white.

Gin Rickey

juice and rind of ½ lime

2 ounces gin

soda water

Pour lime juice and gin over ice cubes in highball glass and stir. Fill with soda water and drop lime rind into drink.

Gin and Tonic

1½ ounces gin

6 ounces tonic

Pour over ice cubes in highball glass and stir. Squeeze lime wedge and drop into drink.

Harvey Wallbanger

1 ounce vodka

6 ounces orange juice

½ ounce Galliano liqueur

Pour vodka and orange juice over ice cubes in highball glass and stir. Float liqueur on top.

Highland Cooler

juice of ½ lemon

1 teaspoon sugar

1½ ounces Scotch whisky

2 dashes aromatic bitters

ginger ale

Shake lemon juice, powdered sugar, whisky, and bitters well and pour over ice cubes in Collins glass. Fill with ginger ale.

Variations: Gin, rum, or vodka may be substituted for the Scotch whisky.

Hot Buttered Rum

This is the classic warmer-upper of colonial days, and it is still popular today. It is guaranteed to take away cold stiffness if you have been skating, skiing, or out in the cold too long. We do not recommend it if you are going back out into the freezing cold weather.

1 teaspoon sugar

1½ ounces dark rum

5 ounces boiling water

1 pat hard butter

nutmeg or cloves

1 cinnamon stick

Rinse an 8-ounce mug or cup with hot water. Put in the sugar, rum, and boiling water. Float the pat of butter on the surface and sprinkle with nutmeg. Use the cinnamon stick as a stirrer. Inhale the wonderful aroma and drink while the mixture is good and hot.

Irish Coffee

This drink was made famous by the Buena Vista Cafe at San Francisco's Fisherman's Wharf shortly after World War II. It has since become popular all over the world.

1 teaspoon sugar

1½ ounces Irish whiskey

5 ounces very hot, strong black coffee

whipped cream

Rinse an 8-ounce stemmed goblet with very hot water. Place the sugar in the glass and pour in the Irish whiskey and coffee. Stir to dissolve sugar and top with whipped cream.

Kir

4 ounces chilled dry white Burgundy wine

½ ounce créme de cassis (or to taste)

Pour over ice cubes in wineglass or highball glass and stir.

Mimosa

2 ounces orange juice

6½ ounces (a split) Champagne

1 teaspoon Grand Marnier (optional)

Pour over ice cubes in highball glass and stir.

Mint Julep

In a Collins glass or pewter tankard, dissolve 1 teaspoon sugar in just enough water to cover it. Fill with shaved ice. Pour in Bourbon whisky to within a half-inch of the top. Stir until glass is thoroughly frosted. Decorate generously with fresh mint.

If you want a more pronounced mint flavor, crush a

sprig of mint together with the sugar and water and leave it in the glass. Then pack with ice, add the Bourbon, stir, and decorate.

Moscow Mule

1½ ounces vodka

juice of ½ lime

ginger beer

Pour vodka and lime juice over ice cubes in an 8-ounce copper mug and stir. Fill with ginger beer. Garnish with wedge of lime.

Piña Colada

1½ ounces cream of coconut

3 ounces pineapple juice

3 ounces light rum

Blend with shaved ice and strain into Collins glass. Serve with a straw.

Planter's Punch

1 ounce lime juice

1 teaspoon sugar

2 ounces Jamaican rum

Dissolve the sugar in the lime juice in a bar glass. Put in the rum and cracked ice and shake well. Strain into a highball glass that is half filled with finely cracked ice. Decorate with maraschino cherry, sliver of fresh pineapple, half a slice of orange, and sprig of mint. Serve with a straw.

Port Wine Sangaree

2¼ ounces port wine

½ ounce simple syrup

Pour over ice cubes in highball glass and stir. Grate nutmeg on top.

Rum Swizzle

juice of 1 lime

1 teaspoon powdered sugar

1½ ounces light rum

2 dashes bitters

soda water

Shake lime juice, sugar, rum, and bitters well and pour over ice cubes in highball glass. Fill with soda water. Serve with swizzle stick.

Variations: Brandy, gin, or whisky may be substituted for the rum.

Rum Toddy

1 cube sugar

1½ ounces dark rum

boiling water

1 cinnamon stick

lemon slice

cloves

Place sugar cube and rum in toddy glass and fill with boiling water. Insert one small piece of cinnamon and one slice of lemon garnished with cloves. Stir. Serve with a spoon and a small pitcher of hot water on the side.

Screwdriver

1½ ounces vodka

5 ounces orange juice

Pour over ice cubes in highball glass and stir.

Sherry Cobbler

2 ounces sweet sherry

¾ ounce simple syrup

Pour over shaved ice in stemmed goblet and stir. Decorate with fresh fruits, cubed or slice, cocktail cherry, and sprig of mint. Serve with a straw.

Variations: Whisky or port may be substituted for the sherry.

Singapore Sling

1 ounce lime juice

1 ounce cherry liqueur

2 ounces gin

soda water

Shake lime juice, cherry liqueur, and gin well and pour over ice cubes in Collins glass. Fill with soda water. Decorate with orange slice and sprig of mint. Then add through the middle with a dropper:

4 drops Bénédictine (or 8 drops B & B)

4 drops brandy

This recipe is said to be the original from the Raffles Hotel in Singapore. Modern versions include bitters, grenadine, pineapple juice, and Cointreau.

Sloe Gin Fizz

¾ ounce lemon juice

1 teaspoon sugar

1½ ounces sloe gin liqueur

soda water

Shake lemon juice, sugar, and sloe gin liqueur well and pour over ice cubes in highball glass. Fill with soda water.

Tom Collins

¾ ounce lemon juice

1 teaspoon sugar

1½ ounces gin soda water

Shake lemon juice, sugar, and gin well and pour over ice cubes in Collins glass. Fill with soda water.

Variation: For a Vodka Collins, substitute vodka for the gin.

Tom and Jerry

1 egg, separated

1 teaspoon sugar

1 ounce brandy

1 ounce dark rum

hot milk or boiling water

In an 8-ounce cup mix the yolk of the egg with the sugar. Pour in a brandy and rum. Stir thoroughly. Put in the beaten white of egg and, while stirring, pour in hot milk or boiling water to fill the cup. Sprinkle nutmeg on top.

Vermouth Cassis

1½ ounces dry vermouth

½ ounce créme de cassis

soda water

Pour vermouth and créme de cassis over ice cubes in highball glass and stir. Fill with soda water.

Ward Eight

1 ounce lemon juice

1½ ounces whisky

1 teaspoon grenadine

soda water

Shake lemon juice, whisky, and grenadine well and pour over ice cubes in highball glass. Fill with soda water.

Zombie

The original recipe is supposedly still a closely guarded secret of Don the Beachcomber.

¾ ounce lime juice

¾ ounce pineapple juice

1 teaspoon Falernum or simple syrup

1 ounce light rum

2 ounces medium rum

1 ounce Jamaican rum

½ ounce 151-proof Demeraran rum

½ ounce apricot liqueur

Shake well and pour into 14-ounce Zombie glass half-filled with shaved ice. Garnish with slice of orange and several sprigs of mint. Serve with a straw.

PUNCHES AND WINE CUPS

Brandy Milk Punch

1 pint brandy

1 quart milk

4 teaspoons sugar

Stir together in a punch bowl. Add a small block of ice and dust top liberally with nutmeg. Serves twelve.

Champagne Cup

1 tablespoon sugar

4 ounces brandy

2 ounces Curaçao

1 ounce maraschino

1 ounce Grand Marnier

1 bottle Champagne

Stir together in a pitcher or bowl. Add a small block of ice and decorate with slices of orange and pineapple, one piece of cucumber rind, and sprigs of mint. Serve in a stem glass or punch cup.

Variations: Claret, Rhine wine, or Sauternes may be substituted for the Champagne.

Egg Nog

12 eggs, separated

1 cup sugar

1 quart milk

1 quart heavy cream

1 quart rum, Bourbon, or brandy

Beat egg yolks until light and beat in sugar. Beat in milk and rum, Bourbon, or brandy. Chill. Whip cream until stiff and fold into mixture. Shortly before serving, beat egg whites until stiff and fold in. Sprinkle top with nutmeg.

Fish House Punch

¾ pound loaf sugar

1 to 2 quarts water

1 quart lemon juice

2 quarts Jamaican rum

1 quart Cognac

4 ounces peach liqueur

Dissolve loaf sugar in the water in punch bowl. When entirely dissolved, add lemon juice, then all the other ingredients. Put a large piece of solid ice in the punch bowl and allow the mixture to steep for about two hours, stirring occasionally. In winter, when ice melts slowly, more water may be used; in summer, less. The melting ice dilutes the mixture sufficiently. This will make 1½ gallons, depending on dilution.

This is the original Fish House Punch, made by the Fish House Club, now called the State in Schuylkill, founded in 1732. We are indebted to Anna Wetherill Reed, in whose *Philadelphia Cook Book of Town and Country* this recipe appears.

Maywine Punch

½ package Waldmeister

13 bottles German or Alsatian wine

1 bottle Champagne

2 ounces Bénédictine

2 ounces Cognac

¼ pound sugar

1 quart soda water

Soak Waldmeister (sweet-scented woodruff—a European woodland herb) six hours in 1 bottle of wine. Strain and mix with 12 remaining bottles. Add Champagne, Bénédictine, and Cognac. Dissolve sugar in soda water and add. Decorate with strawberries and fresh Waldmeister. When sufficiently cold, serve in wineglasses from a punch bowl. To keep the punch cold, place a pitcher full of shaved ice in the center of the bowl. This will serve approximately 100 cups of 3½ ounces each.

Mulled Red Wine

2 cups water

1 cup sugar

4 cinnamon sticks

4 cloves

2 lemons

1 bottle claret or Burgundy

Boil the water with the sugar, cinnamon, and cloves for five minutes. Then add the lemons sliced very thin, cover, and let stand for ten minutes. Add the wine and heat gradually, but do not allow to boil. Serve very hot in a pitcher or brown jug. A spoon placed in each glass will prevent it from cracking.

Sangria

Throughout the Spanish-speaking world one of the traditional ways of enjoying wine is in the form of a wine cup, the Sangria. The recipe given is more time-consuming than using bottled Sangria, but the fresh fruit flavor more than compensates.

¼ cup sugar (or to taste)

1 cup water

1 orange, thinly sliced

1 lime, thinly sliced

1 bottle red or white wine

6 ounces soda water

Dissolve sugar in water in large pitcher. Add fruit and wine, plus 12 or more ice cubes. Stir until cold. Add sparkling water. Serve, putting some of the fruit in each glass.

Wassail Bowl

2 cups water

1 teaspoon freshly ground nutmeg

2 teaspoons ground ginger

2-inch stick of cinnamon

6 whole cloves

6 allspice berries

4 coriander seeds

4 cardamom seeds

2 bottles cream sherry or Madeira

2 quarts ale

4 cups sugar

12 eggs, separated

1 cup Cognac or brandy

12 roasted slices of apples or 12 tiny roasted apples

Combine water and spices in a saucepan and simmer for 10 minutes. Add sherry and ale and stir in sugar. Heat, but do not boil. Beat 12 egg yolks until they are pale and thick;

fold in 12 stiffly beaten egg whites. Strain half the ale and sherry mixture over the eggs. Turn into a warmed punch bowl. Bring the remaining ale and sherry to a boil and strain it into the punch bowl. Add Cognac and roasted apples or apple slices.

A Yard of Flannel

1 quart ale

2 egg whites

4 egg yolks

4 tablespoons brown sugar

½ tablespoon nutmeg

Stir brown sugar and nutmeg into beaten egg yolks. Fold in beaten egg whites. Boil ale and gradually stir in egg-sugar-nutmeg mixture. Then pour it rapidly back and forth between two pans until the drink is smooth and finely frothed. Serve hot.

Prepared Cocktails

Certain mixed drinks whose ingredients include wine and spirits can very easily be prepared in large quantities and stored and distributed in bottles and cans. These prepared cocktails are practical for those who do not have facilities in the home for mixing them fresh. They have the advantage of being uniform, and they can be put in the refrigerator until needed. Many come in convenient one- or two-portion containers.

The most popular varieties are Martinis, Manhattans, Sours, and Daiquiris. But prepared cocktails also include Tequila Sours, Margaritas, Vodka Martinis, Scotch Mists, Banana Daiquiris, Black Russians, Gin Collinses and Sours, Gimlets, Screwdrivers, Side Cars, Stingers, and many others. Bottled Sangria is probably the most widely sold wine cocktail.

The liquor industry had to overcome many obstacles

in making prepared cocktails that would keep a long time. The aim was to make drinks that were uniform in quality, that would taste the same a week after the bottle was opened, and in which the sugar would not change flavor or crystallize. With the development of nondairy creamers that need no refrigeration, a new field of prepared drinks has opened up for the liquor industry. Prepared eggnogs, Brandy Alexanders, and Grasshoppers are examples of drinks that formerly had to be made with fresh cream but can now be purchased as finished beverages.

Cocktail mixes

Cocktail mixes are expertly prepared cocktails with all the necessary ingredients except the liquor. To create a Manhattan, for example, add whisky to the appropriate mix.

There are two main types of cocktail mixes now on

the market: liquid and dry powder. The liquid mix, to which you just add liquor to make the appropriate drink, has been in existence for decades, although the range of cocktails has increased tremendously. The dry mix is a powder to which water and liquor are added to dissolve the powder and create the drink. Recently freeze-dried fruit has been added to dry mixes, making for fresher flavor.

Frozen cocktail mixes offer the advantages of fresh-tasting fruit juices. The most popular is the frozen Daiquiri mix, which is made with fresh lime juice, and is approved by the Puerto Rican rum producers. Refrigerated egg nog mix, sold around the holiday season, needs only liquor and a dusting of nutmeg.

In addition to being convenient, mixes allow the home bartender to be creative. He can add Scotch to the Manhattan mix and get a Rob Roy. The Daiquiri mix is a starting point for a Planter's Punch, Pink Lady, Clover Club, Ward Eight, or Gin Fizz. In addition, of course, the host or hostess can choose which brands of liquor they want to use.

Bar Operation

Bar profits depend on the economical and practical operation of the bar. In most instances a bar represents a substantial investment in plant, furniture, and decoration. This investment must be protected by maintaining a standard of service and quality of beverages on a par with the decor and the investment.

The recent American interest in tasting many different wines, combined with innovations in wine packaging, storage, and wine service, have led to the popularity of wine bars. Additionally, since many have a glass of wine as a substitute for a cocktail, eventually the desire to know just what wine was being poured and, if possible, to have a selection from which to choose, became important.

Wine bars with simple food menus have been responding to this interest. Instead of just being restaurants with extensive wine lists, a selection of wines are offered by the glass each day. In this way, the patron gets to taste or compare many different wines, without having to order a whole bottle.

The advantages to the customer are numerous: if he or she is considering buying the wine for a home cellar, it may be tasted with little risk to the budget. If a group of people are dining together, it is not necessary for all to agree on the wine. Each may have what he or she wants. It is also possible to have a glass of white wine with the first course, and then change to a glass of rosé or red for the main course. Dessert wines may also be available by the glass.

In addition, some wine bars even offer half portions, or tasting portions, so that a person doesn't even have to risk the price of a whole glass before deciding on what wine to have. It is possible to have tasting portions of several wines.

In the past, many restaurateurs have hesitated to open expensive or rare bottles, because of the possibility of the wine's oxidizing before being used up. New equipment, however, that uses nitrogen to blanket the wine in the bottle, thus keeping oxygen away from the wine, has enabled wine bar owners to serve a wider variety of costly wines. The Cruvinet, from France, is the most famous and expensive nitrogen system, but many wine bars have improvised their own. Blind taste-tests confirm that the nitrogen does not affect the taste of the wine, and does keep it stable.

Since the wines are poured at the bar and served in wine glasses, it is important for the owner to instruct the staff not to mix up the glasses when bringing them to the table.

Restaurants that do a large business in one single wine can also make use of nitrogen technology. At La Colline, in Washington, D.C., for example, the house wine is purchased in 3-liter containers, and put in 5-gallon stainless steel transfer tanks with sealed lines. Nitrogen replaces the wine as it is pumped to the bar. White wines remain fresh, and red wines, which sell less than whites, do not oxidize, and the tank does not have to be continually topped off.

There are two basic types of spirits bars: the front, or stand-up, bar, where drinks are made in front of the patrons; and the service bar never seen by the patrons, from which drinks are dispensed. A service bar is sometimes called a back bar. The space behind a front bar is also sometimes called a back bar, although we prefer to call it the back-of-the-bar space.

The working arrangement of a bar is of the utmost importance. This matter is too often overlooked when the installation plans are made, and nine times out of ten the people who work behind the bar are not consulted. The space between the front and the back of the bar should be wide enough so that two bartenders can pass each other without jostling. The front section should not be too low, but so arranged that the bartender can reach ice, mixing glass, and bottles with ease.

In laying out a bar, try to keep the working stations well off the floor. Plumbing repairs will have to be made, and if there is plenty of working space the repairs will be completed in less time and at much less expense. More importantly, people will have to work in the fairly cramped space between the front and the back of the bar. In practically every new large bar layout we have observed over the years the bartender's comfort has been forgotten. The fact that a man must be on his feet for eight hours or longer is not taken into account. Wooden or plastic racks or cushioned rubber on the floor makes the difference between a smiling, efficient bartender and one who is tired and grouchy after a couple of hours of standing on a cold cement floor.

Floor racks can be built using clear pine laths three inches wide by one inch thick by three feet long; allow a one-inch separation between laths and hold the rack together by crosspieces of the same laths. This produces racks with a two-inch clearance off the floor. If the racks are longer than three feet, they become too heavy to lift for cleaning the floor.

If the bar is oval or some other shape whereby the customers standing on one side can see the working stations on the other, a cover should be hung in front of the stations to conceal the pipes and other equipment. Under the same circumstances, special thought must be given to the floor covering.

The working space between the front and the back of the bar should be at least thirty inches, and thirty-six inches is ideal. Doors of refrigerators set into the back-of-the-bar space should not be so wide that they block traffic when opened.

The back-of-the-bar space should also have storage cabinets and shelves to hold bottles.

Do not have a lighting system that consists of electric bulbs under glass shelves on which bottles are placed. The heat generated by the lights will be detrimental to the liquid contents.

For service bars out of public sight, there need be no back work space. This space will be occupied by large refrigerators, while the bottles that ordinarily would be on the back of the bar are placed on overhead shelves above the counter.

The working space between the service bar and the back wall line must be at least ten feet, particularly if the bar services banquets. This provides the extra space needed for stacking cases of wines, liquors, and waters when they are to be served in quantities exceeding the capacity of the regular storage space.

A service bar should have one entrance and one exit. Some establishments prefer a turnstile at the entrance. If there is none, the rule must be enforced that once a waiter reaches the bar there can be no turning around and going out the way he came in. The waiter should exit past the service-bar manager.

The Bartender's Job

Beverage dispensing should be done quietly and with dignity, creating an atmosphere of refinement and good taste. The job of the bartender is no different from that of any other retail salesman except that, because of the character of the goods he is selling, extra care should be taken to please customers and look after their welfare.

The bartender's day really starts the night before, for without sufficient rest he cannot do his best work on the job.

The bartender is often in close contact with the guest, and it is therefore imperative that he practice scrupulous personal hygiene.

Uniform coats or vests, as appropriate for the operation, should be provided by the employer, but it is the responsibility of the bartender to provide a white shirt, black tie, and dark trousers, or a white blouse and dark skirt for women. The full uniform must always be kept clean and pressed. Colored shirts should never be worn unless they are part of a uniform. Jewelry should be limited. Aprons are not considered in good form today, unless they are part of a specific uniform.

Care of the feet is important for the bartender. He cannot show the customer a happy face if his feet are tired and aching. It is a good idea to have two pairs of comfortable shoes and change once or twice during the day. Shoes with built-in arches are available and help prevent fatigue. Rubber heels also relieve the strain.

When not busy, the bartender should not slouch or stand around with his hands in his pockets. The bartender should refrain from smoking while on duty. Customers as a rule do not like smoking behind the bar, and smoking while handling food or drink is extremely unsanitary. The same is true of drinking—do not drink while on duty. Many times the bartender is asked to take a drink with a customer, but he should pass it up.

The first duty of the day, of course, is to report for work on time, whether the bartender is to open the bar or to relieve someone else. The bar should be inspected to see that it is spotlessly clean, that the floor, walls, windows, and furniture for table service are in perfect condition, that the room temperature is right, and that there are no offensive odors.

At the bar the woodwork should be polished, the back of the bar dusted, and bottles and glasses neatly arranged. The mirrors should be clean and shining. Liquor bottles should be wiped off with a damp cloth each morning.

The work area sinks and drain board and the storage cabinets under the bar should be clean and ready for use.

Supplies of wines and liquors should be carefully checked so that the stock is up to par for the day. Any orders should be sent to the storeroom and followed up to make sure all supplies are on hand before the first customer arrives. Ice boxes should be filled with ice. Bottles of liquor should be in the speed racks or in their proper places on the shelves. Then the working equipment and the draft beer system should be checked.

There should be a supply of clean towels, which are properly kept behind the bar, not stuck into the belt or over the shoulder of the bartender.

Next, the fruit and other garnishes should be prepared. These include oranges, lemons, limes, pineapples, olives, cherries, cocktail onions, and any special items that are ordered frequently or that are unique to the operation.

This should be done just before opening time so that the garnishes will be as fresh as possible. If the bar opens an hour or two before lunch, it is well to prepare only the fruits for which there will be a call during the luncheon hour. During the afternoon lull there is time to prepare such additional fruits as might be necessary for the cocktail hour and the evening.

Oranges should be of uniform size—about 216 to the crate is a good size—and either California or Florida fruit may be used. Floridas have more juice, but Californias have a better color, which is better for slices and peel. Cut orange slices in half from top to bottom, about one-fourth inch thick, and discard the end pieces. Slices should be kept together as much as possible until used, to preserve their freshness. The main supply should be covered with a moist napkin and kept, if possible, in a refrigerator.

Lemon slices should also be about a quarter-inch thick. Begin by cutting the lemon in half in the middle as for juicing. Then slice each half, throwing the ends away.

Limes should be cut in wedges large enough to grasp and squeeze the juice into the drink. A forty-eight-to-fifty-four count lime (forty-eight to fifty-four to the crate) should yield eight wedges. Begin by cutting each lime in half as for juicing. Place the flat side on the cutting board and cut into four equal wedges. Keep the finest fruits for slicing and peeling, reserving the less perfect fruit for squeezing.

Where twists of lemon or orange peel are called for, start at one end of the whole fruit and cut a strip about three-quarters of an inch wide, skin deep, the length of the fruit to the other end. If a long spiral piece of lemon or orange peel is called for, start at one end and cut a strip about three-quarters of an inch wide spirally, as when peeling an apple, until the other end is reached.

Fresh pineapple should be used for punches and special drinks. The best method of preparing this fruit is to cut it into strips about three inches long.

Olives and cherries should be placed in handy containers so they may be reached easily. Only small pitted green olives, especially prepared for cocktails, should be used, never stuffed olives. Maraschino cherries especially prepared for cocktail use, pitted but with the stems left on, are the best. No broken fruit should be used.

Never use anything but tongs or picks when serving ice or fruit. It is unsanitary and undignified to use the fingers.

Juices needed for most situations are lemon, orange, pineapple, tomato, and sometimes grapefruit. Freshly squeezed orange and lemon juices yield superior cocktails, but because of cost and/or convenience, frozen orange concentrate and frozen or bottled lemon juice are widely used.

Lemon juice mixes can be purchased presweetened with sugar or artificial sweetener. The artificially sweetened ones often leave a bitter aftertaste, so it is best to sample them in a cocktail before purchasing them in any significant quantity.

Tomato, pineapple, and grapefruit juices are usually purchased canned. It is best to transfer the liquid to a pitcher or bottle if it is to be kept opened for any length of time without being used.

The appearance of a drink should have great eye appeal, since eye appeal is a factor in your guests' enjoyment as well as in merchandising. The professional touch is given when a drink is well garnished with fruit. The glass should be filled to within one-eighth to one-fourth inch of the brim. Filling the glass to the brim or allowing it to overflow is sloppy.

Finally, the dishes on the bar should be filled with whatever appetizers the rules of the house call for—pretzels, cheese crackers, cheese, nuts, and so forth. One of the functions of these salty foods is to stimulate the guests to further beverage consumption and they should be placed within reach without guests' having to ask for them.

Some Rules for the Bartender

1. Your manners will be reflected in your sales. After you have served a drink, step back from your customer or move away. Never appear to listen to a conversation and never take part in it unless you are directly addressed.
2. Cultivate a good memory for the faces and tastes of your regular customers and greet them pleasantly when they come in.
3. Handle complaints courteously. At the bar the customer is always right. If he complains about his drink, fix it or mix another. A bar quickly gets a reputation for fine drinks and courteous service—and it can lose it just as quickly.
4. Never hurry a customer or show that you are impatient. Don't show by your manner that you think a customer is drinking too much—or too little. If he is intoxicated he

should be refused service courteously. It may be against the law to serve him and you could lose your license to sell alcoholic beverages if you do so.

5. If you must answer a telephone at the bar, do so quietly. If the call is for a patron, never say that he is there. Instead, say that you will inquire and leave it up to the patron to decide whether or not he wishes to answer the telephone.
6. Be cooperative and friendly with the other employees.
7. Be sure you know how to mix standard cocktails without referring to a book. A helpful trick in starting is to take a glass cutter and make a few tiny marks on the outside of the bar glass, showing where the main ingredients for Martinis and Manhattans come to for one, two, three, and four drinks. It is simpler to gauge ingredients if you put them in before adding the ice. Practice until you can fill four glasses to just the right height and not have a drop left over in your bar glass.

8. When a drink is ordered, first place the required glass on top of the bar. If more than one drink is ordered, place the glasses in a straight row with the rims touching. Then place your mixing glass on the bar and pour the ingredients into it where the customer can see. Allow for ice melting during the shaking process.
9. In pouring more than one drink, run your mixing glass back and forth over the row of glasses, filling them all first quarter full, then half full, then full. Never fill one glass first and then another.
10. As soon as you have mixed a drink, put the bottles back in their proper places, no matter how rushed you are. Discard the ice, rinse your bar glass, shaker, and strainer, and you are ready for the next one. Good, efficient work habits will save time in the long run.
11. As a rule, follow standard recipes, but you should also study regular patrons' likes and dislikes and make their drinks the way they prefer.

12. Many houses now require the use of the shot glass or jigger, as modern bar controls make it necessary to account for every drink. An inexperienced bartender often has a little left over in the shaker, which goes down the sink. This waste is trifling on one drink, but if it is repeated often during a day, the loss is substantial. Therefore, measure to be sure.
13. When preparing standard cocktails such as the Martini and Manhattan, use cracked ice or ice cubes. Finely shaved ice melts too rapidly and dilutes the cocktail too much.
14. Cocktails that are shaken should be shaken briskly and not too long, since the ice melts and weakens the drink.
15. In the past it was proper to wipe all glasses twice, one to dry and again to give them a polish. In view of present-day sanitation codes, however, it is best that all glasses air dry on racks to avoid unsanitary handling by wiping.

Closing Procedures

1. Put all bottles in their proper places and lock the liquor cabinet if required.
2. Clean all bar tools and utensils.
3. Wash all dirty glasses and ashtrays.
4. Wipe down the bar and clean your station thoroughly, including the outside of ice bins, beer boxes, and so forth.
5. Drain and wipe off the sinks and drain boards.
6. Write up your liquor order for the next day's operation.
7. Count out and turn in your receipts for the night.
8. Turn out lights and lock up after making sure that all tables have been cleaned off and wiped down by the person responsible.

Implements For The Bar

Aside from the necessary glassware the person behind the

bar needs a number of tools of the trade, some of which are stationary, some movable. The stationary equipment is the province of the architects who design the bar.

The principal implements needed in a bar are:

Bar spoons—assorted sizes
Beer can openers
Beer scraper
Bottle openers, cap lifters
Cocktail picks
Cocktail shakers
Corkscrews—automatic and waiter's type
Cutting board
Electric blender
Electric drink mixer
Electric juice extractor
Fruit knives
Fruit tongs
Ice crusher
Ice pick
Ice scoops
Ice tongs
Lemon and lime squeezers
Mixing glasses—large and small
Muddlers—wooden

Nutmeg shakers or graters
Pitchers
Saltshakers
Speed pourers
Strainers
Sugar bowls
Swizzle sticks
Towels

SUGGESTIONS FOR MANAGERS

1. When you find a good bartender, make every effort to keep him.
2. It pays to listen to the bartender's suggestions.
3. If you have no confidence in your bartender, don't keep him on the job.
4. A good bartender is worth a good salary in the added business he brings you.
5. Show the bartender you are interested in him.
6. Set policy and guidelines, but avoid overly rigid rules,

since exceptions are often necessary to please a customer.

7. Many organizations find they do better by training their own bartenders. After several weeks of group training, the best is gradually given more responsibility in accordance with his abilities.

Dos and Don'ts in Mixing

Do not make up more cocktails than are needed to fill the exact number of glasses. "Dividends," the remains in the shaker, are usually tasteless and watery from melting ice.

Cocktails taste better when freshly made. If allowed to stand, some of the ingredients will separate. This is particularly the case with mixed drinks that contain fruit juices and sugar.

Cocktails made of liquor and wine may be prepared in

quantity in advance of a party, but those that include fruit juices are better if mixed just before drinking.

If the recipe calls for lime juice, use fresh green limes for best results. The only exception to this rule is the frozen Daiquiri mix. In many tests we have found it the equal of fresh lime juice and we recommend it highly. Do not substitute lemon juice for lime juice in a drink. This is particularly important with rum drinks, such as the Daiquiri, Planter's Punch, or Swizzle. Lemon juice will not give the sharp acid tang necessary for best results with rum.

GLOSSARY

The abbreviations Aus., Eng., Fr., Hun., It., Port., Sp., and Yug. represent the countries of origin Austria, England, France, Hungary, Italy, Portugal, Spain, and Yugoslavia respectively.

abboccato (It.). Semidry.

Abfüllung, Abf. (Ger.). Bottling.

Abstich (Ger.). Racking.

acerbe (Fr.). Green, acid.

acid, acidity. Compounds in wine that provide a tart freshness and contribute to the wine's ability to age.

acqua vita, aqua vitae (It., Latin). Water of life—spirits.

adega (Port.). Equivalent of *bodega*, wine warehouse.

aftertaste. The taste in the back of the throat after a wine has been swallowed. A lingering after taste is an indication of a complex wine.

agrafes (Fr.). Metal clips used in Champagne cellars to hold the temporary corks in place.

aguardiente (Sp.). Spirits, primarily brandy or whisky.

aigre (Fr.). An acid undertone.

albariza (Sp.). Chalky-white soil of best Jerez sherry vineyards in Spain.

alcohol (ethyl). Chemically C_2H_5OH, one of the results of fermenting liquids containing sugar.

aldehydes. By-products of alcoholic liquids resulting from the combination of alcohol, acid, and air.

alembic, *alambic, alambique* (Eng., Fr., Sp.). Still.

alt (Ger.). Old.

amabile (It.). Semisweet.

amaro (It.). Bitter or very dry.

amélioré (Fr.). Improved, usually by the addition of sugar to the must before fermentation.

amertume (Fr.). Bitter.

amontillado (Sp.). Dry type of sherry.

amoroso (Sp.). Medium-dry type of sherry.

ampelography. Science of grapevine culture.

añada (Sp.). Wine of one vintage.

ansprechend (Ger.). Attractive, engaging.

aperitif. Appetizer wine or spirit.

Appellation d'Origine Contrôlée (Fr.). Term that appears on labels of fine French wines signifying origin and right to the name it bears, guaranteed by French law.

âpre (Fr.). Harsh, rough.

arenas (Sp.). Sandy soils of the Jerez sherry vineyards in Spain.

arome, aroma (Fr., Sp.). Odor or bouquet of a wine or spirit.

arroba (Sp.). Wine measure holding 16½ liters.

arrope (Sp.). Concentrated wine used to sweeten and give color to sherries. See also *vino de color*.

artig (Ger.). Smooth, rounded.

asciato (It.). Dry.

astringence. Puckering or drying sensation in the mouth after drinking certain tannic wines.

aszú (Hun.). Sweeter type of Tokay wine.

Auslese (Ger.). A wine made from selected grapes.

balance. The harmony of a wine in which none of the components is overly apparent.

Balthazar. Oversize Champagne bottle, holding 16 regular bottles, or 416 ounces.

Banvin, Ban de Vendange (Fr.). Ancient French custom of fixing the date when the gathering of the grapes might begin.

barrique, barrica (Fr., Sp.). Hogshead, cask.

barros (Sp.). Clayish soils of the Jerez sherry vineyards in Spain.

basto (Sp.). Coarse.

B.A.T.F. Bureau of Alcohol, Tobacco, and Firearms, U.S. Treasury Department.

Baumé. Measurement of the degree of sweetness in wines and spirits. Hydrometer and scales invented by the French chemist Antoine Baume.

Beerenauslese (Ger.). A wine made from individually

selected, perfectly ripe grapes.

beste (Ger.). Best.

bianco (It.). White.

binning. Storing wines in bins in a cellar for development.

blanc de blancs (Fr.). Wine made from the juice of white grapes only.

blanco (Sp.). White.

blending. Marrying two or more similar products to obtain a better and more uniform quality.

Blume (Ger.). Bouquet, aroma.

blumig (Ger.). Good bouquet.

Bocksbeutel (Ger.). Squat, flasklike bottle used for Frankenwein.

bocoy (Sp.). Large cask holding approximately 162 gallons.

bodega (Sp.). Ground-level wine warehouse.

body. The term employed to describe the consistency of beverages. For example, a thin wine has less body than a full one.

bond, in. A wine or spirit on which duty and Internal Revenue tax has not been paid must remain under government supervision as "bond" that same will be paid.

bonded warehouse. Warehouse under government supervision.

bon goût (Fr.). Good or pleasant taste.

bor (Hun.). Wine. *Fehérbor* is white wine. *Vörösbor* is red wine. Both are pluralized with the suffix *-ok*, as in *borok*.

bota (Sp.). Butt, sherry cask, holding 132 gallons.

bottle, *bouteille*, *botella* (Eng., Fr., Sp.). A wine bottle containing from 23 to 26 ounces.

Bottled in Bond. U.S.: Term signifying a straight whisky, at least four years old, bottled at 100 proof, under government supervision, before taxes have been paid on same. **Canada:** Term signifying a blended whisky, at least three years old, bottled at 100 proof, under government supervision, before taxes have been paid on same.

bouchonné (Fr.). Corky, as a wine that has taken on an unpleasant taste of cork.

bouquet. Aroma or fragrance of a wine or spirit.

Bowle (Ger.). Wine cup prepared with fresh fruit, wine, herbs, and liqueurs or brandy.

brandewijn, Branntmein (Dutch, Ger.). Brandy; literally, "burned wine."

breed. The character or degree of excellence a wine attains.

brouilli (Fr.). The middle distillate (about 24 to 32 percent alcohol), collected for the second distillation in Cognac.

brut (Fr.). Dry. Also, the driest type of Champagne.

bukettreich (Ger.). Rich, pronounced bouquet.

butt. Standard shipping cask for sherry, 132 gallons.

Cabinet-wein (Ger.). Term used before 1971 to denote the finest quality of certain Rhine wines specially reserved and so marked.

cantina (It.). Cellar, winery, or bar.

cantina sociale (It.). Wine growers' cooperative.

capataz (Sp.). Foreman or *bodega* master in Jerez.

capiteux (Fr.). Spirity, heady.

capsule. Protector made of metal or plastic for wine and spirit bottle cork.

caque (Fr.). Basket in which grapes are carried from the vineyard to the press.

casco (Sp.). Cask or large barrel, usually made of oak, used for developing (aging) and/or shipping wines and spirits.

cask. Large container, usually made of oak, for wines or spirits.

casse (Fr.). Chemical disease of wines resulting from excess iron.

catalyst. Chemical agent that induces chemical changes in other substances by its presence but itself remains unchanged.

cave, celler, cellier (Fr.). Warehouse (usually underground) or cellar for storing wines and/or spirits.

cellar. Warehouse for storing wines.

centiliter. 1/100 part of a liter.

cep (cépage), cepa (Fr., Sp.). The vinestock.

chat (Fr.). Ground-level or aboveground warehouse, usually kept totally dark, for wines and/or spirits.

chambrer (Fr.). To bring red wine to room temperature (65-68 degrees Fahrenheit) gradually.

chaptalization. The practice of increasing the natural sugar content of the grape juice, before fermentation begins, by the addition of sugar or concentrated grape must when there is such a deficiency, especially in poor vintage years.

charnu (Fr.). Full bodied.

château-bottled. Wine bottled at the château estate, or vineyard where grapes from which it was made are grown. Applies to Bordeaux wines primarily.

chiaretto (It.). Very light red.

clarete (Sp.). Light red or dark rose.

classified growths. Bordeaux wines listed according to merit in 1855, 1955, and 1959.

climat (Fr.). Vineyard.

cochylis. A disease of the vine.

collage (Fr.). Fining or clearing a wine.

commune (Fr.). Parish, a subdivision of a district.

Confréries (Fr.). Wine and gastronomic fraternities, mostly of ancient "guild" origin such as Burgundy's *Confrérie des Chevaliers du Tastevin* (Brotherhood of Gentlemen of the Tasting Cup) and the *Confrérie de la Chaîne des Rôtisseurs* (Fraternity of the Turners of the Roasting Spit).

consejo regulator (Sp.). Organization for the control and promotion of the *Denominacion de Origen.*

consorzio (It.). Local growers' association with legal standing.

consumo (Port., Sp.). Ordinary wine for local consumption.

cordial. See liqueur.

corks. Stoppers for bottles made from the spongy bark of the cork oak. Portuguese cork is the finest for this purpose.

corky wine. A wine with an unpleasant odor imparted by a diseased cork. This can happen to even the finest wines.

corps (Fr.). Body, richness in alcohol and other substances.

corsé (Fr.). Full bodied.

cosecha (Sp.). Crop or vintage.

coulant (Fr.). Easy, pleasant.

couleur, color (Fr., Sp.). The color of a wine.

coupage (Fr.). Blending or mixing of wines.

coupé (Fr.). A blended wine.

courtier, corredor (Fr. Sp.). Wine broker.

crémant (Fr.). Crackling or slightly sparkling. Given appellation status by I.N.A.O.

criadera (Sp.). Nursery stage in the sherry maturing system.

criado y embotellado por (Sp.). Grown and bottled by.

cru (Fr.). Vineyard, growth.

cru classé (Fr.). See classified growths.

crust. The heavy deposit thrown off by red wines that have been long in bottles. Applies principally to Vintage Portos.

cuit, cotto (Fr., It.). A wine that has been heated or "cooked."

cup. Iced wine flavored with fresh fruits, brandy, liqueurs, and/or herbs.

cuvaison (Fr.). The period of first or violent fermentation during which the must remains in contact with the grape skins to obtain its color. Applies only to red wines.

cuvée (Fr.). The blend.

decanter. A glass bottle or container into which wines or spirits are poured from their original containers, for serving.

decanting. Transferring a wine or spirit from one bottle to another.

dégorgement (Fr.). Disgorging process used in production of Champagne to remove the sediment.

délicat (Fr.). Delicate, not harsh or coarse.

delimited area. A certain area whose regional name by law is given to the wine or spirit produced within the geographical limits of the region.

demi (Fr.). Half.

demijohn. A fat-bellied, wicker-encased bottle holding 4 to 10 gallons.

demi-muid (Fr.). Cask holding 157 gallons used in Cognac.

demi-queue (Fr.). A Burgundy cask measuring 228 liters, a half-*queue*.

demi-sec (Fr.). Semidry. Also, a fairly sweet type of Champagne.

Denominacion de Origen (Sp.). Guarantee of origin and authenticity of a wine.

density. See specific gravity.

deposit. Normal sediment precipitated by a wine as it

matures in the bottle.

dépôt (Fr.). Natural sediment that all wines deposit; more visible in red wines.

dextrin. One of the sugars resulting from starch being exposed to the action of malt.

diastase. The enzyme, formed by malting barley, that causes the starch in grains to be converted into sugars.

dolce (It.). Sweet.

domaine (Fr.). Followed by a name, it denotes ownership. For example, Domaine de la Romanée-Conti.

Domäne (Ger.). Usually a state-owned and/or state-managed vineyard property.

dosage (Fr.). The amount of sugar used in preparing Champagne.

douil (Fr.). An open cask holding 7 to 8 hectoliters in which the grapes are carted from the vineyard to the pressing house in the Bordeaux wine region.

doux (Fr.). Sweet. Also, the sweetest type of Champagne.

dry. The opposite of sweet, literally, lacking in sugar.

duftig (Ger.). Fragrant, fine bouquet.

dulce (Sp.). Sweet.

dulce apagado (Sp.). See *mistelle*.

dunder. Sugarcane juice remains, used in making full-bodied rums.

dur (Fr.). Hard, harsh.

earthy. A flavor in wines reminiscent of earth or soil, highly prized in Burgundy where it is called *goût de terroir*.

eau de vie (Fr.). Spirits, generally brandy. Literally, "water of life."

eau de vie de marc (Fr.). A brandy distilled from the fermented pomace or husks of grapes after they have been pressed for wine.

echt (Ger.). Genuine.

edel (Ger.). Noble, extra fine.

Edelbeerenauslese (Ger.). Term used before 1971 to denote an especially fine Beerenauslese.

Edelfäule (Ger.). Noble mold that settles on over ripe grapes. See also *pourriture noble*.

Edelsüsse (Ger.). Great natural, noble sweetness.

edes (Hun.). Sweet.

égrappage (Fr.). Process of destemming grapes before they are pressed.

égrappoir (Fr.). Apparatus used to perform the egrappage.

Ehrwein (Ger.). Very fine wine.

Eigene abfüllung (Ger.). Bottled by the producer.

Eiswein (Ger.). A wine produced from perfectly ripened grapes that have been partially frozen while still hanging on the vine. Eiswein used to be very rare, appearing perhaps once every twenty or twenty-five years. It is now made more often but only in very limited quantities. Eiswein is quite elegant and very rich and may be considered between an Auslese and an Edelbeerenauslese.

élégance (Fr.). A term used to denote a wine of a poor vintage with delicacy and lightness but that does not promise longevity.

éleveur (Fr.). See *négociant-éleveur*.

élixir (Fr.). Old term used in France for liqueur.

enology, oenology. The science or study of wines.

enzymes. The organic catalysts of yeasts and other substances, which cause various reactions, including alcoholic or vinous fermentation.

Erben (Ger.). Heirs of, or estate of.

erdig (Ger.). Earthy.

espumoso (Sp.). Sparkling.

Essenz, Eszencia (Hun.). Essence. The rarest and richest Tokay wine.

estate-bottled. Produced and bottled by the vineyard owner-producer, traditionally in Burgundy.

esters. The volatile compounds formed by the combination of organic acids with the alcohols. Esters give the bouquet of a wine or spirit.

estufa (Port.). Hothouses or heated cellars where Madeiras are baked when young.

ether. A sweet-smelling compound that contributes to the bouquet of a wine, formed by the dehydration of alcohol molecules.

ethyl alcohol. The principal alcohol found in alcoholic beverages.

extra sec. Extra dry. Also, a type of dry Champagne, somewhat sweeter than *brut*.

fad (Ger.). Insipid.

faible (Fr.). Thin, weak.

Fass (Ger.). A cask of 600-liter capacity employed in all German wine regions except the Moselle, where the cask is called *Fuder*.

fein, feine, feinste (Ger.). Fine, very fine, finest.

feints. The first and last parts of a distillation, also called the heads and tails.

ferme (Fr.). Firm, full.

fermentation. The chemical process whereby sugars are broken down into ethyl alcohol, carbon dioxide, and other by-products.

fett (Ger.). Full, big; literally, fat.

fiasco (It.). Raffia-wrapped flask employed for bottling Chianti, Orvieto, and some other Italian wines. Plural *fiaschi*.

filter. To clarify liquids by passing them through a fine screen or permeable membrane.

finage (Fr.). All of the vineyards of a given sub-district.

fine. To clarify wine by adding materials that combine with the particles floating in it and, after a short period, settle to the bottom, leaving the wine clear.

fine maison (Fr.). The house brandy served in a restaurant.

finesse (Fr.). Fineness, delicacy.

fino (Sp.). The driest type of sherry.

flagon. An ancient wine flask.

flask. A flat-sided bottle usually holding 12½ ounces but with a capacity of anywhere from 8 to 32 ounces.

flinty. See *pierre-à-fusil*.

flor (Sp.). See flower.

flower, flowering. Unique property of the yeast in the Jerez sherry region of Spain. Multiplying profusely, the yeast forms a film on the surface of the wine in the cask, especially in the case of the drier, more delicate fino types, giving sherry its nutty character. A similar flowering of the yeast also occurs in the casks of the *vin jaune* and *vin de paille* of Chateau-Châlon and Chateau d'Arlay, in the Côtes de Jura region of France, and in South Africa.

flowery. A pleasing, fragrant perfume in some white wines.

fort (Fr.). Strong, with high alcohol.

fortified wines. Wines whose natural alcoholic strength is increased by the addition of brandy. Term not recognized by the B.A.T.F.

foudre (Fr.). A large storage cask for wines.

foxiness. The very pronounced grapey flavor found in wines produced from American grapes in the eastern United States.

franc (Fr.). Natural-tasting, clean.

frappé (Fr.). Iced. A liqueur served with finely cracked ice.

Freiherr (Ger.). Baron.

frisch (Ger.). Fresh, sprightly.

frizzante (It.). Semisparkling, crackling.

fruity, *fruité, fruchtig* (Eng., Fr., Ger.). Describes the frank taste of the grape found in good wines.

Fuder (Ger.). A Moselle wine cask holding 1,000 liters.

Fülle (Ger.). Richness, fullness.

fumet (Fr.). A pronounced bouquet.

fumeux (Fr.). Spirited, heady.

fungus. Mold that appears when wine is kept carelessly and when the most careful hygiene is not observed.

Fürst (Ger.). Prince.

fusel oil. The higher alcohols found in all spirits.

gallon. A liquid measure containing 128 fluid ounces.

Gay Lussac. French inventor of the alcoholometer and the standard metric measures of alcoholic strengths, in use today, that bear his name.

gefällig (Ger.). Pleasing, harmonious.

gefüllt (Ger.). Full, rich.

Gemarkung (Ger.). The boundary of a district in which wine is grown.

généreux (Fr.). Generous, warming.

Gewächs (Ger.). Growth or vineyard. Always followed by the name of the proprietor, to denote ownership.

gezuckert (Ger.). Sugared or improved.

glatt (Ger.). Smooth.

goût (Fr.). Taste.

goût américain (Fr.). Sweet Champagne to please the South American market.

goût anglais (Fr.). A very dry Champagne for the English market.

goût de bois (Fr.). Woody taste.

goût de bouchon (Fr.). Corky taste.

goût de paille (Fr.). Straw, musty taste.

goût de pique (Fr.). Vinegary taste.

goût de terroir (Fr.). Earthy taste.

goût d'évent (Fr.). Flat, lifeless taste.

gradi, gradi alcool, grado alcoolico (It.). Followed by a number, percentage of alcohol by volume.

Graf (Ger.). Count.

grain spirits. Patent still spirits obtained from malted and unmelted grain.

grappa (It.). Brandy distilled from grape pressings in Italy and California. See also *marc*.

green. Very young, light, such as *vinho verde* ("green wine") of Portugal.

gros producteur (Fr.). A vine variety that produces large quantities of grapes but not fine-quality wines.

grossier (Fr.). Harsh, coarse.

growth. A vineyard (*cru* in French).

grün (Ger.). Young, green, immature.

gut (Ger.). Good.

habzó (Hun.). Sparkling.

Halb-fuder (Ger.). The standard Moselle wine cask containing 500 liters, a half-*Fuder*.

Halb-stück (Ger.). The standard Rhine wine cask containing 600 liters, a half-***Stück***.

harmonisch (Ger.). Harmonious, well-balanced.

hart (Ger.). Hard, acid, even vinegary.

heads. The spirits obtained at the beginning of distillation.

hecho (Sp.). Made. A completed wine ready for bottling and shipping.

hectare. 100 ares, equaling 2.47 acres.

hectoliter. 100 liters, equaling 26.418 gallons.

herb (Ger.). Bitter.

high wines. The useful spirits obtained in distillation after eliminating heads and tails.

Hochgewächs (Ger.). Superior vineyard or growth.

Hock. The English abbreviation for Hochheimer that today denotes any Rhine wine.

hogshead. Cask of varying measure. A hogshead of sherry contains 66 gallons.

honigartig (Ger.). Honeylike.

Hospices de Beaune (Fr.). A charitable hospital in Beaune, Burgundy, supported by an annual public sale of wine.

hübsch (Ger.). Nice, delicate.

hydrometer. An apparatus used to measure the density of alcoholic beverages and other liquids.

imbottigliato (It.). Bottled.

impériale (Fr.). An oversize Bordeaux bottle with a capacity of 8 bottles, or 6 liters; known as a Methuselah when used for Champagne.

I.N.A.O. (Fr.). *Institut National des Appellations d'Origine des Vins et Eaux-de-Vie*.

informing grape. The principal grape that gives a wine its varietal character.

isinglass. Substance made from fish gelatine; used as a fining material.

jarra (Sp.). Wooden or metal jar holding 11½ to 12½ liters, used in all sherry blending operations as the basic unit of measure.

Jeroboam or **double magnum**. Oversize Bordeaux or Champagne bottle, holding 4 regular bottles or 104 ounces.

jigger. The standard 1½-ounce measure used in cocktails and mixed drink recipes.

jung (Ger.). Young, immature.

Kabinett (Ger.). The driest wine of Qualitätswein mit Prädikat.

keg. A small, stout cask.

Keller (Ger.). Cellar.

Kellerakfüllung, kellerabzug (Ger.). Bottled at the cellar or estate.

kilogram, kg. 1,000 grams, or 2.2 pounds.

klein (Ger.). Small.

Körper (Ger.). Body.

kräftig (Ger.). Robust, rich in alcohol.

kräusen (Ger.). A method of carbonating beers.

lagar (Sp., Port.). The pressing and treading trough.

Lage (Ger.). Vineyard site.

lager. To store beer for aging and sedimentation. All American beers today are lagered.

lebendig (Ger.). Fresh, racy.

lees. The sediment that settles on the bottom of a cask of wine.

léger (Fr.). Light, lacking in body.

levante (Sp.). Hot, searing wind that blows over the sherry region, said to originate in the Sahara Desert.

lias (Sp.). Wine lees.

licoroso (Sp.). Rich, sweet, fortified.

Limousin (Fr.). The oak used for the casks in which Cognac is aged.

liqueur (Fr.). A sweetened, flavored distilled spirit.

***liqueur de tirage* (dosage)** (Fr.). In Champagne, the sugar solution added at the time of bottling to ensure a proper secondary fermentation.

liqueur d'expédition (Fr.). In Champagne, the sugar solution added at the time of disgorging to give the varying degrees of sweetness.

liquoreux (Fr.). Rich, sweet.

lodges. The warehouses where Porto wines are stored in Vila Nova de Gaia, Portugal. Also, the warehouses where Madeira wines are stored in Funchal, Madeira.

low wines. In pot still distillation, the spirits obtained from the first operation.

maderisé (Fr.). A white wine that has become very dark and taken on a woody character because of oxidation and exposure to heat.

mager (Ger.). Thin, lacking in body, undistinguished.

magnum. A double-size bottle.

maigre (Fr.). Thin, weak.

malt. Grain, generally barley, that has been allowed to germinate for a short period so that the enzyme diastase may be formed.

malts. Scotch whisky made entirely from malted barley.

marc (Fr.). The grapes required to load a Champagne press for a pressing; also a distillate of skins, pips, or husks remaining after the grapes have been pressed.

mashing. The operation of mixing ground meal and malt with water to liquefy the starches so they may be converted into sugars by the diastase in the malt.

Master of Wine, M.W. Professional title in England acquired by members of the trade after many years of study and rigorous examinations.

metallic. See *pierre-à-fusil*.

Methuselah. Oversize Champagne bottle, holding 7 to 8 regular bottles or 179 to 208 ounces.

mildew. A disease that attacks the vines in rainy or

damp seasons.

millésime (Fr.). Vintage year.

mise d'origine (Fr.). Bottled by the shipper.

mis en bouteille à la propriété (Fr.). Bottled by the shipper.

mis en bouteille au château (Fr.). Bottled at the chateau where the grapes are grown in Bordeaux.

mis en bouteille au domaine (Fr.). Bottled at the property where it is made in Burgundy; estate-bottled.

mistelle (Fr.). Grape must whose fermentation is halted by adding sufficient brandy to give it an alcohol content of 15 percent. The natural unfermented grape sugar remains as sweetening. *Mistelles* are used as sweetening wines, particularly in making vermouths and aperitif wines.

moelleux (Fr.). Soft, velvety.

Monimpex (Hun.). The Hungarian state export monopoly.

monopole (Fr.). A trademark name.

mou (Fr.). Flabby, lacking in character.

mousseux (Fr.). Sparking.

mûr (Fr.). Balanced, fruity.

must, *moût, Moot, mosto* (Eng., Fr., Ger., Sp.). Grape juice before and during fermentation.

mustimeter. See saccharometer.

musty. Moldy, unpleasant.

muté (Fr.). *Mistelle* or a sweet wine whose fermentation has been inhibited by the addition of brandy.

Mycodermae aceti. The vinegar yeast.

Mycodermae vini. The yeast responsible for vinous fermentation.

Natur, Naturrein, Naturwein (Ger.). Completely natural wine to which no sugar has been added.

nature (Fr.). Term used in Champagne labeling interchangeably with ***brut.*** Also denotes still Champagne.

Nebuchadnezzar. Extraordinary Champagne bottle size holding 20 regular bottles or 520 ounces.

négociant-éleveur (Fr.). A merchant who buys wine from the grower, blends, bottles, and then markets it.

nero (It.). Very dark red.

nerveux (Fr.). Vigorous, with long-keeping qualities.

nervig (Ger.). Good, full-bodied.

neutral spirits. Spirits distilled out from any material at a proof of 190 or more, regardless of whether they are later reduced in proof.

Nicolauswein (Ger.). Denotes a wine produced from grapes gathered on December 6, St. Nicholas Day.

nip. Miniature bottle of spirits.

nose. The bouquet or aroma of a wine or spirit.

nu (Fr.). "Bare." Term denoting that the price quoted for a barrel of wine does not include the cost of the cask.

nube (Sp.). Cloudiness.

Öchsle (Ger.). The German scale for measuring the sugar content of the grape must before fermentation. The determination is made by the higher weight in grams of the must in relation to an equal volume of water, or its specific gravity. Twenty-five percent of this greater weight is known to be sugar. Thus, 100 liters of must with a reading of 100 ***Öchsle*** contains 25 kilograms of natural grape sugar.

octave, *octavilla* (Eng., Sp.). An eighth of a cask. In the sherry trade, 16½ gallons.

oeil de perdrix (Fr.). Partridge eye. Describes pale or still pink sparkling wine, usually from Burgundy, Switzerland, or California.

oenology. See enology.

oïdium. A fungus disease that attacks the vines.

ölig (Ger.). Having high consistency that gives wine the impression of being oily as it is poured.

oloroso (Sp.). The full-bodied, deeper-colored sherries. Although very dry in their *soleras*, they are usually shipped as sweet-tasting sherries by blending sweet wines with them.

organoleptic examination. The method of judging the quality of wines, beers, and spirits by the human organs of sight, smell, and taste.

Originalabfüllung, Originalabzug (Ger.). Term used before 1971 to denote original bottling Equivalent to estate bottling.

overproof. A spirit whose alcoholic strength is more than 100 proof.

palma (Sp.). The special chalk marking used to identify a very fine fino sherry (Y).

palo cortado (Sp.). The special marking used to denote *dos rayas*, sherries that have developed fino characteristics (†).

Passe Tout Grains (Fr.). A Burgundy wine made of a mixture of at least one-third Pinot Noir and the balance Camay grapes.

passito (It.). A wine made from partially dried grapes.

Pasteur, Louis (1822-1895). Great French scientist whose studies on malt and vinous fermentations gave the first complete explanation of these phenomena.

pasteurization. A process discovered by Louis Pasteur of arresting, making inactive, or killing the ferments in wine, beer, milk, and other liquids through heating the liquid and holding it for a brief time at 131 to 158 degrees Fahrenheit.

patent still. The two-column or continuous still "patented" by Aeneas Coffey in 1832.

pelure d'oignon (Fr.). Onion skin. The brown tinge that certain red wines take on after aging.

perfume. The fragrance of a wine or spirit.

Perlwein (Ger.). Slightly sparkling wine.

pétillant (Fr.). Crackling or semisparkling.

petit (Fr.). Small, thin.

Pfarrgut (Ger.). Vineyard owned by a church whose product is given to the parson or preacher as part of his remuneration.

Phylloxera vastatrix. The American grape louse.

pièce (Fr.). A cask holding approximately 60 gallons, used in many French wine regions.

pierre-à-fusil (Fr.). Gun flint. A sharp, metallic tang sometimes noticed in bone-dry wines especially those from Chablis.

pikant (Ger.). Attractive, intriguing.

pint. Liquid measure of 16 ounces.

pipe. The cask used in the Porto, Lisbon, and Tarragona wine trades containing 138 gallons and in the Madeira trade where a pipe holds 110 gallons.

piquant (Fr.). A pleasant point of acidity. Generally applied to dry white wines.

piqué (Fr.). A term used to describe a wine that has begun to turn and whose only use is for vinegar.

piquette (Fr.). A common, ordinary wine used in certain parts of France.

pisador (Sp.). One who treads the grapes at vintage time in the sherry region.

plastering. The system of adding *yeso* or gypsum to grapes when they are treaded and pressed in the *lagar* in

Jerez, Spain.

plat (Fr.). Dull, flat, lifeless.

plein (Fr.). Full bodied.

pony. One-ounce brandy or liqueur glass.

portes-greffes (Fr.). The hardy *Phylloxera*-resistant American rootstocks on which the fine vines of Europe are grafted.

pot still. The old-fashioned, fat-bellied, tapered neck steal that requires two distinct operations to produce the spirit that is eventually bottled.

pourriture noble (Fr.). "Noble rot," the state of over-ripeness of the grapes of the Sauternes region of Bordeaux. It is in reality a yeast or mold known scientifically as *Botrytis cinerea*.

précoce (Fr.). Precocious, maturing rapidly.

pressoir, prensa (Fr., Sp.). Wine press.

proof. An arbitrary system of measuring the alcoholic strength of a liquid. In America, a spirit of 100 proof is one that contains exactly 50 percent alcohol by volume at 60 degrees Fahrenheit. Each degree of proof represents ½ percent alcohol.

puncheon. A large cask of varying capacities.

pupitres (Fr.). The special racks used in the Champagne cellars during *remuage* (shaking sediment onto the cork).

puttony (Hun.). The measure in which grapes are gathered in Tokay-Hegyalja. Plural *puttonos*.

Qualitätswein (Ger.). Superior table wine subject to certain controls, from any of eleven designated regions.

Qualitätswein mit Prädikat (Ger.). As above, but with more stringent control and special attributes.

quart. Liquid measure of 32 ounces.

quarter bottle. Wine bottle containing 6 to 6½ ounces, one-fourth the size of a regular bottle.

quarter cask. In cases where the standard cask, pipe, or butt is too large for a merchant, casks containing one-fourth the original are used. Quarter casks vary in contents, depending on the wine region where they are used.

queue (Fr.). Burgundy casks holding 2 *pièces*, a total of 120 gallons or 456 liters.

quinquina (Fr.). Quinine. Most French aperitif wines use the word as a description because they are quinined wines.

quinta (Port.). Vineyard or winery estate in Portugal, similar to chateau in the Bordeaux wine region.

quintal, quintale (Fr., It.). 100 kilograms.

race (Fr.). Breed.

racking. The drawing of wine off its lees into a fresh, clean cask. Also, the transference of any alcoholic beverage from one cask or vat to another.

rancio (Sp.). A term used to describe a sweet fortified wine that has lost some color through age in the bottle. Such a wine acquires a special aroma.

rassig (Ger.). With race and breed.

rauh (Ger.). Raw, harsh.

raya (Sp.). The chalk mark used in the sherry region to identify wines that will become finos or amontillados (/).

récemment dégorgé (Fr.). Recently disgorged.

récolte (Fr.). Vintage.

rectifying. Anything that changes the natural state of a spirit, such as redistilling after it has been barreled or adding coloring matter, sweetening, or any other flavoring material. Adding water to reduce proof does not constitute rectifying.

redondo (Sp.). Round, well-balanced.

reduce. To lower alcoholic strength of a spirit by the addition of water.

red wine. Any wine that has the slightest part of red coloring, obtained from the pigment found on the inside of the grape skin.

refresh. To add young wine to an older one (in cask)

to give the old wine new life. This term is also used in the same manner with respect to spirits, particularly brandies.

Rehoboam. Oversize Champagne bottle holding 6 regular bottles or 156 ounces.

reif (Ger.). Ripe, fine, sweet.

rein (Ger.). Pure.

reintönig (Ger.). Well-balanced, very good.

remuage (Fr.). The "shaking-down" operation employed in the production of Champagne, whereby the bottles are placed head downward and periodically shaken and turned slightly to cause the sediment to settle on the cork. In the United States the term used is *riddling*.

Rentamt (Ger.). Collection office.

reserva (Sp.). Mature quality.

riche (Fr.). Having a generous bouquet, flavor, and fullness of body.

rick. Framework or rack in a warehouse in which barrels

of distilled spirits are stored for aging. Also, to place or rack barrels.

riddling. See *remuage*.

riserva (It.). Mature quality.

robe. The sheen of color left on the inside of a glass from a highly pigmented red wine.

rociar (Sp.). To refresh an old *solera* with young new wine.

rondeur (Fr.). Roundness.

rosé, *rosato, rosado* (Eng., It., Sp.). A pale red wine obtained by removing the grape skins as soon as the required amount of color has been attained.

rosso (It.). Red.

Rotwein (Ger.). Red table wine.

ruby. A port of a very deep red color, usually quite young, in contrast to one that has been aged for some time in wood and has become "tawny," pale in color, through repeated finings.

rund (Ger.). Round, harmonious.

saccharometer. Instrument used to measure the sugar content of must or of wines or liqueurs.

saftig (Ger.). Juicy, succulent.

Salmanazar. Oversize Champagne bottle holding 10 to 12 regular bottles or 270 to 312 ounces.

sancocho (Sp.). Syrup produced by simmering or cooking must to one-third its original volume. Used in the sherry blend to sweeten and color the wine.

sauber (Ger.). Clean, pure.

scantling. The stout wooden beams or supports on which the casks rest in the cellar.

schal (Ger.). Musty, bred.

Schaumwein (Ger.). Sparkling wine.

Schloss (Ger.). Castle.

schlossabzug (Ger.). Bottled at the castle's cellars, equivalent to estate-bottled.

schnapps. Generic Dutch and German term denoting spirituous liquors.

Schwefel (Ger.). Sulfur smell in the bouquet of the wine.

sec (Fr.). Dry. Also, a medium-sweet Champagne.

secco, seco (It., Sp.). Dry.

sediment. The natural deposit found in wines as they mature, formed by the crystallization and settling or precipitation of bitartrates, tannins and pigments.

Sekt (Ger.). Sparkling wine.

self whiskies. Used in the Scotch whisky trade to denote a "straight" or unblended Scotch malt whisky.

sève (Fr.). Sappy, aromatic, vigorous.

Sikes (Sykes). Hydrometer and tables for measuring alcoholic strengths that are in use in England; invented by Bartholomew Sikes.

skunky. Describing the off aroma in beer that has been exposed to excessive light and heat.

slatko (Yug.). Sweet.

solear (Sp.). Sunning. The exposure of the grapes to the sun (*sol*) for 24 to 48 hours in the sherry region.

solera (Sp.). The system of tiered casks used to blend sherry.

sophistiquer (Fr.). To falsify a wine or to ameliorate a defective wine with anything that will cover up its defects.

souche (Fr.). *Cep* or vine rootstock.

sour mash. Yeasting process in which at least one quarter of the working yeast from a previous fermentation and fresh yeast may be added to the mash to induce fermentation.

soutirer (Fr.). To rack clear wine from one cask in to a fresh one.

soyeux (Fr.). Silky, smooth, soft roundness. Lacking in roughness.

Spätlese (Ger.). Late gathered. A wine made from late-picked bunches of grapes. Generally sweeter than wine made from grapes gathered earlier.

specific gravity. A measure of the density of a liquid or solid; the ratio of the weight of any volume of a liquid or solid to the weight of an equal volume of water.

spirits. The generic term for distilled beverages.

split. See quarter bottle.

spritzig (Ger.). Prickling, slightly effervescent.

spumante (It.). Sparkling.

stahlig (Ger.). Steely, austere.

still. The apparatus in which, by application of heat, the alcohol in a liquid may be separated and recovered. Pot still is the original form of still or alembic; Coffey still, patent still, and double-column still are three names applied to the continuous-operation still.

still wine. Table wine without any additional alcohol, carbon dioxide, or flavorings.

stirrup-cup. A cup for the parting drink. The name comes from an old custom of having a last drink with a guest after he had mounted his horse.

stolno vino (Yug.). Table wine.

Stück, Stückfasser (Ger.). The standard of cask measure, used in the Rhine, containing 1200 liters.

suho (Yug.). Dry.

süss (Ger.). Sweet.

sweet mash. Yeasting process in which fresh yeast is added to the mash to induce fermentation.

Tafelwein (Ger.). Ordinary table wine from any of the five Tafelwein regions.

tannin, tannic. Organic compound found mostly in red grapes, their woody stems, and new wood casks used for aging wines. They give the wine astringency and some bitterness when young and they give the wine the ability to develop and age. Tannin is a large part of the sediment that eventually forms in sturdy red wines.

tawny. The quality of paleness that Portos acquire when matured in wood. This loss of red color comes from repeated finings. Such wines are Tawny Portos.

teinturier (Fr.). Grapes used primarily for the abundance of color they contribute to the must.

tendre (Fr.). A rather light and delicate wine, usually a young wine.

tête de cuvée (Fr.). Outstanding growth; generally used in Burgundy.

tierce, terzo, tercero (Fr., It., Sp.). A cask holding one-third of a butt or pipe.

tilts. Bars used for adjusting casks or scantlings to the desired position.

tinto (Sp.). Red.

tirage (Fr.). Drawing off wines or spirits into other containers, usually from casks into bottles.

tonelero (Sp.). Cooper.

tonneau (Fr.). Tun. Term used in the Bordeaux wine trade representing 4 *barriques* of 225 liters or 900 liters. This is the unit of measure in which wines are sold in the bulk trade, the equivalent of 96 cases of finished wine.

Traube (Ger.). Bunch of grapes.

Traubenkelter (Ger.). Hydraulic grape press.

trocken (Ger.). Dry.

Trockenbeerenauslese (Ger.). Wine made from individually selected, dry, raisinlike grapes. Weather conditions must be perfect throughout the summer and the late vintage season for a Trockenbeerenauslese wine to be made. It is very rare and very sweet.

uisgebeatha, uisgebaugh (Celtic). Water of life, whisky.

ullage. The air space in a cask or bottle due to evaporation or leakage. May result in deterioration of contents.

underproof. Describes a spirit whose alcoholic strength is below proof. In the United States this is a spirit of less than 100 proof, as opposed to an overproof spirit having a strength of over 100 proof.

ungazuckert (Ger.). Unsugared, pure.

usé (Fr.). A wine that has passed its peak and is on the decline.

uva (Sp.). Grape.

vats. The containers in which alcoholic beverages are fermented or blended.

vatting. Mixing or blending in a vat.

velouté (Fr.). Rich, mellow, velvety, soft.

vendange (Fr.). Grape harvest.

vendange tardif (Fr.). Late-picked wine, implying more strength and/or sweetness.

vendangeur (Fr.). Grape harvester.

vendemmia, vendimia (It., Sp.). Vintage or harvest.

venencia (Sp.). The special cup used for drawing samples from the sherry butts in the *bodega*. It is a cylindrical silver cup attached to a long, flexible strip of whalebone.

viejo (Sp.). Old.

vif (Fr.). Lively, brisk.

vigne (Fr.). Vine.

vigneron (Fr.). Vine grower.

vignoble (Fr.). Vineyard.

vin (Fr.). Wine.

viña (Sp.). Vine. Also, vineyard in Argentina and Chile.

vin blanc (Fr.). White wine.

vin cuit (Fr.). A concentrated wine used to improve thin wines.

vin de garde (Fr.). A wine worth keeping, for laying down.

vin de goutte (Fr.). Wine made from the last pressing. It is generally of poor quality.

vin de messe (Fr.). Altar wine.

vin de paille (Fr.). White wine made from grapes that have been spread on straw (*paille*) mats to dry in the sun, before pressing.

vin de pays (Fr.). Small wines of each region, consumed locally.

vin doux (Fr.). A sweet wine.

vine. Climbing plant, one variety of which produces grapes.

viñedo (Sp.). Vineyard.

vineux (Fr.). Vinosity.

vin gris (Fr.). A pale pink wine made in Lorraine.

vinho (Port.). Wine.

vinho claro (Port.). Natural wine.

vinho estufado (Port.). Madeira wine after it has been baked in the *estufa*.

vinho generoso (Port.). Fortified wine.

vinho surdo (Port.). Fortified wine. According to Portuguese law, Porto wine must be a *vinho surdo*.

vinho verde (Port.). Light, young white or red wine produced in northern Portugal.

viniculture. The science of making wine.

vini tipici (It.). Typical or standard wines.

vin mousseux (Fr.). Sparkling wine.

vin nature (Fr.). Natural, unsweetened wine.

vino (It., Sp.). Wine.

vino corriente (Sp.). Ordinary wine for local consumption.

vina crudo (Sp.). Young or immature wine.

vino de añada (Sp.). Young wine of one vintage, ready for the *criadera* reserves.

vino de color (Sp.). Concentrated wine used in the sherry *bodega* to give color and sweetness to the final blend.

vino de crianza (Sp.). A suitable wine destined to become sherry.

vino de mesa (Sp.). Table wine.

vino frizzante (It.). A lightly sparkling type of wine in Italy.

vino liquoroso (It.). Very sweet wine.

vino maestro (Sp.). Master wine. A sweet, full wine used to lend character and body to weaker thinner wine.

vin ordinaire (Fr.). Ordinary cheap wine for immediate consumption.

vinosity. The character of a wine, the balance of its bouquet, flavor, and body.

vino spumante (It.). Sparkling wine.

vinous. Pertaining to wine.

vin rosé (Fr.). Pink wine.

vin rouge (Fr.). Red wine.

Vin (Vino) Santo (It.). Sweet white wine produced from dried grapes in the Chianti region of Tuscany.

vin sec (Fr.). Dry wine.

vintage. Gathering the grape crop and making the wine. Also, the year when the wine is made which often appears on wine labels.

vintage wine. In certain wine regions, particularly Champagne and Porto, the product of exceptional years only is dated. In other regions wines are dated each year.

virgin brandy. Unblended Cognac brandy.

viticulture. The science of growing grapes.

vitis (Latin). Vine.

vornehm (Ger.). Noble, aristocratic.

vörös (Hun.). Red.

Wachstum (Ger.). See *Gewächs*.

wash. In a distillery (usually whisky), the fermented liquor when it is ready to go to the still. In a Scotch distillery, the still that receives the wash is known as the wash still.

weepers. Bottles that show leakage through the cork.

Wein (Ger.). Wine.

Weinbau (Ger.). Viticulture.

Weingut (Ger.). Vineyard or estate.

Weinkeller (Ger.). Wine cellar.

Weisswein (Ger.). White wine.

wernig (Ger.). Vinous, vinosity.

wine. The fermented juice of fruit, usually grapes unless otherwise specified. Ideally, wine is the naturally fermented juice of freshly gathered ripe grapes that have been pressed at or near the place where gathered.

wine broker. An intermediary who acts for buyers and for a vineyard owner.

Winzergenossenschaft (Ger.). Wine growers' cooperative.

woody. The taste of a wine or spirit that has spent too much time in wood, sometimes called *goût de bois*.

wormwood. A perennial herb, *Artemisia absinthium*, aromatic, tonic, and bitter. Formerly used in the preparation of absinthe, certain liqueurs, and vermouths.

würzig (Ger.). Spicy, desirable, flowery.

yayin. A biblical Hebrew term for wine.

yeast. The plant organism whose fermentative qualities cause sugars to break down into alcohol and carbon dioxide gas.

yema (Sp.). The must resulting from the treading before the grapes are subjected to pressure. *Yema* in Spanish means "yolk of an egg" or the core of any product.

yeso (Sp.). Powdered gypsum (calcium sulfate) sprinkled on the grapes in the *lagar* at the time of treading and pressing to fix the tartaric acid during fermentation of the must into sherry wine.

zapatos de pisar (Sp.). Special nail-studded shoes worn by the men who tread the grapes in the *lagar* in the Jerez sherry region.

zymase. The enzyme in yeast cells that causes vinous fermentation and whose catalytic action converts sugars into alcohol and carbon dioxide gas.

APPENDIX A

Quick Guide to Wines and Spirits

Any wine can accompany any food, and you should choose a wine according to personal preference. Certain combinations of wine and food have developed, however, because they are generally pleasing. These are listed here for general guidance but should not be taken as hard and fast rules. Remember also that many chilled wines, either still or sparkling may be enjoyed by themselves, as hospitality wines, or as aperitifs.

Service temperature: *—Room temperature / **—Slightly Chilled / ***— Cold

Serve with: AD—After dinner / BD—Before dinner / C—Cocktails / Ch—Cheese / F—Fish / Fr—Fruits / G—Game / H—Highballs / Hosp—Hospitality / LM—Light meats / P—Poultry / Pun—Punches / RM—Red meats / S—Straight

1855 classification: 1st—First growth / 2nd—Second growth, etc.; *wines of Burgundy*: GC—*Grand Cru* / PC—*Premier Cru*

Name	Phonetic Spelling	Source	Type	Color	Taste	Serv.Temp.	Serve With
Adabag	ah-DAH-bah	Turkey	Table wine	Red	Dry	*	Ch, G, & RM
Adom Atic	ah-DOHM ah-TEEK	Israel	Table wine	Red	Dry	*	Ch, G, & RM
Advocaat	AHD-voh-kaht	Holland	Prepared eggnog	Yellow	Sweet	* or ***	AD
Afames	ah-FAHM-ees	Cyprus	Table wine	Red	Dry	*	Ch, G, & RM
Affentaler	AH-fen-tah-lehr	Baden, Ger.	Table wine	Red	Dry	*	RM
Aigle	AY-gul	Switzerland	Table wine	White	Med. dry	***	F, P, & LM
Albana di Romagna	ahl-bahn-eh dee ro-MAHN-yeh	Emilia, It.	Table wine	White	Dry to med.	***	F, P
Ale		Various	Malt beverage	Straw to dark amber	Bittersweet	***	Hosp
Aleatico	ah-leh-AH-tee-koh	California & Italy	Dessert wine	Red	Sweet	*	AD
Alella	ah-LAY-yah	Spain	Table wine	Red or white	Dry	* or ***	Varies with color
Aloxe-Corton	ah-lohs-kor-toh(n)	Côte de Beaune, Fr.	Table wine	Red	Dry	*	Ch, G, & RM
Amarone della Valpolicella	ah-mah-roh-neh deh-lah vahl-poh-lee-CHAY-lah	Veneto, It.	Table wine	Red	Dry	*	Ch, G, & RM
Amer Picon	ah-mehr pee-koh(n)	France	Aperitif	Dark	Bitter	***	BD

Name	Phonetic Spelling	Source	Type	Color	Taste	Serv.Temp.	Serve With
Amontillado	ah-mohn-tee-YAH-dah	Jerez, Sp.	Sherry	Amber	Dry	**	Hosp
Angelica	ahn-JEL-ee-kah	California	Fortified wine	Gold	Sweet	*	Hosp
Angostura Bitters	ahn-gus-TOO-rah	Trinidad	Aromatic bitters	Reddish brown	Bitter	*	C & Pun
Anisette	ah-nee-zet	Various	Liqueur	White	Aniseed	*	AD
Anjou	ah(n)-zhoo	Loire, Fr.	Table wine	White or pink	Med. sweet	***	F, P, & LM
Anninger Perle	on-ing-ehr PEHR-luh	Austria	Table wine	White	Dry	***	F, P, & LM
Applejack		U.S.	Apple brandy	Amber	Dry, fruity	*	AD
Apricot liqueur		Various	Liqueur	Amber	Sweet,fruity	*	AD
Aquavit	AHK-wa-veet	Denmark	Spirit	White	Caraway	***	BD
Armagnac	ar-mahn-yahk	Ger., Fr.	Brandy	Amber	Dry	*	AD
Assmannshausen	AHS-mahnz-howz-en	Rheingau, Ger.	Table wine	Red	Dry	*	RM
Asti Spumante	ahs-tee spoo-MAHN-teh	Piedmont, It.	Sparkling wine	White	Sweet	***	Desserts
Aurora	oh-RORE-uh	New York State	Table wine	White	Dry	***	F, P, & LM
Avdat	AHV-daht	Israel	Table wine	Red or white	Dry	* or ***	Varies with color
Baco Noir	bah-koh nwahr	New York State	Table wine	Red	Dry	*	P & RM

Name	Phonetic Spelling	Source	Type	Color	Taste	Serv.Temp.	Serve With
Badacsonyi Rizling	BAHD-ah-choh-nee reez-ling	Hungary	Table wine	White	Dry	***	F, P, & LM
Badacsonyi Szürkebarát	BAHD-ah-choh-nee tsoor-keh-BAH-raht	Hungary	Table wine	White	Med. dry	***	F, P, & LM
Banyuls	bah-nyuls	Banyuls, Fr.	Fortified wine	White	Sweet	*	AD
Barack Palinka	BAR-ahks PAH-leen-kah	Hungary	Apricot brandy	Orange	Dry	*	AD
Barbaresco	bar-bah-REHZ-koh	Piedmont, It.	Table wine	Red	Dry	*	Ch, G, & RM
Barbera	bar-BEH-rah	Piedmont, It., California	Table wine	Red	Dry	*	Ch, G, & RM
Bardolino	bar-doh-LEEN-oh	Veneto, It.	Table wine	Red	Dry	*	Ch, G, & RM
Barolo	bah-ROH-loh	Piedmont, It.	Table wine	Red	Dry	*	Ch, G, & RM
Barsac	bar-sahk	Barsac, Fr.	Table wine	White	Sweet	***	Fr & desserts
Batard-Montrachet (GC)	bab-tar-moh(n)rah-shay	Côte de Beaune, Fr.	Table wine	White	Dry	***	F, P, & LM
Batavia arak	bah-TAY-vee ah AHR-ahk	Java, Indonesia	Spirit	Straw	Dry, aromatic	***	C, Pun,& H
Beaujolais	boh-zhoe-lay	Beauplais, Fr.	Table wine	Red	Dry	* or **	All foods
Beaune	bone	Côte de Beaune, Fr.	Table wine	Red	Dry	*	Ch, G, & RM

Name	Phonetic Spelling	Source	Type	Color	Taste	Serv.Temp.	Serve With
Beaune-Grèves (PC)	bone-grehv	Côte de Beaune, Fr.	Table wine	Red	Dry	*	Ch, G, & RM
Beaune-Les Fèves (PC)	bone-lay-fohv	Côte de Beaune, Fr.	Table wine	Red	Dry	*	Ch, G, & RM
Beer, lager	LAH-gur	Various	Malt beverage	Pale gold	Dry	***	Hosp
Bénédictine	bay-nay-deck-teen	Fécamp, Fr.	Liqueur	Gold	Spicy, sweet	*	AD
Bernkasteler Doctor	behrn-kahs-tel-ehr DAWK-tohr	Moselle, Ger.	Table wine	White	Med. dry	***	F, P, & LM
Bianco di Custoza	bee-AHN-koh dee kus-TOES-eh	Veneto, It.	Table wine	White	Dry	***	F, P
Bienvenue-Bâtard Montrachet (GC)	bya(n)-veh-noo-bah-tahr-moh(n)-rah-sbay	Côte de Beaune, Fr.	Table wine	White	Dry	***	F, P, & LM
Binger Scharlachberg	bing-ehr SHAHR-lahk-behrk	Rheinhessen, Ger.	Table wine	White	Dry	***	F, P, & LM
Bitters		Various	Spirit	Reddish brown	Bitter	***	C, H, & Pun
Blackberry liqueur		Various	Liqueur	Dark red	Sweet, fruity	*	AD
Blanc de Blancs	blah(n) duh blah(n)	Champagne, Fr.	Sparkling wine	White	Dry	***	All foods & Hosp

Name	Phonetic Spelling	Source	Type	Color	Taste	Serv.Temp.	Serve With
Bonnes Mares, Les (GC)	lay bun mahr	Côte de Nuits, Fr.	Table wine	Red	Dry	*	Ch, G, & RM
Bordeaux Blanc	bor-dah blah(n)	Bordeaux, Fr.	Table wine	White	Dry, semisweet	***	F, P, & LM
Bordeaux Rouge	bor doh roozh	Bordeaux, Fr.	Table wine	Red	Dry	*	Ch, G, & RM
Bourbon whisky		U.S.	Spirit	Brown	Dry		S, C, H, & Pun
Bourgogne Blanc	boor-gun-yeh blah(n)	Burgundy, Fr.	Table wine	White	Dry	***	F, P, & LM
Bourgogne Rouge	boor-gun-yeh roozh	Burgundy, Fr.	Table wine	Red	Dry	*	Ch, G, & RM
Brachetto	brah-KET-oh	Piedmont, It.	Table wine	Red	Dry	*	Ch, G, & RM
Brandy	BRAN-dee	Various	Fruit spirit	Amber	Dry, fruit	*	BD, C, & H
Brauneberger Juffer	brown-uh-behrk-ehr YOO-fehr	Moselle, Ger.	Table wine	White	Dry	***	F, P, & LM
Brouilly	brwee-yee	Beaujolais, Fr.	Table wine	Red	Dry	*	Ch, G, & RM
Brunello di Montalcino	broo-NEHL-oh dee mohn-tahl-CHEE-noh	Tuscany, It.	Table wine	Red	Dry	*	Ch, G, & RM
Bual (Boar)	boo whal	Madeira	Fortified wine	Gold	Sweet	*	Hosp
Bucelas	boo-SEL-ush	Portugal	Table wine	White	Med. sweet	***	LM & Fr
Buzbag	BOOZ-bah	Turkey	Table wine	Red	Dry	*	Ch, G, & RM

Name	Phonetic Spelling	Source	Type	Color	Taste	Serv.Temp.	Serve With
Cabernet Sauvignon	kah-behr-nay soh-vee-nyoh(n)	Various	Table wine	Red	Dry	*	Ch, G, & RM
Calvados	kahl-vah-dohs	Normandy, Fr.	Apple brandy	Brown	Dry, fruit	*	AD
Campari	kahm-PAR-ee	Italy	Aperitif	Red	Bitter	***	BD
Canadian whisky		Canada	Spirit	Brown	Dry, rich	* or ***	C, H, Pun, & S
Capri	KAH-pree	Capri, It.	Table wine	White	Dry	***	F, P, & LM
Carcavelos	kar-sah-VEL-ush	Portugal	Fortified wine	White	Sweet	***	AD
Carema	kah-RAY-mah	Piedmont, It.	Table wine	Red	Dry	*	Ch, G, & RM
Carruades de Château Lafite-Rothschild	kah-rwahd duh shah-toh lah-feet-roh-sheeld	Médoc, Fr.	Table wine	Red	Dry	*	Ch, G, & RM
Catawba	kuh-TAW-bah	New York State & Ohio	Table or sparkling wine	White	Sweet	***	Fr & Hosp
Cava	cah-vah	Spain	Sparkling	White	Dry	***	Hosp
Chablis	shah-blee	Chablis, Fr.	Table wine	White	Dry	***	Oysters, P, & LM
Chablis Blanchots (GC)	shahblee blah(n)-shoh	Chablis, Fr.	Table wine	White	Dry	***	Oysters, P, & LM
Chablis Bougros (GC)	shah-blee boo-groh	Chablis, Fr.	Table wine	White	Dry	***	Oysters, P, & LM

Name	Phonetic Spelling	Source	Type	Color	Taste	Serv.Temp.	Serve With
Chablis Grenouilles (GC)	shah-blee grah-nwee	Chablis, Fr.	Table wine	White	Dry	***	Oysters, P, & LM
Chablis Les Clos (GC)	shah-blee lay kloh	Chablis, Fr.	Table wine	White	Dry	***	Oysters, P, & LM
Chablis Les Preuses (GC)	shah-blee lay pruhz	Chablis, Fr.	Table wine	White	Dry	***	Oysters, P, & LM
Chablis Valmur (GC)	shah-blee vahl-moor	Chablis, Fr.	Table wine	White	Dry	***	Oysters, P, & LM
Chablis Vaudésir (GC)	shah-blee voh-day-zeer	Chablis, Fr.	Table wine	White	Dry	***	Oysters, P, & LM
Chambertin, Le (GC)	lah shah(m)-behr-ta(n)	Côte de Nuits, Fr.	Table wine	Red	Dry	*	Ch, G, & RM
Chambertin-Clos de Bèze (GC)	shah(m)-behr-ta(n)-klohd-behz	Côte de Nuits, Fr.	Table wine	Red	Dry	*	Ch, G, & RM
Chambolle-Musigny	shah(m)-bohl-moo-see-nyee	Côte de Nuits, Fr.	Table wine	Red	Dry	*	Ch, G, & RM
Chambollo-Musigny-Les Amoureuses (PC)	shah(m)-bohl-moo-see-nyee layz-ah-mohr-uhz	Côte de Nuits, Fr.	Table wine	Red	Dry	*	Ch, G, & RM
Champagne	shah(m)-pah-nye	Champagne, Fr.	Sparkling wine	White or light red	Dry to sweet	***	All foods & Hosp

Name	Phonetic Spelling	Source	Type	Color	Taste	Serv.Temp.	Serve With
Chapelle-Chambertin (GC)	shah-pohl-shah(m)-behr-ta(n)	Côte de Nuits, Fr.	Table wine	Red	Dry	*	Ch, G, & RM
Charbono	shar-BOH-noh	California	Table wine	Red	Dry	*	Ch, G, & RM
Chardonnay	shahr-doh-NAY	Various	Table or sparkling wine	White	Dry	***	F, P, & LM
Charmes-Chambertin (GC)	shahrm-shah(m)-behr-ta(n)	Côte de Nuits, Fr.	Table wine	Red	Dry	*	Ch, G, & RM
Chartreuse	shahr-truhz	Voiron, Fr.	Liqueur	Yellow or green	Spicy, sweet	*	AD
Chassagne-Montrachet	shah-sah-nyuh-moh(n)-rah-shay	Côte de Beaune, Fr.	Table wine	White or red	Dry	* or ***	Varies with color
Château Ausone	shah-toh oh-sohn	Saint-Émilion, Fr.	Table wine	Red	Dry	*	Ch, G, & RM
Château Batailley (5th)	shah-toh bah-tie-yay	Médoc, Fr.	Table wine	Red	Dry	*	Ch, G, & RM
Château Beauséjur	shah-toh boh-say-zhew	Saint-Émilion, Fr.	Table wine	Red	Dry	*	Ch, G, & RM
Château Belair	shah-toh bel-ehr	Saint-Émilion , Fr.	Table wine	Red	Dry	*	Ch, G, & RM
Château Belgrave (5th)	shah-toh bel-grahv	Médoc, Fr.	Table wine	Red	Dry	*	Ch, G, & RM

Name	Phonetic Spelling	Source	Type	Color	Taste	Serv.Temp.	Serve With
Château Bellevue	shah-toh bel-vuh	Saint-Émilion, Fr.	Table wine	Red	Dry	*	Ch, G, & RM
Château Beychevelle (4th)	shah-toh baysh-vehl	Médoc, Fr.	Table wine	Red	Dry	*	Ch, GM & RM
Château Bouscaut	shah-toh boo-skoh	Graves, Fr.	Table wine	Red or white	Dry	* or ***	Varies with color
Château Boyd-Cantenac (3rd)	shah-toh bwahd-kah(n)-teh-nahk	Médoc, Fr.	Table wine	Red	Dry	*	Cb, G, & RM
Château Branaire-Ducru (4th)	shah-toh brah-nehr-doo-croo	Médoc, Fr.	Table wine	Red	Dry	*	Ch, G, & RM
Château Brane-Cantenac (2nd)	shah-toh brahn kah(n)-teh-nahk	Médoc, Fr.	Table wine	Red	Dry	*	Ch, G, & RM
Château Broustet (2nd)	shah-toh broo-stay	Barsac, Fr.	Table wine	White	Sweet	***	Desserts
Château Caillou (2nd)	shah-toh kah-yoo	Barsac, Fr.	Table wine	White	Sweet	***	Desserts
Château Calon-Ségur (3rd)	shah-toh kah-loh(n) say-goor	Médoc, Fr.	Table wine	Red	Dry	*	Ch, G, & RM
Château Camensac (5th)	shah-toh kah-men-sahk	Médoc, Fr.	Table wine	Red	Dry	*	Ch, G, & RM

Name	Phonetic Spelling	Source	Type	Color	Taste	Serv.Temp.	Serve With
Château Canon	shah-toh kah-noh(n)	Saint-Émilion, Fr.	Table wine	Red	Dry	*	Ch, G, & RM
Château Cantemerle (5th)	shah-toh kha(n)-teh-mehrl	Médoc, Fr.	Table wine	Red	Dry	*	Ch, G, & RM
Château Cantenac-Brown (3rd)	shah-toh kha(n)teh-nahk-brown	Médoc, Fr.	Table wine	Red	Dry	*	Ch, G, & RM
Château Carbonnieux	shah-toh car-boh-nyuh	Graves, Fr.	Table wine	Red or white	Dry	* or ***	Varies with color
Château Certan-Giraud	shah-toh sehr-ta(n)zhee-roh	Pomerol, Fr.	Table wine	Red	Dry	*	Ch, G, & RM
Château Châlon	shah-toh-shah-loh(n)	Jura, Fr.	Table wine	White	Dry	***	BD
Château Cheval-Blanc	shah-toh sheh-vahl-blah(n)	Saint-Émilion, Fr.	Table wine	Red	Dry	*	Ch, G, & RM
Château Clerc-Mil-on-Mondon (5th)	shah-toh klehr-mee-loh(n)-moh(n)-doh(n)	Médoc, Fr.	Table wine	Red	Dry	*	Ch, G, & RM
Château Climens (1st)	shah-toh klee-mah(n)	Barsac, Fr.	Table wine	White	Sweet	***	Desserts

Name	Phonetic Spelling	Source	Type	Color	Taste	Serv.Temp.	Serve With
(Château) Clos Fourtet	shah-toh kloh foor-tay	Saint-Émilion, Fr.	Table wine	Red	Dry	*	Ch, G, & RM
(Château) Clos Haut-Peyraguey (1st)	shah-toh kloh oh-pay-rah-gay	Sauternes, Fr.	Table wine	White	Sweet	***	Desserts
Château Cos d'Estournel (2nd)	shah-toh kob deb-toor-nel	Médoc, Fr.	Table wine	Red	Dry	*	Ch, G, & RM
Château Cos-Labory (5th)	shah-toh koh-lah-boh-ree	Médoc, Fr.	Table wine	Red	Dry	*	Ch, G, & RM
Château Couhins	shah-toh kwah(n)	Graves, Fr.	Table wine	White	Dry	***	F, P, & LM
Château Coutet (1st)	shah-toh koo-tay	Barsac, Fr.	Table wine	White	Sweet	***	Desserts
Château Croizet-Bages (5th)	shah-toh krwah-zeh-bahzh	Médoc, Fr.	Table wine	Red	Dry	*	Ch, G, & RM
Château d'Arche (2nd)	shah-toh dahrsh	Sauternes, Fr.	Table wine	White	Sweet	***	Desserts
Château Dauzac (5th)	shah-toh dah-zahk	Médoc, Fr.	Table wine	Red	Dry	*	Ch, G, & RM
Château de Malle (2nd)	shah-toh duh mahl	Sauternes, Fr.	Table wine	White	Sweet	***	Desserts

Name	Phonetic Spelling	Source	Type	Color	Taste	Serv.Temp.	Serve With
Château d'Issan (3rd)	shah-toh dee-sah(n)	Médoc, Fr.	Table wine	Red	Dry	*	Ch, G, & RM
Château de Rayne-Vigneau (1st)	shah-toh duh rayn-vee-nyoh	Sauternes, Fr.	Table wine	White	Sweet	***	Desserts
Château Doisy-Daene (2nd)	shah-toh dwah-zee-dan	Barsac, Fr.	Table wine	White	Sweet	***	Desserts
Château Doisy-Vedrines (2nd)	shah-toh dwah-zee-vay-dreen	Barsac, Fr.	Table wine	White	Sweet	***	Desserts
Château Ducru-Beaucaillou (2nd)	shah-toh doo-croo-boh-kah-yoo	Médoc, Fr.	Table wine	Red	Dry	*	Ch, G, & RM
Château-Duhart-Milon-Rothschild (4th)	shah-toh doo-ar-mee-loh(n)-roh-sheeld	Médoc, Fr.	Table wine	Red	Dry	*	Ch, G, & RM
Château Durfort-Vivens (2nd)	shah-toh duhr-for-vee-vah(n)	Médoc, Fr.	Table wine	Red	Dry	*	Ch, C, & RM
Château du Tertre (5th)	shah-toh doo tehrtr	Médoc, Fr.	Table wine	Red	Dry	*	Ch, G, & RM
Château d'Yquem (1st)	shah-toh dee-kem	Sauternes, Fr.	Table wine	White	Sweet	***	Desserts

Name	Phonetic Spelling	Source	Type	Color	Taste	Serv.Temp.	Serve With
Château Ferrière (3rd)	shah-toh fehr-yehr	Médoc, Fr.	Table wine	Red	Dry	*	Ch, G, & RM
Château Fieuzal	shah-toh fyuh-zahl	Graves, Fr.	Table wine	Red	Dry	*	Ch, G, & RM
Château Figeac	shah-toh fee-zhahk	Saint-Émilion, Fr.	Table wine	Red	Dry	*	Ch, G, & RM
Château Filhot (2nd)	shah-toh fee-loh	Sauternes, Fr.	Table wine	White	Sweet	***	Desserts
Château Gazin	shah-toh gah-za(n)	Pomerol, Fr.	Table wine	Red	Dry	*	Ch, C, & RM
Château Giscours (3rd)	shah-toh zhis-koor	Médoc, Fr.	Table wine	Red	Dry	*	Ch, G, & RM
Château Grand-Puy-Ducasse (5th)	shah-toh grah(n)-pwee-doo-kahs	Médoc, Fr.	Table wine	Red	Dry	*	Ch, G, & RM
Château Grand-Puy-Lacoste (5th)	shah-toh grah(n)-pwee-lah-kohst	Médoc, Fr.	Table wine	Red	Dry	*	Ch, G, & RM
Château Grillet	shah-toh gree-yay	Côtes du Rhône, Fr.	Table wine	White	Dry	***	F, P, & LM
Château Gruaud-Larose (2nd)	shah-toh groo-oh-lah-rohz	Médoc, Fr.	Table wine	Red	Dry	*	Ch, G, & RM
Château Guiraud (1st)	shah-toh zhwee-roh	Sauternes, Fr.	Table wine	White	Sweet	***	Desserts

Name	Phonetic Spelling	Source	Type	Color	Taste	Serv.Temp.	Serve With
Château Haut-Bages-Libéral (5th)	shah-toh oh-bahzh-lee-beh-rahl	Médoc, Fr.	Table wine	Red	Dry	*	Ch, G, & RM
Château Haut-Bailly	shah-toh oh-bay-yee	Graves, Fr.	Table wine	Red	Dry	*	Ch, C, & RM
Château Haut-Batailley (5th)	shah-toh oh-bah-tie-yay	Médoc, Fr.	Table wine	Red	Dry	*	Gh, G, & RM
Château Haut-Brion (1st)	shah-toh oh-bree-oh(n)	Graves, Fr.	Table wine	Red	Dry	*	Ch, G, & RM
Château Haut-Brion Blanc	shah-toh oh-bree-oh(n) blah(n)	Graves, Fr.	Table wine	White	Dry	***	F, P, & LM
Château Kirwan (3rd)	shah-toh kir-wah(n)	Médoc, Fr.	Table wine	Red	Dry	*	Ch, G, & RM
Château La Conseillante	shah-toh lah koh(n)-say-ah(n)t	Pomerol, Fr.	Table wine	Red	Dry	*	Ch, G, & RM
Château Lafaurie-Peyraguey (1st)	shah-toh lah-foh-ree-pay-rah-gay	Sauternes, Fr.	Table wine	White	Sweet	***	Desserts
Château Lafite-Rothschild (1st)	shah-toh lah-feet-roh-sheeld	Médoc, Fr.	Table wine	Red	Dry	*	Ch, G, & RM
Château La Fleur-Pétrus	shah-toh lah fluhr-pay-troos	Pomerol, Fr.	Table wine	Red	Dry	*	Ch, G, & RM

Name	Phonetic Spelling	Source	Type	Color	Taste	Serv.Temp.	Serve With
Château Lafon-Rochet (4th)	shah-toh lah-foh(n)-roh-shay	Médoc, Fr.	Table wine	Red	Dry	*	Ch, G, & RM
Château La Gaffelière	shah-toh lah gah-fel-yehr	Saint-Émilion, Fr.	Table wine	Red	Dry	*	Ch, G, & RM
Château La Garde	shah-toh lah gahrd	Graves, Fr.	Table wine	Red	Dry	*	Ch, G, & RM
Château Lagrange (3rd)	shah-toh lah-grah(n)zh	Médoc, Fr.	Table wine	Red	Dry	*	Ch, G, & RM
Château La Lagune (3rd)	shah-toh lah lah-goon	Médoc, Fr.	Table wine	Red	Dry	*	Ch, G, & RM
Château La Mission Haut Brion	shah-toh lah mee-syoh(n) oh bree-oh(n)	Graves, Fr.	Table wine	Red	Dry	*	Ch, G, & RM
Château Lamothe (2nd)	shah-toh lah-moht	Sauternes, Fr.	Table wine	White	Sweet	***	Desserts
Château Langoa-Barton (3rd)	shah-toh lah(n)-gah ahbahr-toh(n)	Médoc, Fr.	Table wine	Red	Dry	*	Ch, G, & RM
Château Laroze	shah-toh lah-rohz	Saint-Émilion, Fr.	Table wine	Red	Dry	*	Ch, G, & RM
Château Larrivet Haut Brion	shah-toh lah-ree-veh oh-bree-oh(n)	Graves, Fr.	Table wine	White	Dry	***	F, P, & LM

Name	Phonetic Spelling	Source	Type	Color	Taste	Serv.Temp.	Serve With
Château Lascombes (2nd)	shah-toh lahs-coh(m)b	Médoc, Fr.	Table wine	Red	Dry	*	Ch, G, & RM
Château Latour (1st)	shah-toh lah-toor	Médoc, Fr.	Table wine	Red	Dry	*	Ch, G, & RM
Château La Tour-Blanche (1st)	shah-toh lah toor-blah(n)sh	Sauternes, Fr.	Table wine	White	Sweet	***	Desserts
Château La Tour-Carnet (4th)	shah-toh lah to or-car-n ay	Médoc, Fr	Table wine	Red	Dry	*	Ch, G, & RM
Château La Tour Haut Brion	shah-toh lah toor oh bree-oh(n)	Graves, Fr.	Table wine	Red	Dry	*	Ch, G, & RM
Château La Tour-Martillac	shah-toh lah toor-mahr-tee-yahk	Graves, Fr.	Table wine	Red or white	Dry	* or ***	Varies with color
Château Latour-Pomerol	shah-toh lah toor-pohm-rohl	Pomerol, Fr.	Table wine	Red	Dry	*	Ch, G, & RM
Château Laville Haut Brion	shah-toh lah-vee yoh bree-oh(n)	Graves, Fr.	Table wine	White	Dry	***	F, P, & LM
Château Léoville-Barton (2nd)	shah-toh lay-oh-veel-bar-toh(n)	Médoc, Fr.	Table wine	Red	Dry	*	Ch, G, & RM
Château Léoville-Lascases (2nd)	shah-toh lay-oh-veel-lahs-kahz	Médoc, Fr.	Table wine	Red	Dry	*	Ch, G, & RM

Name	Phonetic Spelling	Source	Type	Color	Taste	Serv.Temp.	Serve With
Château Léoville-Poyferré (2nd)	shah-toh lay-oh-veel-pwah-feh-ray	Médoc, Fr.	Table wine	Red	Dry	*	Ch, G, & RM
Château L'Evangile	shah-toh lay-vah(n)-zheel	Pomerol, Fr.	Table wine	Red	Dry	*	Ch, G, & RM
Château Lynch-Bages (5th)	shah-toh leensh-bahzh	Médoc, Fr.	Table wine	Red	Dry	*	Ch, G, & RM
Château Lynch-Moussas (5th)	shah-toh leensh-moo-sah	Médoc, Fr.	Table wine	Red	Dry	*	Ch, G, & RM
Château Magdelaine	shah-toh mahg-duh-lehn	Saint-Émilion, Fr.	Table wine	Red	Dry	*	Ch, G, & RM
Château Malartic-Lagravière	shah-toh mah-lahr-teek-lah-grahv-yehr	Graves, Fr.	Table wine	Red or white	Dry	***	Varies with color
Château Malescot-Saint-Exupéry (3rd)	shah-toh mah-lebs koh-sa(n) tex-oo-peh-ree	Médoc, Fr.	Table wine	Red	Dry	*	Ch, G, & RM
Château Margaux (1st)	shah-toh mahr-goh	Médoc, Fr.	Table wine	Red	Dry	*	Ch, G, & RM
Château Marquis d'Alesme-Becker (3rd)	shah-toh mahr-kee dah-lehm-beh-ker	Médoc, Fr.	Table wine	Red	Dry	*	Ch, G, & RM

Name	Phonetic Spelling	Source	Type	Color	Taste	Serv.Temp.	Serve With
Château Marquis de Terme (4th)	shdh-toh mahr-kee duh tehrm	Médoc, Fr.	Table wine	Red	Dry	*	Ch, G, & RM
Château Montrose (2nd)	shah-toh moh(n)-rohz	Médoc, Fr.	Table wine	Red	Dry	*	Ch, G, & RM
Château Mouton-Baron-Philippe (5th)	shah-toh moo taw(n)-bah-roh(n)-fee-leep	Médoc, Fr.	Table wine	Red	Dry	*	Ch, G, & RM
Château Mouton-Rothschild (1st)	shah-toh mootaw(n)-roh-sheeld	Médoc, Fr.	Table wine	Red	Dry	*	Ch, G, & RM
Château Myrat (2nd)	shah-toh mee-rah	Barsac, Fr.	Table wine	White	Sweet	***	Desserts
Château Nairac (2nd)	shah-toh nay-rahk	Barsac, Fr.	Table wine	White	Sweet	***	Desserts
Château Nenin	shah-toh nuh-neen	Pomerol, Fr.	Table wine	Red	Dry	*	Ch, G, & RM
Châteauneuf-du-Pape	shah-toh-nuf-doo-pop	Rhône, Fr.	Table wine	Red	Dry	*	Ch, G, & RM
Château Olivier	shah-toh oh-lee-vyay	Graves, Fr.	Table wine	Red or white	Dry	* or ***	Varies with color
Château Palmer (3rd)	shah-toh pahl-mehr	Médoc, Fr.	Table wine	Red	Dry	*	Ch, G, & RM
Château Pape-Clement	shah-toh pop-klay-mah(n)	Graves, Fr.	Table wine	Red	Dry	*	Ch, G, & RM

Name	Phonetic Spelling	Source	Type	Color	Taste	Serv.Temp.	Serve With
Château Pavie	shah-toh pah-vee	Saint-Émilion, Fr.	Table wine	Red	Dry	*	Ch, G, & RM
Château Pédesclaux (5th)	shah-toh pay-dehs-kloh	Médoc, Fr.	Table wine	Red	Dry	*	Ch, G, & RM
Château Petit-Village	shah-toh puh-tee-vee-lahzh	Pomerol, Fr.	Table wine	Red	Dry	*	Ch, G, & RM
Château Pétrus	shah-toh peh-troos	Pomerol, Fr.	Table wine	Red	Dry	*	Ch, G & RM
Château Pichon-Longueville (Baron) (2nd)	shah-toh pee-shoh(n)-loh(n)g-veel (bah-roh(n))	Médoc, Fr.	Table wine	Red	Dry	*	Ch, G & RM
Château Pichon-Longueville-Comtesse (2nd)	shah-toh pee-shoh(n)-loh(n)g-vee-coh(m)-tehs	Médoc, Fr.	Table wine	Red	Dry	*	Ch, G, & RM
Château Pontet-Canet (5th)	shah-toh poh(n)-teh-kah-neh	Médoc, Fr.	Table wine	Red	Dry	*	Ch, G, & RM
Château Pouget (4th)	shah-toh poo-zhay	Médoc, Fr.	Table wine	Red	Dry	*	Ch, G, & RM
Château Prieuré-Lichine (4th)	shah-toh pree-uh-ray-lee-sheen	Médoc, Fr.	Table wine	Red	Dry	*	Ch, G, & RM
Château Rabaud-Promis (1st)	shah-toh rah-boh-proh-mee	Sauternes, Fr.	Table wine	White	Sweet	***	Desserts

Name	Phonetic Spelling	Source	Type	Color	Taste	Serv.Temp.	Serve With
Château Rausan-Ségla (2nd)	shah-toh roh-zah(n)-say-glah	Médoc, Fr.	Table wine	Red	Dry	*	Ch, G, & RM
Château Rauzan-Gassies (2nd)	shah-toh roh-zah(n)-gah-see	Médoc, Fr.	Table wine	Red	Dry	*	Ch, G, & RM
Château Rieussec (1st)	shah-toh ree-uh-sehk	Sauternes, Fr.	Table wine	White	Sweet	***	Desserts
Château Ripeau	shah-toh ree-poh	Saint-Émilion, Fr.	Table wine	Red	Dry	*	Ch, G, & RM
Château Romer (2nd)	shah-toh roh-mehr	Sauternes, Fr.	Table wine	White	Sweet	***	Desserts
Château Saint-Pierre (4th)	shah-toh sa(n)-pyehr	Médoc, Fr.	Table wine	Red	Dry	*	Ch, G, & RM
Château Sigalas-Rabaud (1st)	shah-toh see-gah-lah-rah-boh	Sauternes, Fr.	Table wine	White	Sweet	***	Desserts
Château Smith-Haut-Lafitte	shah-toh smith-oh-lah-feet	Graves, Fr.	Table wine	Red	Dry	*	Ch, G, & RM
Château Suau	shah-toh soo-oh	Barsac, Fr.	Table wine	White	Sweet	***	Desserts
Château Suduiraut (1st)	shah-toh soo-dwee-roh	Sauternes, Fr.	Table wine	White	Sweet	***	Desserts
Château Talbot (4th)	shah-toh tahl-boh	Médoc, Fr.	Table wine	Red	Dry	*	Ch, G, & RM

Name	Phonetic Spelling	Source	Type	Color	Taste	Serv.Temp.	Serve With
Château Trimoulet	shah-toh tre-moo-lay	Saint-Émilion, Fr.	Table wine	Red	Dry	*	Ch, G, & RM
Château Troplong-Mondot	shah-toh troh-loh(ng)-moh(n)-doh	Saint-Émilion, Fr.	Table wine	Red	Dry	*	Ch, G, & RM
Château Trotanoy	shah-toh trwah-tahn-wah	Pomerol, Fr.	Table wine	Red	Dry	*	Ch, G, & RM
Château Trottevieille	shah-toh troht-vyay	Saint-Émilion, Fr.	Table wine	Red	Dry	*	Ch, G, & RM
(Château) Vieux Château Certan	(shah-toh) vyuh shah-toh sehr-ta(n)	Pomerol, Fr.	Table wine	Red	Dry	*	Ch, G, & RM
Chefoo	chay-foo	China	Dessert wine	Red or white	Sweet	***	Desserts
Chelois	shel-wah	New York State	Table wine	Red	Med. dry	**	P & RM
Chenin Blanc	sheh-neen blah(n)	California & France	Table wine	White	Med. dry	**	F, P, & LM
Cherry liqueur		Various	Liqueur	Red	Sweet, cherry	*	AD
Chevalier-Montrachet (GC)	sheh-vahl-yay moh(n)-rah-shay	Côte de Beaune, Fr.	Table wine	White	Dry	***	F, P, & LM
Chianti	kee-AHN-tee	Tuscany, It.	Table wine	Red	Dry	*	All foods

Name	Phonetic Spelling	Source	Type	Color	Taste	Serv.Temp.	Serve With
Chiaretto del Garda	kee-ah-RET-oh del gar-dah	Veneto, It.	Table wine	Pink	Med. dry	***	All foods
Cider		Spain & England	Sparkling or still wine	Straw	Sweet, fruity	***	Hosp
Clos de la Roche (GC)	kloh duh lah rohsh	Côte de Nuits, Fr.	Table wine	Red	Dry	*	Ch, G, & RM
Clos des Lambrays (PC)	kloh day lah(m)-bray	Côte de Nuits, Fr.	Table wine	Red	Dry	*	Ch, G, & RM
Clos des Mouches (PC)	kloh day moosh	Côte de Beaune, Fr.	Table wine	Red	Dry	*	Ch, G, & RM
Clos de Tart (GC)	kloh-duh tahr	Côte de Nuits, Fr.	Table wine	Red	Dry	*	Ch, G, & RM
Clos de Vougeot (GC)	kloh duh voo-zhoh	Côte de Nuits, Fr.	Table wine	Red	Dry	*	Ch, G, & RM
Clos Saint-Denis (GC)	kloh sa(n)-duh-nee	Côte de Nuits, Fr.	Table wine	Red	Dry	*	Ch, G, & RM
Clos Sainte-Odile	kloh sa(n)-toh-deel	Alsace, Fr.	Table wine	White	Med. dry	***	All foods
Clos Saint-Jacques (PC)	kloh sa(n)-zhahk	Côte de Nuits, Fr.	Table wine	Red	Dry	*	Ch, G, & RM
Cognac	koh-nyahk	Cognac, Fr.	Brandy	Brown	Dry	*	AD

Name	Phonetic Spelling	Source	Type	Color	Taste	Serv.Temp.	Serve With
Cointreau	kwa(n)-troh	Angers, Fr.	Liqueur	White	Sweet, orange	*	AD
Colares	Loh-LAHR-esh	Portugal	Table wine	Red	Dry	*	Ch, G, & RM
Combettes, Les (PC)	lay co(m)-bet	Côte de Beaune, Fr.	Table wine	White	Dry	***	F, P, & LM
Commandaria	koh-maim dah-REE-ah	Cyprus	Dessert wine	White	Sweet	*	AD
Cortaillod	kohr-tie-oh	Switzerland	Table wine	Red	Dry	*	Ch, & RM
Cortese di Gavi	kohr-TAY-zee	Piedmont, It.	Table wine	White	Dry	***	F, P, & LM
Corton, Le (GC)	lah kohr-toh(n)	Côte de Beaune, Fr.	Table wine	Red	Dry	*	Ch, G, & RM
Corton-Charlemagne (GC)	kor-toh(n)-shahr-leh-mah-nyuh	Côte de Beaune, Fr.	Table wine	White	Dry	***	F, P, & LM
Corton-Clos du Roi (GC)	kor-toh(n)-kloh doo rwah	Côte de Beaune, Fr.	Table wine	Red	Dry	*	Ch, G, & RM
Corton-Pougets (GC)	kor-toh(n)poo-zheh	Côte de Beaune, Fr.	Table wine	Red	Dry	*	Ch, G, & RM
Corvo	kohr-vah	Sicily, It.	Table wine	Red or white	Dry	* or ***	Varies with color
Côteaux de la Loire	koh-toh dub lah lwahr	Loire, Fr.	Table wine	White	Med. sweet	***	All foods

Name	Phonetic Spelling	Source	Type	Color	Taste	Serv.Temp.	Serve With
Côte Rôtie	koht roh-tee	Rhône, Fr.	Table wine	Red	Dry	*	Ch, G, & RM
Cotnari Grasa	koht-NAR-ee GRAH-sah	Romania	Dessert wine	Gold	Sweet	***	Desserts, AD
Crème de bananes	krehm deh bah-nahn	Various	Liqueur	Gold	Sweet, banana	*	AD
Crème de cacao	krehn duh kah-kah oh	Various	Liqueur	Brown or white	Sweet, chocolate	*	AD
Crème de cassis	krehm duh kah-sees	Various	Liqueur	Red	Sweet, currant	***	H & C, aperitifs
Crème de menthe	krehm duh mah(n)t	Various	Liqueur	White or green	Sweet, mint	***	AD
Crème de noyaux	krehm duh noy-oh	Various	Liqueur	Cream	Sweet, nut	*	AD
Crème de violettes	krehm duh vee-oh-let	Various	Liqueur	Violet	Sweet,violet	*	AD
Crème Yvette	krehm ee-vet	Connecticut	Liqueur	Blue or violet	Sweet,violet	*	AD
Criots-Bâtard-Montrachet (GC)	kree-ut-bah-tahr-moh(n)-rah-shay	Côte de Beaune, Fr.	Table wine	White	Dry	***	F, P, & LM
Csopaki Furmint	CHO-pah-kee foor-mint	Hungary	Table wine	White	Dry	***	P, P, & LM
Curaçao	kuh-rah-soh	Various	Liqueur	Orange	Sweet, orange	*	AD

Name	Phonetic Spelling	Source	Type	Color	Taste	Serv.Temp.	Serve With
Cynar	CHEE-nar	Italy	Aperitif	Brown	Bitter	***	BD
Danziger Goldwasser	dahnt-zeeg-ehr GOHLD-vahs-ehr	Danzig, Ger.	Liqueur	White	Sweet	*	AD
Dão	dow	Portugal	Table wine	Red or white	Dry	* or ***	Varies with color
Debröi Hárslevelü	DEH-broy harsh-leh vel-yoo	Hungary	Table wine	White	Med. sweet	***	All foods
Deidesheimer Leinhöhle	die-dehs-hie-mehr-LINE-hoyl-eh	Rheinpfalz, Ger.	Table wine	White	Med. dry	***	F, P, & LM
Demeraran rum	demeh-RAH-rahn	Guyana	Spirit	Dark brown	Med sweet	***	C, H, Pun & S
Demestica	deh-MES-tee-kah	Greece	Table wine	Red or white	Dry	* or ***	Varies with color
Dézaley	day-zah-lay	Switzerland	Table wine	White	Dry	***	F, P, & LM
Dolcetto	dohl-CHET-oh	Piedmont, It.	Table or sparkling wine	Red	Dry or sweet	* or ***	All foods
Dôle de Sion	dohl duh see oh(n)	Switzerland	Table wine	Red	Dry	*	Ch, G, & RM
Domaine de Chevalier	duh-men duh sheh-vahl-yay	Graves, Fr.	Table wine	Red or white	Dry	* or ***	Varies with color
Drambuie	dram-BOO EE	Scotland	Liqueur	Gold	Sweet, spicy	*	AD
Dubonnet	doo-boh-nay	France & U.S.	Aperitif	Red or white	Sweet	***	BD

Name	Phonetic Spelling	Source	Type	Color	Taste	Serv.Temp.	Serve With
Dürkheimer Michelsberg	doork-hie-mehr MEEK-els-behrk	Rheinpfalz, Ger.	Table wine	White	Med. dry	***	F, P, & LM
Dürkheimer Spielberg	doork-hie-mehr SHPEEL-behrk	Rheinpfalz, Ger.	Table wine	White	Med. dry	***	F, P, & LM
Eau de Vie de Marc	ode-vee duh mahr	France	Brandy	Brown	Dry	*	AD
Eau de Vie de Poire	ode-vee duh pwahr	Various	Pear brandy	White	Dry, pear	***	AD
Echézeaux, Les (GC)	lays ay-sheh-zoh	Côte de Nuits, Fr.	Table wine	Red	Dry	*	Ch, G, & RM
Egri Bikavér	eg-ree BEE-kah-vehr	Hungary	Table wine	Red	Dry	*	Ch, G, & RM
Eiswein	ICE-vine	Rhine & Moselle, Ger.	Table wine	White	Sweet	***	Desserts
Erbacher Marcobrunn	EHR-bahk-ehr MAHR-koh-bruhn	Rheingau, Ger.	Table wine	White	Med. dry	***	F, P, & LM
Erdener Treppchen	ehrd-eh-nehr TREPF-shen	Moselle, Ger.	Table wine	White	Med. dry	***	F, P, & LM
Escherndorfer Lump	eh-shehrn-dorf-ehr LOOMP	Franconia, Ger.	Table wine	White	Med. dry	***	F, P, & LM
Est! Est!! Est!!!	ehst-ehst-EHST	Latium, It.	Table wine	White	Dry	***	F, P, & LM
Falerno	fah-LEHR-noh	Campania, It.	Table wine	Red or white	Dry	* or ***	Varies with color

Name	Phonetic Spelling	Source	Type	Color	Taste	Serv.Temp.	Serve With
Fendent de Sion	fah(n)-dah(n) duh see oh(n)	Switzerland	Table wine	White	Dry	***	F, P, & LM
Fernet Branca	fohr-net BRAHN-kah	Italy & U S.	Bitters	Reddish brown	Bitter	*	C & H
Fiano di Avellino	FYAN-oh dee ab-veh-LEEN-oh	Campania, It.	Table wine	White	Dry	***	F, P, LM, or Ch
Fino	FEE-noh	Jerez, Sp.	Sherry	Straw	Dry	**	BD
Fior d'Alpe	fyor DAHL-pay	Italy	Liqueur	Gold	Sweet	*	AD
Fleurie	fluh-ree	Beaujoiais, Fr.	Table wine	Red	Dry	*	All foods
Folle Blanche	fohl blah(n)sh	California	Table wine	White	Dry	***	F, P, & LM
Forster Kirchenstück	forsb-ter KEER(KH)-en-shtuk	Rheinpfalz, Ger.	Table wine	White	Med. dry	***	F, P, & LM
Forster Ungeheuer	forsb-ter OONG eh-hoy-er	Rheinpfalz, Ger.	Table wine	White	Med. dry	***	F, P, & LM
Fraise	frehz	Various	Strawberry brandy	White	Dry	***	AD
Framboise	frah(m)-bwahz	Various	Raspberry brandy	White	Dry, raspberry	***	AD
Frascati	frahs-KAH-tee	Latium, It.	Table wine	White	Med. sweet	***	F, P, & LM
Frecciarossa	frehchah-ROH-sah	Lombardy, It.	Table wine	Red or white	Dry	* or ***	Varies with color

Name	Phonetic Spelling	Source	Type	Color	Taste	Serv.Temp.	Serve With
Freisa	FRAY-sah	Piedmont, It.	Table wine	Red	Dry	*	Ch, G, & RM
French vermouth		Midi, Fr.	Aromatized wine	White	Dry	***	BD & C
Galestro	gah-LEHS-troh	Tuscany, It.	Table wine	White	Dry	***	F, P, LM
Galliano	gahl-YAH-noh	Milan, It.	Liqueur	Gold	Sweet	*	AD
Gamay	gah-may	Framce & California	Table wine	Red	Dry	**	Ch, G, & RM
Gamay Beaujolais	Gam-aye boh-zhoe-lay	California	Table wine	Red	Dry	*	P, LM, & Ch
Gattinara	gah-tee-NAH-rah	Piedmont, It.	Table wine	Red	Dry	*	Ch, G, & RM
Gavi	GAH-vee	Piedmont, It.	Table wine	White	Dry	**	F, P, LM, & Ch
Geisenheimer Mäuerchen	gie-zen-hie-mehr MOY-er-shen	Rheingau, Ger.	Table wine	White	Med. dry	***	F, P, & LM
Geisenheimer Rothenberg	gie-zen-bie-mehr RAHTH-en-behrk	Rheingau, Ger.	Table wine	White	Med. dry	***	F, P, & LM
Genever (gin)		Holland	Spirit	White	Dry	**	BD, S, & H
Gevrey-Chambertin	zhev-ray-shah(m)-behr-ta(n)	Côte de Nuits, Fr.	Table wine	Red	Dry	*	Ch, G, & RM
Gewurztraminer	geh-VURTZ-trah-meen-er	Alsace, Fr., & California	Table wine	White	Med. dry	***	All foods

Name	Phonetic Spelling	Source	Type	Color	Taste	Serv.Temp.	Serve With
Gin, dry	jin	Various	Spirit	White	Dry	***	C, H, & S
Girò	zhee-roh	Sardinia, It.	Dessert wine	Red	Sweet	*	AD
Graacher Himmebeich	grah-kehr HIM-el-rie(kh)	Moselle, Ger.	Table wine	White	Med. dry	***	F, P, & LM
Gragnano	grah-NYAH-noh	Campania, It.	Table wine	Red	Dry	*	Ch, G, & RM
Grand Marnier	grah(n) mahr-nyay	Cognac, Fr.	Liqueur	Orange	Sweet, orange	*	AD
Grands Echézeaux, Les (GC)	lay grah(n) zay-sheh-zoh	Côte de Nuits, Fr.	Table wine	Red	Dry	*	Ch, G, & RM
Graves	grahv	Bordeaux, Fr.	Table wine	Red or white	Dry	* or ***	Varies with color
Greco di Tufo	greh-koh dee TOO-foh	Campania, It.	Table wine	White	Med. dry	***	F, P, & LM
Grenadine	GREHN-ah-deen	Various	Syrup	Red	Sweet	***	C & Pun
Grignolino	gree-nyoh-LEE-noh	Piedmont, It.	Table wine	Red	Dry	*	Ch, G, & RM
Grinzinger	GRINT-zing-ehr	Austria	Table wine	White	Dry	***	F, P, & LM
Griotte-Chambertin (GC)	gree-ut-shah(m)-behr-ta(n)	Côte de Nuits, Fr.	Table wine	Red	Dry	*	Ch, G, & RM
Grumello	groo-MEL-oh	Lombardy, It.	Table wine	Red	Dry	*	Ch, G, & RM
Gumpoldskirchner	GOOM-pohls-keer(kh)-nehr	Austria	Table wine	White	Dry	***	F, P, & LM

Name	Phonetic Spelling	Source	Type	Color	Taste	Serv.Temp.	Serve With
Haitian rum	hay-shum	Haiti	Spirit	Straw	Dry	***	C, Pun, H, & S
Hallgartener Schönhell	hahl-gar-ten-ehr SHOYN-hel	Rheingau, Ger.	Table wine	White	Med. dry	***	F, P, & LM
Hattenheimer Nussbrunnen	haht-ten-hie-mehr NOOS-broon-en	Rheingau, Ger.	Table wine	White	Med. dry	***	P, & LM
Hermitage	ehr-mee-tahzh	Rhône, Fr.	Table wine	Red or white	Dry	* or ***	Varies with color
Hochheimer Domdechaney	hok-hie-mehr DOHM-deh-shah-nay	Rheingau, Ger.	Table wine	White	Med. dry	***	F, P, & LM
Hochheimer Kirchenstück	hok-hie-mehr KEER(KH)-en-shtuk	Rheingau, Ger.	Table wine	White	Med. dry	***	F, P, & LM
Hohenwarther	HOH-hen-vahr-tehr	Austria	Table wine	White	Dry	***	F, P, & LM
Hollands (gin)		Holland	Spirit	White	Dry	*	BD, S, & H
Hospices de Beaune	ohs-pees duh bone	Côte de Beaune, Fr.	Table wine	Red or white	Dry	* or ***	Varies with color
Inferno	een-FEHR-noh	Lombardy, It.	Table wine	Red	Dry	*	Ch, G, & RM
Iphofener Julius-Echter-Berg	ip-hah-fehn-er YOOL-yuhs-eh(kh)t-ehr-behrk	Franconia, Ger.	Table wine	White	Dry	***	F, P, & LM
Irish whiskey		Ireland	Spirit	Brown	Dry, rich	* or ***	C, H, AD, & S

Name	Phonetic Spelling	Source	Type	Color	Taste	Serv.Temp.	Serve With
Ischia	EESK-yah	Campania, It.	Table wine	White	Dry	***	F, P, & LM
Italian vermouth		Italy	Aromatized wine	Red	Bittersweet	***	C & BD
Jamaican rum	jah-MAY-kuh	Jamaica, W.I.	Spirit	Dark brown	Med. sweet	***	C, H, Pun, & S
Johannisberger Erntebringer	yoh-hahn-is-behrk-ehr EHRN-teh-bring-ehr	Rheingau, Ger.	Table wine	White	Med. dry	***	F, P, & LM
Johannisberg Riesling	yoh-hahn-is-behrk REES-ling	California	Table wine	White	Med. dry	***	F, P, & LM
Juliénas	yoo-lee-eh-nahs	Beaujolais, Fr.	Table wine	Red	Dry	*	All foods
Kadmon	KAHD-mahn	Israel	Dessert wine	Amber	Sweet	*	AD
Kahlúa	kah-LOO-ah	Mexico	Liqueur	Brown	Sweet, coffee	*	AD
Kalebag	kab-LAY-bah	Turkey	Table wine	Red	Dry	*	Ch, G, & RM
Kéknyelü	KAYK-nee-el-yoo	Hungary	Table wine	White	Dry	***	F, P, & LM
Kirsch	keersh	Various	Cherry brandy	White	Dry, cherry	***	AD
Kirschwasser	KEERSH-vah-sehr	Various	Cherry brandy	White	Dry, cherry	***	AD
Klosterneuburger	klos-tir-NOY-boorg-ehr	Austria	Table wine	White	Dry	***	F, P, & LM

Name	Phonetic Spelling	Source	Type	Color	Taste	Serv.Temp.	Serve With
Knipperlé	k nip-ehr-lay	Alsace, Fr.	Table wine	White	Dry	***	All foods
Kokineli	koh-kee-NAY-lee	Cyprus	Table wine	Red	Dry, non-resinated	*	Ch, G, & RM
Kokineli	koh-kee-NAY-lee	Greece	Table wine	Red	Dry, resinated	**	F, P, & LM
Kremser	KREHM-zer	Austria	Table wine	White	Dry	***	F, P, & LM
Kröver Nacktarsch	kroy-vehr-NAHK-tarsh	Moselle, Ger.	Table wine	White	Med. dry	***	F, P, & LM
Kummel	KUHM-mel	Various	Liqueur	White	Sweet, caraway	*	AD
Lacryma Christi	lah-creem-ah KREES-tee	Campania, It.	Table wine	White	Med. dry	***	All foods
Lambrusco	lahm-BROOS-coh	Emilia, It.	Sparkling wine	Red	Med. sweet	***	All foods
Latricières-Chambertin (GC)	lah-tree-syehr-shah(m)-behr-ta(n)	Côte de Nuits, Fr.	Table wine	Red	Dry	*	Ch, G, & RM
Leányka Edes	LAY-ahn-kyah a-dehsh	Hungary	Table wine	White	Med. sweet	***	F, P, & LM
Leányka Szaras	LAY-ahn-kyah ZHAH-rahzh	Hungary	Table wine	White	Dry	***	F, P, & LM
Liebfraumilch	LEEB-frow-mil(kh)	Rhine, Ger.	Table wine	White	Med. dry	***	F, P, & LM

Name	Phonetic Spelling	Source	Type	Color	Taste	Serv.Temp.	Serve With
Lillet	lee-lay	France	Aperitif	White	Bitter	***	BD
Lugana	loo-GAHN-ah	Veneto, It.	Table wine	White	Dry	***	F, P, & LM
Mâcon	mah-coh(n)	Burgundy, Fr.	Table wine	White	Dry	***	F, P, & LM
Madeira	mah-DEHR-ah	Madeira	Fortified wine	Dark brown	Dry or sweet	*	Hosp
Málaga	MAH-lah-gah	Málaga, Sp.	Fortified wine	Dark brown	Sweet	*	Hosp
Malmsey	MALM-zee	Madeira	Fortified wine	Dark brown	Sweet	*	Hosp
Malvasia	mahl-vay-see ah	Sicily, It.	Fortified wine	Gold	Sweet	*	Hosp
Manzanilla	mahnt-sah-NEE-yah	Sanlúcar, Sp.	Sherry	Straw	Dry	**	Hosp
Maraschino	mah-rahs-KEE-no	Various	Liqueur	White	Sweet, cherry	*	AD
Marsala	mabr-SAH-lah	Sicily, It.	Dessert wine	Brown	Sweet	*	Hosp
Mastikha	MAHS-tee-kah	Greece	Liqueur	Cloudy white	Sweet	***	BD & H
Mavrodaphne	mahv-roh-DAHF-nee	Greece	Dessert wine	Red	Sweet	*	AD
Maximim Grünhauser Herrenberg	mahx-ee-meen GRUHN-hoyz-ehr HEHR-ehn-behrk	Moselle, Ger.	Table wine	White	Med. dry	***	F, P, & LM
May wine		Germany & U.S.	Table wine	White	Med. sweet	***	All foods
Mazis-Chambertin (GC)	mah-zee-shah(m)-behr-ta(n)	Côte de Nuits, Fr.	Table wine	Red	Dry	*	Ch, G, & RM

Name	Phonetic Spelling	Source	Type	Color	Taste	Serv.Temp.	Serve With
Médoc	may-dohk	Médoc, Fr.	Table wine	Red	Dry	*	Ch, G, & RM
Mercurey	mehr-kyu-ray	Chalonnais, Fr.	Table wine	Red	Dry	*	Ch, G, & RM
Merlot	mehr-LOH	Various	Table wine	Red	Dry	*	Ch, P, LM, & RM
Meursault	muhr-soh	Côte de Beaune, Fr.	Table wine	White	Dry	***	F, P, & LM
Meursault-Charmes (PC)	mohr-soh-shahrm	Côte de Beaune, Fr.	Table wine	White	Dry	***	F, P, & LM
Meursault-Genevrières (PC)	mohr-soh-zhah(n)-eh-vryehr	Côte de Beaune, Fr.	Table wine	White	Dry	***	F, P, & LM
Meursault-Perrières (PC)	muhr-soh-pehr-yehr	Côte de Beaune, Fr.	Table wine	White	Dry	***	F, P, & LM
Mirabelle	mee-rah-bel	Alsace, Fr.	Plum brandy	White	Dry, plum	***	AD
Montilla	mohn-TEE-yah	Cordoba, Sp.	Aperitif wine	Straw	Dry	***	Hosp & BD
Montrachet, Le (GC)	luh moh(n)-rah-shay	Côte de Beaune, Fr.	Table wine	White	Dry	***	F, P, & LM
Moore's Diamond		New York State	Table wine	White	Dry	***	F, P, & LM
Moscatel de Setúbal	mohs-kah-tel duh seh-TOO-bahl	Portugal	Fortified wine	Gold	Sweet	***	AD
Moscatel de Sitges	mohs-kahtel duh SEET-yes	Catalonia, Sp.	Fortified wine	Gold	Sweet	*	Hosp

Name	Phonetic Spelling	Source	Type	Color	Taste	Serv.Temp.	Serve With
Moscato di Salento	mohs-KAH-toh dee sah-LEN-toh	Apulia, It.	Fortified wine	Gold	Sweet	*	Hosp
Moscato Fior d'Arancio	mohs-KAH-toh fyor dah-RAHN-choh	Sicily, It.	Fortified wine	Gold	Sweet	*	Hosp
Moselblümchen	MOH-zel-bloom-shehn	Moselle, Ger.	Table wine	White	Med. dry	***	F, P, & LM
Moulin-à-Vent	moo-la(n)-ah-vah(n)	Beaujolais, Fr.	Table wine	Red	Dry	*	Ch, G, & RM
Muscadet	moo-skah-day	Loire, Fr.	Table wine	White	Dry	***	F, P, & LM
Muscatel	mus-kah-tel	California	Fortified wine	Gold	Sweet	*	AD
Musigny, Les (GC)	lay moo-see-nyee	Côte de Nuits, Fr.	Table wine	Red	Dry	*	Ch, G, & RM
Muskotaly	MOOSH-koh-tah-lee	Hungary	Table wine	White	Dry	***	F, P, & LM
Nackenheimer Rothenberg	nok-en-hie-mehr ROTH-ehn-behrk	Rheinhessen, Ger.	Table wine	White	Med. dry	***	F, P, & LM
Nebbiolo	nehb-yoh-loh	Piedmont, It.	Table wine	Red	Dry	*	Ch, G, & RM
Neuchâtel	nah-shah-tel	Switzerland	Table wine	White	Dry	***	F, P, & LM
Niersteiner Auflangen	neer-shtine-ehr OWF-lahngen	Rheinhessen, Ger.	Table wine	White	Med. dry	***	F, P, & LM
Niersteiner Heiligenbaum	neer-shtine-ehr HIE-lee-gen-bowm	Rheinhessen, Ger.	Table wine	White	Med. dry	***	F, P, & LM

Name	Phonetic Spelling	Source	Type	Color	Taste	Serv.Temp.	Serve With
Niersteiner Hipping	neer-shtine-ehr HIP-ing	Rheinhessen, Ger.	Table wine	White	Med. dry	***	F, P, & LM
Niersteiner Oelberg	neer-shtine-ehr OHL-behrk	Rheinhessen, Ger.	Table wine	White	Med. dry	***	F, P, & LM
Niersteiner Rehbach	neer-shtine-ehr RAY-bahkh	Rheinhessen, Ger.	Table wine	White	Med. dry	***	F, P, & LM
Nuits-Saint-Georges	nwee-sa(n)-zhorzh	Côte de Nuits, Fr.	Table wine	Red	Dry	*	Ch, G, & RM
Nussberger	NOOS-behrk-ehr	Austria	Table wine	White	Dry	***	F, P, & LM
Oeil de Perdrix	Oy duh pehr-dree	Burgundy, Fr., Switzerland, & U.S.	Sparkling or still wine	Pale pink	Med. dry	***	All foods
Oloroso	oh-loh-ROH-soh	Jerez, Sp.	Sherry	Gold	Sweet	*	Hosp
Opol	Oh-POHL	Yugoslavia	Table wine	Light red	Dry	***	All Foods
Oppenheimer Daubhaus	ah-pen-hie-mehr DOWB-howss	Rheinhessen, Ger.	Table wine	White	Med. dry	***	F, P, & LM
Oppenheimer Herrenberg	ah-pen-hie-mehr HEHR-en-behrk	Rheinhessen, Ger.	Table wine	White	Med. dry	***	F, P, & LM
Oppenheimer Kreuz	ah-pen-hie-mehr KROYTS	Rheinhessen, Ger.	Table wine	White	Med. dry	***	F, P, & LM

Name	Phonetic Spelling	Source	Type	Color	Taste	Serv.Temp.	Serve With
Oppenheimer Sackträger	ah-pen-hie-mehr ZAHK-tray-gehr	Rheinhessen, Ger.	Table wine	White	Med. dry	*	F, P, & LM
Orgeat	or-zhah	France	Syrup	Gray	Sweet, almond	***	C & Pun
Orvieto (abboccato)	orv-YEHT-oh (ah-boe-KAHT-oh)	Umbria, It.	Table wine	White	Dry (or semisweet)	***	F, P, & LM
Othello	oh-THEL-loh	Cyprus	Table wine	Red	Dry	*	Ch, G, & RM
Ouzo	OO-zoh	Greece	Liqueur	Cloudy white	Sweet, licorice	*	H & C
Partom	PAR-tohm	Israel	Dessert wine	Red	Sweet	*	Desserts, AD
Passito	pahs-EET-oh	Italy	Fortified wine	Amber	Sweet	**	Fr, AD
Pastis de Marseilles	pahs-tees duh mahr-say	Marseilles, Fr.	Liqueur	Cloudy white	Sweet, licorice	***	H & BD
Pavillon Blanc du Château Margaux	pah-vee-yoh(n) blah(n) doo shah-toh mahr-goh	Médoc, Fr.	Table wine	White	Dry	***	F, P, & LM
Peach liqueur		Various	Liqueur	Brown	Sweet, fruity	*	AD
Perlan	pohr-lah(n)	Switzerland	Table wine	White	Dry	***	F, P, & LM
Pernand-Vergelesses	pehr-nah(n)-vehrzh-uh-les	Côte de Beaune, Fr.	Table wine	Red	Dry	*	Ch, G, & RM

Name	Phonetic Spelling	Source	Type	Color	Taste	Serv.Temp.	Serve With
Pernod	pehr-noh	France	Liqueur	Green gold	Sweet, licorice	***	BD & H
Perry		England	Sparkling or still pear wine	Straw	Sweet	***	Desserts
Peter Heering		Denmark	Liqueur	Red	Sweet, cherry	*	AD
Petit Sirah	puh-tee sih-rah	California	Table wine	Red	Dry	*	Ch, G, & RM
Pfaffstätter	FAHF-shtay-tehr	Austria	Table wine	White	Dry	***	F, P, & LM
Picolit	PEE-coh-leet	Friuli, It.	Table wine	White	Sweet	***	Ch, Fr
Piesporter Goldtröpfchen	pees-port-ehr GOHLD-trehpf-shen	Moselle, Ger.	Table wine	White	Med. dry	***	F, P, & LM
Pineau des Charentes	pee-noh day shah-rah(n)t	Cognac, Fr.	Fortified wine	White	Sweet	***	BD
Pinot Blanc (Bianco)	pee-noh blah(n) (bee-yahn-koh)	France, Italy, California	Table wine	White	Dry	***	F, P, & LM
Pinot Grigio	pee-noh gree-zho	Italy	Table wine	White	Dry	***	F, P, & LM
Pinot Noir	pee-noh nwahr	Various	Table wine	Red	Dry	*	Ch, G, & RM
Pisco	PEES-koh	Pisco, Peru	Brandy	Gold	Dry	*	AD & Pun
Pommard	poh-mahr	Côte de Beaune, Fr.	Table wine	Red	Dry	*	Ch, G, & RM

Name	Phonetic Spelling	Source	Type	Color	Taste	Serv.Temp.	Serve With
Pommard-Clos-de-la-Commareine (PC)	poh-mahr-kloh-duh-lah-kuhm-ah-rehn	Côte de Beaune, Fr.	Table wine	Red	Dry	*	Ch, G, & RM
Pommard-Garollières (PC)	poh-mahr-gah-rohl-yehr	Côte de Beaune, Fr.	Table wine	Red	Dry	*	Cb G, & RM
Pommard-Les-Epenots (PC)	poh-mahr-layzay puh-noh	Côte de Beaune, Fr.	Table wine	Red	Dry	*	Ch, G, & RM
Pommard-Platière (PC)	poh-mahr-plaht-yehr	Côte de Beaune, Fr.	Table wine	Red	Dry	*	Ch, G, & RM
Pommard-Rugiens (PC)	poh-mahr-roo-zhyens	Côte de Beaune, Fr.	Table wine	Red	Dry	*	Ch, G, & RM
Port		U.S.	Fortified wine	Red	Sweet	*	Hosp
Porter		England & Ireland	Malt beverage	Dark brown	Bitter	**	Hosp
Porto		Portugal	Fortified wine	Red	Sweet	*	Hosp
Pouilly-Fuissé	pwee-yee-fwee-say	Mâconnais, Fr.	Table wine	White	Dry	***	F, P, & LM
Pouilly-Fumé	pwee-yee-foo-may	Loire, Fr.	Table wine	White	Med. sweet	***	F, P, & LM
Pousse-Café	poos-kah-fay	France	Liqueur	Various	Sweet	*	AD
Prunelle	proo-nel	France	Liqueur	Brown	Sweet, plum	*	AD
Puerto Rican rum		Puerto Rico	Spirit	White	Dry	***	C, H, Pun, & S

Name	Phonetic Spelling	Source	Type	Color	Taste	Serv.Temp.	Serve With
Puligny-Montrachet	poo-lee-nyee-moh(n)-rah-shay	Côte de Beaune, Fr.	Table wine	White	Dry	***	F, P, & LM
Quetsch	kwehtch	Alsace, Fr.	Plum brandy	White	Dry	***	AD
Quinquina	ka(n)-ka(n)-nah	France	Aperitif	Red or white	Bittersweet	***	BD
Raki	RAHK-ee	Turkey	Liqueur	White	Sweet, licorice	***	AD
Randersackerer Teufelskeller	rahn-dehr-zahk-ehr-ehr TOY-fels-kel-ehr	Franconia, Ger.	Table wine	White	Dry	***	F, P, & LM
Rauenthaler Baiken	row-en-tahl-ehr BY-ken	Rheingau, Ger.	Table wine	White	Med. dry	***	F, P, & LM
Rauenthaler Gehrn	row-en-tah-lehr GAYRN	Rheingau, Ger.	Table wine	White	Med. dry	***	F, P, & LM
Rauenthaler Langenstück	row-entahl-ehr LAHNG-en-shtak	Rheingau, Ger.	Table wine	White	Med. dry	*	F, P, & RM
Rauenthaler Wülfen	rowen-tahl-ehr VIL-fen	Rheingau, Ger.	Table wine	White	Med. dry	***	F, P, & LM
Recioto	reh-chee-OH-toh	Veneto, It.	Table wine	Red	Sweet	**	All foods
Retsina	reht-SEE-nah	Greece	Table wine	White	Dry, resinated	***	All foods
Rhodity	roh-DEE-tis	Greece	Table wine	White red	Dry	***	All foods

Name	Phonetic Spelling	Source	Type	Color	Taste	Serv.Temp.	Serve With
Ricard	ree-kahr	France	Liqueur	Brown	Semisweet	***	BD
Richebourg, Le (GC)	luh reesh-boor	Côte de Nuits, Fr.	Table wine	Red	Dry	*	Ch, G, & RM
Riesling	REES-ling	Various	Table wine	White	Dry or sweet	***	Varies with sweetness
Rioja	ree-OH-hah	Spain	Table wine	Red or white	Dry	* or ***	Varies with color
Rizning Szemelt	REEZ ling tseh-mehlt	Hungary	Table wine	White	Dry	***	F, P, & LM
Romanée, La (GC)	lah roh-mah-nay	Côte de Nuits, Fr.	Table wine	Red	Dry	*	Ch, G, & RM
Romanée-Conti (GC)	roh-mah-nay-kah(n)-tee	Côte de Nuits, Fr.	Table wine	Red	Dry	*	Ch, G, & RM
Romanée-Saint-Vivant (GC)	roh-mah-nay-sa(n)-vee-vain(n)	Côte de Nuits, Fr.	Table wine	Red	Dry	*	Ch, G, & RM
Rubesco	roo-BEHS-coh	Umbria, It.	Table wine	Red	Dry	*	Ch, G, & RM
Ruby Porto		Portugal	Fortified wine	Red	Sweet	*	Hosp
Ruchottes-Chambertin (GC)	roo-shot-shah(m)-behr-ta(n)	Côte de Nuits, Fr.	Table wine	Red	Dry	*	Ch, G, & RM
Rüdesheimer Berg Rottland	roo-des-hie-mehr behrk ROHT-lahnt	Rheingau, Ger.	Table wine	White	Med. dry	***	F, P, & LM

Name	Phonetic Spelling	Source	Type	Color	Taste	Serv.Temp.	Serve With
Rüdesheimer Berg Schlossberg	roo-des-hie-mehr behrk SHLAWS-behrk	Rheingau, Ger.	Table wine	White	Med. dry	***	F, P, & LM
Rüdesheimer Klosterberg	roo-des-hie-mehr KLOHS-tehr-behrk	Rheingau, Ger.	Table wine	White	Med. dry	***	F, P, & LM
Rum		Various	Spirit	Various	Slightly sweet	***	C, H, Pun, & S
Ruppertsberger Hoheburg	roo-pehrts-behrk-ehr HOH-heh-boorg	Rheinpfalz, Ger.	Table wine	White	Med. dry	***	F, P, & LM
Ruppertsberger Nussbien	roo-pehrts-behrk-ehr NOOS-been	Rheinpfalz, Ger.	Table wine	White	Med. dry	***	F, P, & LM
Saint-Amour	sa(n)-tah-moor	Beaujolais, Fr.	Table wine	Red	Dry	*	Ch, G, & RM
Saint-Emilion	sa(n)-tay-meel-yohn	Saint Émilion, Fr.	Table wine	Red	Dry	*	Ch, G, & RM
Saint-Estèphe	sa(n)-tehs-tef	Médoc, Fr.	Table wine	Red	Dry	*	Ch, G, & RM
Saint-Julien	sa(n)-zhul-yen	Médoc, Fr.	Table wine	Red	Dry	*	Ch, G, & RM
Saint-Raphaël	sa(n)-rah-fah-el	France	Aperitif	Red	Bitter	***	BD
Saké	SAH-kee	Japan	Rice beer	White	Dry	100°F	All foods
Sancerre	sa(n)-sehr	Loire, Fr.	Table wine	White	Dry	***	F, P, & LM
Santenay	sa(n)-teh-nay	Côte de Beaune, Fr.	Table wine	Red	Dry	*	Ch, G, & RM

Name	Phonetic Spelling	Source	Type	Color	Taste	Serv.Temp.	Serve With
Sassella	sah-SAY-lah	Lombardy, It.	Table wine	Red	Dry	*	Ch, G, & RM
Saumur	soh-moor	Anjou, Fr.	Still or sparkling wine	White	Med. sweet	***	F, P, & LM
Sauterne	soh-tehrn	U.S.	Table wine	White	Dry	***	All foods
Sauternes	soh-tehrn	Sauternes, Fr.	Table wine	White	Sweet	***	Desserts
Sauvignon Blanc	soh-vee-nyoh(n) blah(n)	California & France	Table wine	White	Dry or sweet	***	F, P, & LM
Scharzhofberg	shartz-huf-behrg	Moselle, Ger.	Table wine	White	Med. dry	***	F, P, Hosp
Schaumwein	SHOHM-vine	Germany	Sparkling wine	White	Dry or sweet	***	All foods
Scheidam (gin)	SKEE-dahm	Holland	Spirit	White	Dry	***	S & H
Schloss-Böckelheimer-Mühlberg	shlawss-BUHK-el-hie mehr-mewl-behrk	Nahe, Ger.	Table wine	White	Dry	***	F, P, & LM
Schloss Johannisberg	shlawss yoh-hahn-is-behrk	Rheingau, Ger.	Table wine	White	Med. dry	***	F, P, & LM
Schloss Vollrads	schlawss FAWL-rahds	Rheingau, Ger.	Table wine	White	Med. dry	***	F, P, & LM
Scotch whisky		Scotland	Spirit	Brown	Dry, smoky	* or ***	C, H, & S
Scuppernong		Southeastern U.S.	Table wine	White	Sweet	***	All foods

Name	Phonetic Spelling	Source	Type	Color	Taste	Serv.Temp.	Serve With
Sekt	sehkt	Germany	Sparkling wine	White	Dry or sweet	***	All foods
Sémillon	seh-mee-yoh(n)	California	Table wine	White	Dry or sweet	***	All foods
Sercial	SIR-shahl	Madeira	Fortified wine	Gold	Med. dry	**	Hosp
Sherry		Jerez, Sp., & various	Fortified wine	Amber	Dry to sweet	* or **	Hosp
Sidra	SEE-drah	Northern Spain	Sparkling cider	Gold	Sweet, apple	***	Hosp
Slivovitz	SHLIV-oh-wits	Various	Plum brandy	Brown	Dry, plum	*	AD
Sloe gin		England & U.S.	Liqueur	Red	Sweet, astringent	* or ***	AD & C
Sonve	suah-veh	Veneto, It.	Table wine	White	Dry	***	F, P, & LM
Somlói Furmint	SHOHM-loy ye foor-mint	Somlósi, Hungary	Table wine	White	Dry	***	F, P, & LM
Spanish brandy		Spain	Brandy	Brown	Med. dry	*	AD
Spanna	SPAHN-neh	Piedmont, It.	Table wine	Red	Dry	*	Ch, G, & RM
Sparkling Burgundy		Burgundy, Fr., & U.S.	Sparkling wine	Red or white	Med. sweet	***	All foods
Steinberger	SHTINE-behrk-ehr	Rheingau, Ger.	Table wine	White	Med. dry	***	F, P, & LM
Stout		England & Ireland	Malt beverage	Dark brown	Bitter	**	Hosp

Name	Phonetic Spelling	Source	Type	Color	Taste	Serv.Temp.	Serve With
Strega	STRAY-gab	Benevento, It.	Liqueur	Gold	Sweet	*	AD
Suze	sooz	France	Aperitif	Brown	Bittersweet	***	BD
Swedish Punsch		Sweden	Liqueur	Yellow	Sweet, rummy	***	AD
Sylvaner (Silvaner)	zil-vah-nehr	Alsace, Fr., & Germany	Table wine	White	Med. dry	***	All foods
Szilvanyi Zold	ZIL-vahn-yuh zuhld	Hungary	Table wine	White	Med. sweet	***	F, P, & LM
Tâche, La (GC)	lah tahsh	Côte de Nuits, Fr.	Table wine	Red	Dry	*	Ch, G, & RM
Taurasi	touw-RAH-zi	Campania, It.	Table wine	Red	Dry	*	Ch, G, & RM
Tavel	tah-vel	Rhône, Fr.	Table wine	Pink	Dry	***	All foods
Tawny Porto		Portugal	Fortified wine	Red	Sweet	*	Hosp
Tequila	teh-KEE-lah	Jalisco, Mex.	Spirit	White	Dry	*	C & S
Tia Maria	tee-ah mah-REE-ah	Jamaica	Liqueur	Brown	Sweet, coffee	*	AD
Tignanello	tee-nyan-EHL-oh	Tuscany, It.	Table wine	Red	Dry	*	Ch, G, & RM
Tocai	tohk-ahye	Friuli, It.	Table wine	White	Dry	***	F, P, & LM
Tokaji Aszú	TOHK-ah ye ah-zoo	Hungary	Dessert wine	Amber	Sweet	**	Hosp & AD

Name	Phonetic Spelling	Source	Type	Color	Taste	Serv.Temp.	Serve With
Tokaji Szamorodni	TOHK-ah ye SAH-mah-rohd-nee	Hungary	Dessert wine	White	Med. dry	***	Hosp
Trakya	TRAHK-yah	Turkey	Table wine	White	Dry	***	F, P, & LM
Triple Sec		Various	Liqueur	White	Sweet, orange	*	AD
Trittenheimer Altärchen	trit-en-hie-mehr AHLT-ehr-shen	Moselle, Ger.	Table wine	White	Med. dry	***	F, P, & LM
Trittenheimer Apotheke	trit-en-hie-mehr ah-poh-TAY-kuh	Moselle, Ger.	Table wine	White	Med. dry	***	F, P, & LM
Tsingtao	TSEENG-tow	China	Malt beverage	Amber	Dry	***	Hosp.
Ürziger Würzgarten	oor-tsee-gehr VURTZ-gahr-ten	Moselle, Ger.	Table wine	White	Med. dry	***	F, P, & LM
Valdepeñas	vahl-day-PAYN-yahs	La Mancha, Sp.	Table wine	Red	Dry	*	Ch, G, & RM
Valgella	vahl-ZHEHL-eh	Lombardy, It.	Table wine	Red	Dry	*	Ch, G, & RM
Valpolicella	vahl-poh-lee-CHAY-lah	Veneto, It.	Table wine	Red	Dry	*	Ch, G, & RM
Valtellina	vahl-tel-LEE-nah	Lombardy, It.	Table wine	Red	Dry	*	Ch, G, & RM
Van Der Hum	VAN der huhm	South Africa	Liqueur	Gold	Sweet	*	AD
Verdelho	vehr-DEL-yo	Madeira	Fortified wine	White	Sweet	*	AD & Hosp

Name	Phonetic Spelling	Source	Type	Color	Taste	Serv.Temp.	Serve With
Verdicchio	vehr-DEEK-yoh	Marches, It.	Table wine	White	Dry	***	Shellfish
Vernaccia	vehr-NAH-chah	Italy	Table wine	White	Dry	*	F & LM
Villányi-Pècs	VIL-ahn-yee-pehch	Hungary	Table wine	Red	Dry	*	G & RM
Vinho Verde	VEE-nyoh vehr-deh	Portugal	Table wine	Red or white	Dry	* or ***	Varies with color
Vin (Vino) Santo	veen (VEE-noh) SAHN-toh	Italy	Table wine	White	Sweet	***	All foods
Vino Nobile di Montepulciano	vee-noh NOH-beel-eh dee mohn-teh-pohl-chi-AHN-oh	Tuscany, It.	Table wine	Red	Dry	*	Ch, G, & RM
Vodka	VAHD-kah	Various	Spirit	White	Dry	***	C, H, & S
Volnay	vuhl-nay	Côte de Beaune, Fr.	Table wine	Red	Dry	*	Ch, G, & RM
Vöslau	FOYS-low	Austria	Table wine	Red	Dry	*	Ch, G, & RM
Vosne-Romanée	vohn-roh-mah-nay	Côte de Nuits, Fr.	Table wine	Red	Dry	*	Ch, G, & RM
Vouvray	voovreh	Loire, Fr.	Table wine	White	Med. sweet or sweet	***	Fr
Wachenheimer Schlossberg	vah(kh)-en-hie-mehr shlawss-behrk	Rheinpfalz, Ger.	Table wine	White	Med. dry	***	F, P, & LM
Wehlener Sonnenuhr	VAY-len-ehr ZAWN-en-oor	Moselle, Ger.	Table wine	White	Med. dry	***	F, P, & LM

Name	Phonetic Spelling	Source	Type	Color	Taste	Serv.Temp.	Serve With
Whisky	WISS-kee	Various	Spirit	Brown	Dry, rich	* or ***	C, H, Pun, & S
White Porto		Portugal	Aperitif	Gold	Sweet	*	Hosp & BD
Wiltinger Schlangengraben	vilt-ing-ehr SHLAHNG-en-grah-ben	Moselle, Ger.	Table wine	White	Med. dry	***	F, P, & LM
Wisniowka	vish-nyoof-kah	Poland	Liqueur	Red	Sweet, cherry	**	AD
Würzburger Stein	vortz-behrk-ehr SHTINE	Franconia, Ger.	Table wine	White	Dry	***	F, P, & LM
Zeller Schwarze Katz	tsel-ehr SHVAHRT-seh kahts	Moselle, Ger.	Table wine	White	Med. dry	***	F, P, & LM
Zeltinger Himmelreich	tsel-ting-ehr HIM-mel-rie(kh)	Moselle, Ger.	Table wine	White	Med. dry	***	F, P, & LM
Zeltinger Schlossberg	tselt-ing-ehr SHLAWSS-behrk	Moselle, Ger.	Table wine	White	Med. dry	***	F, P, & LM
Zeltinger Sonnenuhr	tselt-ing-ehr ZAWN-en-oor	Moselle, Ger.	Table wine	White	Med. dry	***	F, P, & LM
Zinfandel	TZIN-fan-del	California	Table wine	Red	Dry	*	Ch, G, & RM
Zubrowka	zoo-BROHV-kah	Russia & Poland	Flavored spirit	Straw	Dry	***	C, H, & S

APPENDIX B

Vintage Information—France, Italy, Germany, Portugal, and The United States

Every vintage chart is a compilation of many opinions that tends to even out the extremes. There are often exceptional bottles in average years and average bottles in excellent years. The vintage chart must always be considered the indicator of the general quality.

Number ratings:

1 to 10 relate to potential quality when fully mature. A mature wine of modest rating should be preferred to an immature wine whatever its potential quality (10 is finest grade).

Letter code for red Bordeaux and Burgundy:

A = Not at present ready for drinking
B = Can be drunk now but development still to come
C = Fully ready for drinking
D = Approach with caution; could be good, but could be past best

Many of this chart's ratings were collected by the late Gordon Bass.

French and German Vintage Chart

	'59	'60	'61	'62	'63	'64	'65	'66	'67	'68	'69	'70	'71	'72	'73	'74	'75	'76	'77	'78	'79	'80	'81	'82
Red Bordeaux	9C	6D	10C	8C	2D	8C	X	9B	7C	X	6C	9B	8B	5B	6B	6A	10A	8A	5B	8A	8A	8A	8A	10A
Dry White Bordeaux	X	X	X	X	X	9	X	8	X	X	5	9	9	7	7	7	8	7	7	9	8	8	8	9
Sweet White Bordeaux	9D	X	10D	9D	X	X	X	7C	9C	X	7C	9C	9C	6C	6D	6C	9B	7B	7B	6B	8A	8A	9A	8A
Red Côte d'Or Burgundy	9D	X	10C	8C	X	9C	X	8C	6D	X	9B	8C	10B	8C	7C	7C	5C	10B	7B	9B	7B	7A	7A	9A
Red Beaujolais Burgundy	X	X	X	X	X	X	X	X	X	X	X	8D	9D	7C	7C	6C	5B	10B	X	X	9D	6D	8C	8B
White Burgundy	X	X	X	X	X	X	X	9D	7D	X	9D	8D	9C	7D	7D	7D	8C	8C	6C	9B	9B	7B	9B	9A
Loire	X	X	X	X	X	X	X	X	X	X	X	X	X	X	X	X	X	X	4D	9C	8C	7B	8B	8A
Red Rhône	8D	10D	9C	8D	X	8D	X	9C	9C	X	9C	10C	8C	8C	7C	7C	7C	9B	6B	10A	8A	8A	8A	9A
Rhine	X	X	X	X	X	X	X	X	X	X	9D	8D	10C	6D	7D	6D	9C	10C	6D	6D	7B	5D	7C	8A
Mosel-Saar-Ruwer	X	X	X	X	X	X	X	X	X	X	8D	8D	10C	6D	7D	6D	9C	10C	6D	6D	7C	5D	7C	8A

Notes on Red Bordeau Vintages

1945 Very small yield, but quality superb. Excellent to drink now, but will continue to develop.

1946 Generally very light wines.

1947 A great vintage. Big, fine wines that are long lived. Some are starting to decline.

1948 A good vintage that was overshadowed by those of '47 and '49.

1949 An important vintage although the quantity was somewhat below average. Very fine wines.

1950 Abundant vintage. Quality good. Now old.

1951 Small yield, but wines were better than average. Now old.

1952 Wines somewhat hard and slow in developing, long lived. In general a great year.

1953 Big vintage produced under optimum conditions. Wines much softer and earlier developing than the '52s. They are still excellent.

1954 Small crop. Some useful wines but on the whole thin and short lived.

1955 Smaller vintage than '54, but the wines have body. Many good wines and some great wines were produced.

1956 A very small vintage because of severe frosts. Very light, thin wines.

1957 Quantity small. Quality fairly good. Quite hard wines that are now starting to soften.

1958 Quantity small. Light, pleasant, drinkable wines. Now old.

1959 Good harvest. Quality excellent. On the whole big, balanced wines that have developed quickly and are now fully mature.

1960 Better than average quantity. Wines somewhat light and not long lived.

1961 Very small vintage because of rains at time of

flowering. Excellent quality. Wines show concentration and are well balanced. These will be very long lived.

1962 Better than average quantity. Well-made wines, pleasant, soft. At their peak now.

1963 Quality generally poor. A few pleasant light wines were produced.

1964 Rains at harvest time produced wines of variable quality. In Saint-Émilion and Pomerol and in the parts of the Médoc that harvested early some very good wines were made.

1965 A rainy summer produced thin wines.

1966 An excellent year. Big, full-bodied, well-balanced wines. Will be long lived.

1967 A larger harvest than in '66. The wines are lighter than those of '66, maturing earlier, but have charm and elegance.

1968 Generally a very poor year.

1969 Light wines that are generally pleasant.

1970 Very good quantity. Quality excellent. Big wines with character. Will be long lived.

1971 Quantity small but quality excellent. Big, concentrated wines, in many cases comparable to '70s.

1972 Light wines. Many lack fruit and charm. Some pleasant wines. Not long lived.

1973 Very abundant quantity. Variable quality. Some good light wines but will not be long lived.

1974 Good quantity. Quality average. Sound wines that will mature quickly.

1975 Small quantity, less than half that of '74. Quality is excellent. Wines have high alcohol and tannin and should be long lived.

1976 Large quantity. Wines are rich and dark with a great deal of fruit. Lack tannin and consequently may mature early.

1977 Small crop. Quality less than average. Wines

predominantly Cabernet Sauvignon were more successful.

1978 Average crop. Variable vintage with lesser wines disappointing. Wines harvested later were more successful.

1979 Enormous quantity. Early maturation. Quality has some elegance—typically claret.

1980 Less than average quantity. Quality affected by bad weather. Some rot, little fruit, Merlot suffered the most.

1981 Small crop. Better than average quality. Wines are soft and have good color and body.

1982 Very large harvest. Quality good to excellent.

Notes on White Bordeau Vintages

1959 Sauternes excellent—sweet, rich, and luscious. Dry wines were very good.

1960 Dry wines were very good. Sweet wines poor.

1961 Some excellent sweet wines produced. These should be long lived. Dry whites were very good to excellent. High in alcohol.

1962 Very good for sweet wines, many excellent. Good to very good for dry wines, which are now too old.

1963 Fair for dry wines, poor for sweet.

1954 Some good dry wines were produced. Very poor sweet wines.

1965 Very poor year for Sauternes. Dry wines were fair to good.

1966 Some very good sweet wines were produced. The dry wines were good to very good.

1967 Very good Sauternes—sweet, rich, and luscious.

Some very good dry wines were produced.

1968 Generally poor year for sweet and dry wines.

1969 Good dry wines. Sweet wines are variable, but generally good.

1970 An excellent year. Sauternes are rich and elegant, will live long. Graves are well balanced and elegant.

1971 Excellent vintage for Sauternes—elegant, outstanding, long-lived wines. Dry wines also excellent—good depth and character.

1972 Quality is variable. Dry wines generally better than the sweet.

1973 Very large quantity. Dry wines better than the sweet.

1974 Abundant quantity. Quality only fair.

1975 Excellent, luscious sweet wines. Dry wines also excellent and high in alcohol.

1976 September rain washed away the noble rot, and few

quality sweet wines were produced. Some good dry wines, high in acidity, were made from grapes harvested before the rain.

1977 Dry wines better than average. Tiny yield of sweet wines of fair quality.

1978 Very dry year produced less than average yield and quality of sweet wines. Dry whites were very good.

1979 Dry wines were abundant and fruity. Sweet wines were good and in some cases excellent.

1980 Dry wines of good quality but quantity very small. Sweet wines were very fine.

1981 Both dry and sweet wines in short supply. Good noble rot produced great concentration in the sweet wines. Dry wine delicate in style.

1982 Abundant harvest for both whites. Dry whites exemplary. Sweet wines very promising.

Notes on Red and White Burgundy Vintages

1945 Small quantity. A great year. Slow maturing.

1946 Quick-maturing wines.

1947 Wines made with sufficient care were of excellent quality.

1948 A very good vintage.

1949 Excellent vintage.

1950 Above average quantity. Light red wines. White wines good.

1951 Poor quality.

1952 Good, sturdy wines of fine color and bouquet.

1953 Very fine, balanced wines of finesse, body, and flavor.

1954 Very large quantity. Quality variable. Some good wines produced.

1955 Good, well-rounded wines.

1956 Very poor quality. Light wines.

1957 Fair quantity. Good wines of fine color and good body.

1958 Reds fair—some wines have good, fruity flavor. Whites were good.

1959 A great vintage in all respects. One of the best of the century. White wines tend to be overrich.

1960 Fair.

1961 Excellent quality for both red and white wines. Grand Cru reds still excellent for present consumption.

1962 Quality almost up to '61 wines.

1963 Large quantity. Quality variable.

1964 Large quantity. Well-made wines. Early maturing.

1965 Poor quality.

1966 Abundant quantity. Quality was good. Big, full wines. Some fast-maturing wines produced; others will live a long time.

1967 Generally light and fast-maturing wines.

1968 Generally light wines. Whites better than reds.

1969 Low quantity. A great year. Deeply colored, big, full wines. Reds matured faster than expected.

1970 Good quantity. Good quality. Fast-maturing wines.

1971 Small quantity. Full-bodied, concentrated wines. Good color, long lived. Perhaps comparable to the '69s.

1972 Good quantity. Wines somewhat hard, but generally good quality. Will be long lived.

1973 Very large quantity. Variable quality. Many light wines produced. Fast maturing.

1974 A long period of heavy rains lowered the quality.

1975 Quantity small. With good grape selection some good reds were made. Whites tend to be better than the reds, with Chablis producing excellent, full wines.

1976 Average quantity. Very hot summer required early

harvest. Red wines are dark in color, have good alcohol, and are well balanced. They have exceptional potential and should be long lived. Some whites may lack acidity but are very full and round.

1977 Average year. Spotty quality. Taste before you purchase.

1978 Bad weather led to short crop in some areas. Whites very aromatic—reds robust and round. Very good to excellent vintage.

1979 Record crop with whites showing surprisingly high quality for this size yield. Reds show good color but lack body.

1980 Adverse weather reduced crop and produced wines for early maturation. Some reds impressive, while Chablis best of the whites.

1981 White wine year. Short crop but aromatic wines.

1982 Very good weather, abundant harvest and outlook excellent for both reds and whites.

Notes on Champagne Vintages*

1961 Good quantity. Top quality, light and delicate wines.

1962 Good quantity. Excellent quality. Wines are full bodied.

1963 Not a vintage year.

1964 Good quantity. Excellent quality, very full-bodied wines.

1965 Not a vintage year.

1966 Very good quality, well-balanced wines.

1967 Good quality when grapes carefully selected by the producer. Not a vintage year.

1968 Not a vintage year.

1969 Small quantity. Good quality, full-bodied wines.

*Some houses may produce a vintage Champagne in years when the majority of houses do not. The decision is up to each producer. When vintage wines are not produced, the wines of that year are used to replenish blending stocks, so that each house may maintain its unique style and continuity.

1970 Large quantity. Good quality, light, fragrant wines.

1971 Very small quantity. Very good quality, full-bodied wines.

1972 Not a vintage year.

1973 Large quantity. Well balanced wines with good bouquet.

1974 Not a vintage year.

1975 Large quantity. Good quality, very full wines.

1976 Large quantity. Good quality, very full wines. Unusual to have two such years in a row.

1977 Small quantity. Not a vintage year.

1978 Very small crop. High acid wines.

1979 Abundant crop. Quality high.

1980 Not a vintage year. Inadequate crop from devastating weather.

1981 Not a vintage year. Poor weather led to very small yield.

1982 Large quantity. First vintage in several years.

Notes on Rhone Vintages

1945
1949
1952 All long-lived, full-bodied wines.
1955
1957

1959 Selectivity needed in choosing wines.

1960 A very good year.

1961 Good wines produced.

1962 Quantity small. Quality fair.

1963 Quantity very small. Quality poor.

1964 Quality average.

1965 One of the few regions to produce good wines during this year.

1966 An excellent year. Long-lived wines.

1967 Well-balanced, long-lived wines.

1968 Some pleasant, drinkable wines were produced.

1969 Quantity small. Variable quality. Excellent in the north, good in the south.

1970 Large quantity. Excellent quality. Long-lived wines with great potential.

1971 Small quantity. Very good quality. Full body and high alcohol. Need some time.

1972 Big, full-bodied wines. Need time to soften.

1973 Enormous quantity. Most areas suffered from over-production. Most wines pleasant and light. Some good wines produced.

1974 In general, good-quality wines.

1975 Limited quantity and variable quality in the northern Rhône. Good quantity as well as good quality in the south.

1976 Quantity good. Very good quality because of very warm growing conditions. Wines should be long lived with high alcohol and very full body.

1977 Abundant crop. Very good color but lacking fruit.

1978 Superb crop. Superb quality. Superb future.

1979 Generous crop. Wines have fine color, body but less concentration than '78.

1980 Most successful region of this year. Consistently high quality with record-breaking quantity.

1981 Shorter crop than 1980. Good quality overall.

1982 Very abundant crop. Full-bodied, high-alcohol, deeply colored wines.

NOTES ON ALSATIAN VINTAGES

1970 Very large quantity. Quality good.

1971 Excellent quality. Wines high in alcohol.

1972 Quality fair.

1873 Quantity very large. Quality good.

1974 Quality good.

1975 Quantity about average. Quality good. Well-balanced wines.

1976 Average quantity, with above average amount of Beerenauslesen produced. Excellent quality with delicate bouquet and superior elegance.

1977 Light vintage. Ordinary quality.

1978 Mixed harvest. Riesling did well. Gewurztraminer good but small crop.

1979 Fine vintage. All varieties successful.

1980 Poor weather diminished all varieties except for Sylvaner.

1981 Dry season producing all-around fine wines.

1982 Extremely large harvest. Potentially great year, repeating the success of 1981.

RED ITALIAN VINTAGE CHART

	'64	'65	'66	'67	'68	'69	'70	'71	'72	'73	'74	'75	'76	'77	'78	'79	'80	'81	'82
Aglianico del Vulture (Basilicata)							6c	6c	2e	8c	6c	8b	2d	8b	8a	6a	8c	8a	6b
Amarone (Veneto)	10c	5d	7c	8c	6c	8c	6c	6c	6b	6b	8b	7b	6a	8a	6a	8a	7a	6a	10a
Barbaresco (Piedmont)	10c	6e	2e	7d	6d	6c	8c	10b	2e	5c	9b	5b	5b	5b	10a	8a	7a	6a	10a
Barbera (Piedmont)	8d	4e	2e	6d	6d	7d	7c	8c	4e	5d	8c	5c	4b	2e	9a	7a	7b	7b	10a
Bardolino (Veneto)	8e	4e	6e	8e	7e	9e	7e	8e	5e	7e	7e	6e	8e	8e	6d	8c	7c	7c	8c
Barolo (Piedmont)	9c	8c	2e	8d	6d	7b	8b	10a	2e	5c	9a	5b	5b	5b	10a	8a	7a	6a	10a
Brunello di Montalcino (Tuscany)	10c	—	8c	8c	6c	5c	10a	7b	2c	6c	5c	10a	2c	8a	8a	8a	8a	10a	7a
Cannonau (Sardinia)	8e	2e	6d	6d	8d	4d	6d	4d	8c	6c	6c	4c	4c	8c	8c	6c	7c	8c	4c
Carema (Piedmont)							8c	8c	4d	6d	8c	6c	8c	2c	8a	8a	7a	8a	10a
Chianti (Tuscany)	6e	4e	4e	6e	7d	7d	8d	8d	4e	4e	5d	6c	2c	6b	8b	8a	8a	4c	8a
Chianti Classico Riserva (Tuscany)	8d	6d	6d	8c	8c	8c	8c	10c	4e	4d	7c	8b	4c	8b	10a	8b	8a	6b	10a

	'64	'65	'66	'67	'68	'69	'70	'71	'72	'73	'74	'75	'76	'77	'78	'79	'80	'81	'82
Ciro Rosso (Calabria)	4e	6e	—	6d	10c	2e	6d	6d	6c	8c	8b	6c	2d	8b	8b	6b	8b	8b	6b
Friuli-Venezia Giulia Varietals (I)	8e	4e	6e	6e	4e	7e	7e	8d	8d	8d	7d	6c	5c	7c	7c	8c	6c	8c	5c
Gattinara (Piedmont)	10c	6d	4e	6d	8c	8c	8c	4d	2e	4c	10a	6b	8a	4c	6b	8a	7a	6a	10a
Ghemme (Piedmont)	9c	4e	2e	6d	4c	6c	8c	8c	6c	8b	10b	6c	7b	2c	10a	8a	7a	4b	10a
Gutturnio (Emilia-Romagna)	10e	4e	6e	6d	6d	6d	8d	8d	2e	4e	6c	4c	4c	4c	6b	8a	7b	8a	8a
Montepulciano d'Abruzzo (Abruzzo)	2e	8e	6e	6e	10e	2e	4e	4e	4e	8c	8c	8c	4c	8c	6c	8c	8c	6c	5c
Nebbiolo d'Alba (Piedmont)	8e	4e	2e	8e	6e	6e	6e	10c	2e	4d	6c	4c	4c	4c	6b	4b	7a	6a	10a
Sangiovese di Romagna (Emilia-Romagna)	6e	8e	8d	8d	8d	4e	8d	8d	6e	6e	6e	8c	6c	10c	8b	8b	6c	8b	10b
Taurasi (Campania)	8e	6e	8e	8e	10c	6d	8c	8c	6c	8b	6c	8a	6b	10a	6a	8a	8a	8a	10a
Torgiano Rubesco (Umbria)	6d	6d	10c	8c	10c	8c	10c	10c	7c	8c	8b	10a	2d	8a	8a	8a	8a	8a	8a
Trentino-Alto Adige Varietals (II)	9e	2e	6e	6e	5e	10c	8e	8d	4d	5d	6d	8c	7c	6c	5c	5c	8c	6c	6c

	'64	'65	'66	'67	'68	'69	'70	'71	'72	'73	'74	'75	'76	'77	'78	'79	'80	'81	'82
Valpolicella (Veneto)	10e	4e	6e	8e	6e	8e	6e	6e	4e	7e	6e	4e	6d	8c	6c	8c	7c	6c	8c
Valtellina (Lombardy) (III)	10d	2e	4d	6d	4e	8c	7c	8c	4d	6c	4c	6c	4b	2b	8b	6a	6a	6a	10a
Vino Nobile di Montepulciano (Tuscany)	8d	2e	6d	10c	8c	7c	10c	4d	4d	8c	6c	10a	2b	8a	6a	8a	7a	8a	7a

Key to Reading Table

I. Cabernet, Merlot, Pinot Nero, and Refosco are grown in 6 D.O.C. areas: Aquileia, Collio Goriziano or Collio, Colli Orientali de Friuli, Isonzo, and Latisana.

II. Cabernet, Lagrein, Marzemino, Merlot, Pinot Nero, Schiava, and Teroldego are grown in 2 D.O.C. areas: Alto Adige and Trentino.

III. Valtellina embraces 5 sub-denominations: Inferno, Grumello, Sassella, Valgella, and Sfursat.

Number ratings:

2: Less than average vintage
4: Average vintage
6: Good vintage
8: Very good vintage
10: Exceptional vintage

Letter ratings:

a. Best with further aging
b. Can improve with further aging
c. Ready for drinking
d. Caution advised if aged further
e. Wine may be too old to drink

Notes on German Vintages

(1921 was considered one of the greatest vintages ever.)

1971 A great vintage. Edelfäule produced wines of great concentration and depth. Spätlesen and higher will be very long lived.

1972 Generally light, attractive wines. Rhine wines better than Moselles.

1973 Extremely large quantity. Fruity and well-balanced wines best consumed young.

1974 Small quantity. Agreeable but undistinguished.

1975 Average quantity. Great vintage. Extremely high proportion of top-category wines. Almost no Tafelwein was produced.

1976 Small quantity. Long, hot summer produced predominantly Spätlesen and higher-quality wines, but some lack acid.

1977 Generally light wines for quick drinking.

1978 Moderate vintage. Good year for Qualitätswein, and a few late harvest specialties.

1979 Small quantity. Successful Prädikat wines up to Auslese level.

1980 Small quantity of Riesling and Prädikat wines. Rhine wines fared better.

1981 Above average quantity. Good QbA and Kabinett wines.

1982 Superlative vintage in both quantity and quality.

Notes on Porto Vintages

Vintage Porto is made only in fine years, and even then not every producer makes a Vintage Porto. The number of producers who declare a vintage has ranged from two (in 1931) to thirty (in 1927). The average number of producers who declare a vintage is fourteen.

1945 Classic vintage; wines are rich with good color and body.

1947 Good year; wines are fruity and delicate.

1948 Wines are full and powerful with depth.

1950 Lighter wines, faster to mature.

1955 Good year; wines are long lasting and full.

1958 Lighter wines, more delicate.

1960 Good quality, not too dark, can be drunk now.

1963 Big, fat wines, good fruity bouquet, dark color. Drink in 1980s.

1966 Fresh and fruity, not as big as '63s. Drink from 1980 on.

1967 Borderline vintage, few declared; on the light side.

1970 Superb year, good color and body. Drink in the 1990s.

1975 Exceptional year; wines are very dark and intense.

1977 Outstanding year; expected to rank with 1963.

1978 Borderline vintage; most shippers undecided.

1980 Another very good year; many declared due to full, rich wines.

California North Coast Vintage Chart
Second Edition

Napa												
Red Wines	**'68**	**'69**	**'70**	**'71**	**'72**	**'73**	**'74**	**'75**	**'76**	**'77**	**'78**	**'79**
Cabernet Sauvignon	18	17	19	13	12	16	18	16	15	16	17	16
Petite Sirah	16	16	17	14	12	15	16	17	16	15	17	17
Pinot Noir	16	15	17	13	13	14	15	16	17	16	16	17
Zinfandel	18	15	18	14	14	16	17	15	18	17	16	17
White Wines						**'74**	**'75**	**'76**	**'77**	**'78**	**'79**	**'80**
Chardonnay						15	18	15	17	17	18	17
Sauvignon Blanc						15	16	15	16	18	17	18
Chenin Blanc						16	16	15	17	17	16	17
Johannisberg Riesling						14	17	15	16	17	16	18
Sonoma												
Red Wines	**'68**	**'69**	**'70**	**'71**	**'72**	**'73**	**'74**	**'75**	**'76**	**'77**	**'78**	**'79**
Cabernet Sauvignon	17	16	18	14	10	15	17	15	16	16	17	15
Petite Sirah	17	17	17	14	13	15	16	17	16	15	17	16
Pinot Noir	16	15	17	14	13	15	15	16	17	17	16	17
Zinfandel	18	16	18	14	13	16	18	16	19	17	18	17

White Wines						**'74**	**'75**	**'76**	**'77**	**'78**	**'79**	**'80**
Chardonnay						16	17	17	16	18	17	19
Sauvignon Blanc						15	16	17	16	18	16	18
Chenin Blanc						16	16	15	16	16	16	17
Johannisberg Riesling						15	17	17	16	18	17	18
Mendocino												
Red Wines	**'68**	**'69**	**'70**	**'71**	**'72**	**'73**	**'74**	**'75**	**'76**	**'77**	**'78**	**'79**
Cabernet Sauvignon	15	16	16	14	12	15	17	16	15	17	17	16
Petite Sirah	16	17	16	15	13	16	18	18	16	17	18	15
Pinot Noir	16	15	15	14	13	14	15	16	15	16	16	17
Zinfandel	17	15	16	15	14	15	17	15	17	16	17	18
White Wines						**'74**	**'75**	**'76**	**'77**	**'78**	**'79**	**'80**
Chardonnay						17	18	16	17	16	16	17
Sauvignon Blanc						15	16	15	17	17	16	17
Chenin Blanc						17	17	16	17	18	16	18
Johannisberg Riesling						15	16	15	17	17	16	17

Interpretation

20-18 Exceptional
17-16 Very Good
15-14 Average
13-12 Fair
11-10 Poor

APPENDIX C

The Classified Growths of Bordeaux

Official Classification Of 1855

The Official Classification of 1855 listed the red wines of the Médoc and the sweet white wines of the Sauternes in order of quality. The one exception was the inclusion of Château Haut-Brion, from Graves, among the first growths of Médoc. The following list, which uses the current spelling of the names of some of the châteaux, also lists some châteaux that were not originally part of the 1855 classification but which came into existence when a château that had been originally listed was divided up. These wines are shown bracketed, signifying that they were once a single château.

Château Mouton-Rothschild, which is now listed as a first growth, was listed as a second growth from 1855 to 1973, although it always brought prices commensurate with those of the first growths.

Médoc Wines

First Growths

Château Lafite-Rothschild
Château Margaux
Château Latour
Château Haut-Brion
Château Mouton-Rothschild

Second Growths

Château Rausan-Ségla
Château Rauzan-Cassies
Château Léoville-Lascases
Château Léoville-Poyferré
Château Léoville-Barton
Château Durfort-Vivens
Château Gruaud-Larose
Château Lascombes
Château Brane-Cantenac
Château Pichon-Longueville, Baron de Pichon
Château Pichon-Longueville, Comtesse de Lalande
Château Ducru-Beaucaillou
Château Cos d'Estournel
Château Montrose

Third Growths

Château Kirwan
Château d'Issan
Château Lagrange
Château Langoa-Barton
Château Giscours
Château Malescot-Saint-Exupéry
Château Boyd-Cantenac
Château Cantenae-Brown
Château Palmer
Château La Lagune
Château Desmirail
Château Calon-Ségur
Château Ferrière
Château Marquis d'Alesme-Becker

Fourth Growths

Château Saint-Pierre
Château Talbot
Château Branaire-Ducru
Château Duhart-Milon-Rothschild
Château Pouget
Château La Tour-Carnet
Château Lafon-Rochet
Château Beychevelle
Château Prieuré-Lichine
Château Marquis de Terme

Fifth Growths

Château Pontet-Canet
Château Batailley
Château Haut-Batailley
Château Grand-Puy-Lacoste
Château Grand-Puy-Ducasse
Château Lynch-Bages
Château Lynch-Moussas

Château Dauzac
Château Mouton-Baron-Philippe
Château du Tertre
Château Haut-Bages-Libéral
Château Pédesclaux
Château Belgrave
Château Camensac
Château Cos-Labory
Château Clerc-Milon-Mondon
Château Croizet-Bages
Château Cantemerle

Sauternes (Including Barsac)

First Superior Growth

Château d'Yquem

First Growths

Château La Tour-Blanche
[Château Lafaurie-Peyraguoy
[Clos Haut-Peyraguey
Château de Rayne-Vigneau
Château Suduiraut
Château Coutet
Château Climens
Château Guiraud
Château Rieussec
[Château Rabaud-Promis
[Château Sigalas-Rabaud

Second Growths

Château Myrat
[Château Doisy-Daene
[Château Doisy-Dubroca
[Château Doisy-Védrines
Château d'Arche
Château Filhot
[Château Broustet
[Château Nairac
Château Caillou
Château Suau
Château de Malle
[Château Romer (R. Farges, prop.)
[Château Romer (A. du Hayot, prop)
[Château Lamothe
[Château Lamothe-Bergey

Official Classifications Of Other Bordeaux

The wines of Craves and Saint-Émilion were not classified until 1953 and 1955, respectively. The 1955 list still holds for Saint-Émilion, but the Craves list was redone and finalized in 1959. All of these wines are listed in alphabetical order, with the exception of Châteaux Ausone and Cheval-Blanc, which are listed ahead of the other Premiers Grands Crus Classés of Saint-Émilion. In the list of the classified wines of the Graves, Château Haut-Brion appears in Crus Classés—Red, even though it remains listed as a first growth of the 1855 classification.

The wines of Pomerol have never been officially classified. Château Pétrus, however, is considered to be an outstanding growth, equal to the first growths of the Médoc. The rest of the listed Pomerol wines are those generally considered to be the best wines after Château Pétrus.

Graves

1959 Official Classification

CRUS CLASSÉS—RED

Château Bouscaut
Château Carbonnieux
Domaine de Chevalier
Château Fieuzal
Château Haut-Bailly
Château Haut-Brion
Château La Mission Haut Brion
Château La Tour Haut Brion
Château La Tour-Martillac
Château Malartic-Lagravière
Château Olivier
Château Pape-Clément
Château Smith-Haut-Lafitte

CRUS CLASSÉS—WHITE

Château Bouscaut
Château Carbonnieux
Domaine de Chevalier
Château Couhins
Château La Tour-Martillac
Château Laville Haut Brion
Château Malartic-Lagravière
Château Olivier

Saint-Émilion

1955 Official Classification

PREMIERS GRANDS CRUS CLASSÉS

Château Ausone
Château Cheval-Blanc

Château Beauséjour (Lagrosse, prop.)
Château Beauséjour (Fagouet, prop.)
Château Belair
Château Canon
Château Figeac
Château La Gaffelière
Château Magdelaine
Château Pavie
Château Trottevielle
Clos Fourtet

GRANDS CRUS CLASSÉS

Château L'Angélus
Château L'Arrosée
Château Balestard-La Tonnelle
Château Bellevue
Château Bergat
Château Cadet-Bon
Château Cadet-Piola
Château Canon-La Gaffelière

Château Cap-de-Mourlin
Château Chapelle-Madeleine
Château Chauvin
Château Corbin (Giraud, prop.)
Château Corbin (Michotte, prop.)
Château Coutet
Château Croque-Michotte
Château Curé-Bon
Château Fonplégade
Château Fonroque
Château Franc-Mayne
Château Grand-Barrail-Lamarzelle-Figeac
Château Grand-Corbin-Despagne
Château Grand-Corbin-Pécresse
Château Grand-Mayne
Château Grand-Pontet
Château Grandes-Murailles
Château Guadet-Saint-Julien
Château Jean-Faure
Château La Carte
Château La Clotte
Château La Cluzière
Château La Couspaude
Château La Dominique
Château Larcis-Ducasse
Château Lamarzelle
Château Larmande
Château Laroze
Château Lassere
Château La Tour-du-Pin-Figeac (Bélivier, prop.)
Château La Tour-du-Pin-Figeac (Moueix, prop.)
Château La Tour-Figeac
Château Le Châtelet
Château Le Couvent
Château Le Prieuré
Château Mauvezin
Château Moulin-du-Cadet
Château Pavie-Décesse
Château Pavie-Macquin
Château Pavillon-Cadet
Château Petit-Faurie-de-Souchard
Château Petit-Faurie-de-Soutard
Château Ripeau
Château Sansonnet
Château Saint-Georges-Côte-Pavie
Château Soutard
Château Tertre-Daugay
Château Trimoulet
Château Trois-Moulins
Château Troplong-Mondot
Château Villemaurine
Château Yon-Figeac
Clos des Jacobins
Clos La Madeleine
Clos Saint-Martin

Pomerol

CRE EXCEPTIONNEL

Château Pétrus

Premiers Crus

Château Beauregard

Château Certan-Giraud

Château Certan-de-May

Château Gazin

Château La Conseillante

Château La Croix-de-Gay

Château Lafleur

Château La Fleur-Pétrus

Château Lagrange

Château La Pointe

Château Latour-Pomerol

Château L'Église-Clinet

Château L'Évangile

Château Nenin

Château Petit-Village

Château Rouget

Château Trotanoy

(Château) Vieux Château Certan

Source: *Bordeaux et Ses Vins* by Ch. Cocks et Éd. Féret, 12th edition, 1908, 1974.

APPENDIX D

PRINICIPAL VINEYARDS OF THE CÔTE D'OR, BURGUNDY

The ranking of wines of Burgundy has developed by tradition. Over the years, the best wines were judged to be Grands Crus, followed by Premiers Crus. These opinions have generally held to this day.

In this compilation of Grands and Premiers Crus, which is arranged by communes from north to south, Grand Cru vineyards appear in **boldface** type. Where the spelling of a vineyard has changed slightly from the original, the current spelling is used.

Unlike the great châteaux of Bordeaux, the names of Grands Crus vineyards are controlled appellations.

Côte de Nuits

COMMUNE	VINEYARD (CLIMAT)	
Fixin (mostly red)	Les Arvelets	Les Hervelets
	Aux Cheusots	Les Meix-Bas
	Le Clos-du-Chapitre	La Perrière
Gevrey-Chambertin (only red)	**Chambertin**	**Griotte-Chambertin**
	Chambertin-Close de Bèze	**Latricières-Chambertin**
	Chapelle-Chambertin	**Mazis-Chambertin**
	Charmes-Chambertin (Mazoyères-Chambertin)	**Ruchottes-Chambertin**
	Au Closeau	Les Corbeaux
	Aux Combottes	Craipillot
	Bel-Air	Ergots
	Cazetiers	Estournelles
	Champeaux	Le Fonteny
	Champitonnois	Les Gemreaux
	Champonnets	Les Goulots
	Cherbaudes	Issarts
	Clos-du-Chapitre	Lavaut
	Clos-Prieur	La Perrière
	Le Clos Saint-Jacques	Poissenot
	Combe-aux-Moines	Les Véroilles
Morey-Saint-Denis (mostly red)	**Bonnes Mares** (partly in Chambolle-Musigny)	**Clos de Tart**
	Clos de la Roche	**Clos Saint-Denis**

Aux Charmes
Les Bouchots
Calouères
Chabiots
Les Chaffots
Les Charrières
Les Chénevery
Le Clos-Baulet
Clos-Bussière
Clos-des-Lambrays
Le Clos-des-Ormes
Le Clos-Sorbès
Côte Rôtie
Les Façonnières
Les Fremières
Les Froichots
Les Genevrières
Les Gruenchers
Maison-Brûlée
Les Mauchamps
Meix-Rentiers
Les Millandes
La Riotte
Les Ruchots
Les Sorbès

Chambolle-Musigny (mostly red)

Bonnes Mares
Musigny

Les Amoureuses
Aux Beaux-Bruns
Aux Combottes
Les Baudes
Les Bonnes Mares
Les Borniques
Les Charmes
Les Chatelots
Les Combottes
Derrière-la-Grange
Les Fousselottes
Les Fuées
Les Gras
Les Groseilles
Les Gruenchers
Les Hauts-Doix
Les Lavrottes
Les Noirots
Les Plantes
Les Sentiers

Vougeot (mostly red)

Clos de Vougeot

Le Clos-Blanc (white)
Clos-de-la-Perrière
Les Cras
Les Petits-Vougeots

Vosne-Romanée (only red)	**Richebourg**	**Romanée-Saint-Vivant**
	Romanée	**La Tâche**
	Romanée-Conti	
	Aux Brûlées	La Grande Rue
	Aux Malconsorts	Les Petits-Monts
	Les Beaumonts	Les Reignots
	Les Chaumes	Les Suchots
	Le Clos des Réas	
Flagey-Echézeaux (only red)	**Echézeaux**	
	Grands Echézeaux	
Nuits-Saint-Georges (mostly red)	Les Argillats	Clos-des-Forêts
	Aux Argillats	Clos-des-Grandes-Vignes
	Aux Boudots	Le Clos Saint-Marc
	Aux Bousselots	Les Corvées-Paget
	Aux Chaignots	Les Didiers
	Aux Champs-Perdrix	En la Chaine-Carteau
	Aux Cras	Les Hauts-Pruliers
	Aux Crots	La Perrière
	Aux Damodes	Perrière-Noblet
	Aux Murgers	Les Porets
	Aux Perdrix	Les Poulettes
	Aux Thorey	Le Procès
	Aux Vignes-Rondes	Les Pruliers
	Les Cailles	La Richemone
	Les Chaboeufs	La Roncière
	Clos-Arlots	Rue-de-Chaux
	Clos-de-la-Maréchale	Les Saint-Georges
	Clos-des-Argillières	Les Vallerots
	Clos-des-Corvées	Les Vaucrains

Côte de Beaune

COMMUNE	VINEYARD (CLIMAT)	
Aloxe-Corton (mostly red)	**Corton** or **Corton** plus vineyard name: Bressandes, Clos du Roi, Languettes, Perrières, Pougets, Renardes, La Vigne-au-Saint , etc. **Corton-Charlemagne** (white)	
	Les Chaillots	Les Maréchaudes
	En Pauland	Les Meix
	Les Fournières	Les Valozières
	Les Guérets	Les Vercots
Ladoix-Serrigny (mostly red)	Basses-Mourettes	La Maréchaude
	La Coutière	Les Petites Lolières
	Les Grandes-Lolières	La Toppe-au-Vert
Pernand Vergelesses (mostly red)	Les Basses-Vergelesses	En Caradeux
	Creux-de-la-Net	Les Fichots
Savigny-Les-Beaune (mostly red)	Aux Clous	La Dominode
	Aux Fourneaux	Les Hauts-Jarrons
	Aux Grands-Liards	Les Hauts-Marconnets
	Aux Gravains	Les Jarrons
	Aux Guettes	Les Lavières
	Aux Guettes	Les Marconnets
	Aux Petits-Liards	Les Narbantons
	Aux Serpentières	Petits-Godeaux

Aux Vergelesses
Basses-Vergelesses
Bataillière
Les Charnières
Les Peuillets
Redrescuts
Les Rouvrettes
Les Talmettes

Beaune (mostly red)

Les Aigrots
A l'Ecu
Aux Coucherias
Aux Cras
Les Avaux
Le Bas-des-Teurons
Les Blanches-Fleurs
Les Boucherottes
Les Bressandes
Les Cent-Vignes
Champs-Pimont
Les Chouacheux
Le Clos-de-la-Mousse
Le Clos-des-Mouches
Clos-du-Roi
En Genêt
En l'Orme
Les Épenottes
Les Fèves
Les Grèves
Les Marconnets
La Mignotte
Montée-Rouge
Les Montrevenots
Les Perrières
Pertuisots
Les Reversées
Les Seurey
Les Sisies
Sur-les-Grèves
Les Teurons
Tiélandry or Clos-Landry
Les Toussaints
Les Vignes-Franches

Pommard (only red)

Les Argillières
Les Arvelets
Les Bertins
Les Boucherottes
La Chanière
Les Chanlins-Bas
Les Chapponières
Clos-Blanc
Clos-de-la-Commareine
Les Épenots
És-Charmots
Les Fremiers
Les Garollières
Les Petits-Épenots
Les Pézerolles
La Platière
Les Poutures
La Refène

	Clos-du-Verger	Les Rugiens
	Le Clos-Micot	Les Rugiens-Bas
	Les Combes-Dessus	Les Rugiens-Hauts
	Les Croix-Noires	Les Sausilles
	Derrière-Saint-Jean	
Volnay (only red)	Les Angles	En l'Ormeau
	Les Aussy	En Verseuil
	La Barre or Clos-de-la-Barre	Fremiers
	Bousse-d'Or	Les Lurets
	Les Brouillards	Les Mitans
	Caillerets-Dessus	Les Mitans
	Carelle-Dessous	Les Petures (red)
	Carelle-sous-la-Chapelle	Les Pitures-Dessus
	Chanlin	Pointe-d'Angles
	Le Clos-des-Chênes	Robardelle
	Les Clos-des-Ducs	Ronceret
	En Caillerets	Les Santenots (red)
	En Champains	Taille-Pieds
	En Chevret	Village-de-Volnay
Monthélie (mostly red)	Le Cas-Rougeot	Le Meix-Bataille
	Les Champs-Fulliot	Les Riottes
	Le Château-Gaillard	Sur Lavelle
	Le Clos-Gauthey	La Taupine
	Duresse	Les Vignes-Rondes
Auxey-Duresses (predominantly red)	Les Bas-des-Duresses	Les Duresses
	Les Bretterins	Les Écusseaux
	La Chapelle	Les Grands-Champs
	La Chapelle	Reugne
	Clos-du-Val	

Meursault (mostly white)	Aux Perrières Les Bouchères Les Caillerets Les Charmes-Dessous Les Charmes-Dessus Les Cras Les Genevrières-Dessous Les Genevrières-Dessus La Goutte d'Or La Jennelotte	Les Perrières Dessous Les Perrières-Dessus Les Petures La Pièce-sous-le-Bois Le Poruzot Le Poruzot-Dessus Les Santenots-Blancs Les Santenots-du-Milieu Sous-le-dos-d'Ane
Puligny-Montrachet (mostly white)	**Bâtard-Montrachet** (partly in Chassagne-Montrachet) **Bienvenues-Bâtard-Montrachet**	**Chevalier-Montrachet** **Montrachet** (partly in Chassagne-Montrachet)
	Le Cailleret Les Chalumeaux Le Champ-Canet Clavoillons Les Combettes Les Folatières	La Garenne Hameau-de-Blagny Les Pucelles Les Referts Sous-le-Puits
Chassagne-Montrachet (majority red)	**Bâtard-Montrachet** (partly in Puligny-Montrachet) **Criots-Bâtard-Montrachet**	**Montrachet** (partly in Puligny-Montrachet)
	Abbaye-de-Morgeot La Boudriotte Les Brussoles	Grandes-Ruchottes Les Macherelles La Maltroie

	Les Champs-Gain	Morgeot
	Les Chenevottes	La Romanée
	Clos-Saint-Jean	Les Vergers
	En Cailleret	
Saint-Aubin (predominantly red)	Champlot	Les Murgers-des-Dents-de-Chien
	La Chatenière	Sur Gamay
	Les Combes	Sur-le-Sentier-du-Clou
	En Remilly	
	Les Frionnes	
Santenay (mostly red)	Beauregard	Les Gravières
	Beaurepaire	La Maladière
	Clos-de-Tavannes	Le Passe-Temps
	La Comme	

Source: Pierre Poupon and Pierre Forgeot, *The Wines of Burgundy*, 5th ed. (Paris: Presses Universitaires de France, 1974).

Principal Vineyards Of Chablis

Grand Cru Vineyards: Blanchots
Bougros
Grenouilles
Les Clos
Les Preuses
Valmur
Vaudésir

Premier Cru Vineyards (boldface)	Subdivisions (lightface)
Beauroy	**Montée de Tonnerre**
Troesmes	Chapelot
Côte de Léchet	Pieds-d'Aloup
Fourchaume	**Montmains**
Côte de Fontenay	Butteaux
L'Homme Mort	Forêts
Vaulorent	**Monts de Milieu**
Vaupulent	**Vaillons**
Los Fourneaux	Beugnons
Côtes des Prés-Girots	Châtains
Morein	Les Lys
Mélinots	Séché
Les Epinottes	**Vaucoupin**
Roncières	**Vosgros**
	Vaugiraut

PRINCIPAL VINEYARDS OF BEAUJOLAIS

Grand Cru Vineyards: Brouilly
Chénas
Chiroubles
Côte de Brouilly
Fleurie
Juliénas
Morgon
Moulin-à-Vent
Saint-Amour

Source: Pierre Poupon et Pierre Forgeot, *Les Vins de Bourgogne*, 8eme ed. (Paris: Presses Universitaires de France, 1977)

APPENDIX E

D.O.C. Wines, D.O.C.G. Wines, and Principal Grape Varieties of Italy

D.O.C. Wines of Italy (by region from north to south)

Valle d'Aosta

Domnaz
Enfer d'Arvier

Piedmont

Barbaresco
Barbera d'Alba
Barbera d'Asti
Barbera del Monferrato
Barolo
Boca
Brachetto d'Acqui
Bramaterra
Carema
Colli Tortonesi (Barbera, Cortese)
Cortesi dell'Alto Monferrato
Dolcetto d'Acqui
Dolcetto d'Alba
Dolcetto d'Asti
Dolcetto delle Langhe Monregalesi
Dolcetto di Diano d'Alba
Dolcetto di Dogliani
Dolcetto di Ovada
Erbaluce di Caluso or Caluso Passito
Fara
Freisa d'Asti
Freisa di Chieri
Gabiano
Gattinara
Gavi or Cortese di Gavi
Ghemme
Grignolino d'Asti
Grignolino del Monferrato Casalese
Lessona
Malvasia di Casorzo d'Asti
Malvasia di Castelnuovo Don Bosco
Moscato d'Asti Spumante
Moscato Naturale d'Asti
Nebbiolo d'Alba
Rubino di Cantavenna
Sizzano

Lombardy

Botticino
Capriano del Colle (Bianco, Rosso)
Cellatica
Franciacorta Pinot
Franciacorta Rosso
Lugana
Oltrepò Pavese (Barbacarlo, Barbera, Bonarda, Buttafuoco, Cortese, Moscato, Pinot, Riesling, Rosso, Sangue di Giuda)
Riviera del Garda Bresciano (Rosso and Chiaretto)
Tocai di San Martino della Battaglia
Valcalepio
Valtellina (Rosso, Sfursat)
Valtellina Superiore (Inferno, Grumello, Sassella, Valgella)

Trentino-Alto Adige

Alto Adige (Cabernet, Lagrein, Malvasia, Merlot, Moscato Giallo, Moscato Rosa, Müller-Thurgau, Pinot Bianco, Pinot Grigio, Pinot Nero, Riesling Italico, Riesling Renano, Sauvignon, Schiava, Sylvaner, Traminer Aromatico)
Caldaro or Lago di Caldaro
Casteller
Colli di Bolzano
Meranese or Meranese di Collina
Santa Maddalena
Sorni
Terlano
Teroldego Rotaliano
Valdadige
Valle Isarco (Müller Thurgau, Pinot Grigio, Sylvaner, Traminer Aromatico, Veltliner)
Vini del Trentino (Cabernet, Lagrein, Marzemino, Merlot, Moscato, Pinot Bianco, Pinot Nero, Riesling, Traminer Aromatico, Vin Santo)

Veneto

Bardolino
Bianco di Custoza
Breganze (Bianco, Cabernet, Pinot Bianco, Pinot Grigio, Pinot Nero,

Rosso, Vespaiolo)
Colli Berici (Cabernet, Garganega, Merlot, Pinot Bianco, Sauvignon, Tocai Bianco, Tocai Rosso)
Colli Euganei (Bianco, Moscato, Rosso)
Gambellara (Bianco, Recioto, Vin Santo)
Lugana
Montelloe Colli Asolani (Cabernet, Merlot, Prosecco)
Pramaggiore (Cabernet, Merlot)
Prosecco di Conegliano-Valdobbiadene
Soave (Recioto, Soave, Soave Classico)
Tocai di Lison
Valpolicella (Valpolicella, Valpolicella Classico, Recioto, Recioto Amarone)
Vini del Piave (Cabernet, Merlot, Tocai, Verduzzo)

Friuli-Venezia-Giulia

Aquileia (Cabernet, Merlot, Pinot Bianco, Pinot Grigio, Refosco, Riesling Renano, Tocai)
Colli Goriziano or Collio (Bianco Cabernet France, Malvasia, Merlot, Pinot Bianco, Pinot Grigio, Pinot Nero, Riesling Italico, Sauvignon, Tocai Traminer)
Colli Orientali del Friuli (Cabernet Franc, Cabernet Sauvignon, Merlot, Picolit, Pinot Bianco, Pinot Grigio, Pinot Nero, Ribolla, Riesling Renano, Refosco, Sauvignon, Tocai, Verduzzo)
Grave del Friuli (Cabernet Franc, Cabernet Sauvignon, Merlot, Pinot Bianco, Pinot Grigio, Refosco Tocai, Verduzzo)
Isonzo (Cabernet, Malvasia Istriana, Merlot, Pinot Bianco, Pinot Grigio, Riesling Renano, Sauvignon, Tocai, Traminer Aromatico, Verduzzo)
Latisana (Cabernet, Merlot, Pinot Bianco, Pinot Grigio, Refosco, Tocai, Verduzzo)

Liguria

Cinqueterre
Cinqueterre Sciacchetrà
Rossese di Dolceacqua or Dolceacqua

Emilia-Romagna

Albana di Romagna
Biano di Scandiano
Colli Bolognesi (Monte San Pietro or Castelli Medioevali)
Gutturnio dei Colli Piacentini
Lambrusco di Sorbara
Lambrusco Grasparossa di Castelvetro
Lambrusco Reggiano
Lambrusco Salamino di Santa Croce
Monterosso Val d'Arda
Sangiovese di Romagna
Trebbianino Val Trebbia
Trebbiano di Romagna

Tuscany

Bianco della Valdinievole
Bianco di Pitigliano
Bianco Vergine Val di Chiana
Brunello di Montalcino
Carmignano
Chianti (Classico, Colli Aretini, Colli Fiorentini, Colline Pisane, Colline Senesi, Montalbano, Rufina)
Elba (Bianco and Rosso)
Montecarlo
Montescudaio
Morellino di Scansano
Parrina
Rosso delle Colline Lucchesi
Vernaccia di San Gimignano
Vino Nobile di Montepulciano

Marches

Bianchello del Metauro
Bianco dei Colli Maceratesi
Falerio dei Colli Ascolani
Rosso Conero
Rosso Piceno
Sangiovese dei Colli Pesaresi
Verdicchio dei Castelli di Jesi
Verdicchio di Matelica
Vernaccia di Serrapetrona

Umbria

Colli Altotiberini
Colli del Trasimeno
Colli Perugini
Montefalco (Rosso, Sagrantino)
Orvieto
Torgiano (Bianco, Rosso)

Latium

Aleatico di Gradoli
Aprilia (Merlot, Sangiovese, Trebbiano)
Bianco Capena
Cerveteri (Bianco, Rosso)
Cesanese del Piglio or Piglio
Cesanese di Affile or Affile
Cesanese di Olevano Romano or
  Olevano Romano
Colli Albani
Colli Lanuvini
Cori (Bianco, Rosso)
Est! Est!! Est!!! di Montefiascone
Frascati
Marino
Montecompatri Colonna
Orvieto
Velletri (Bianco Rosso)
Zagarolo

Abruzzi and Molise

Montepulciano d'Abruzzo
Trebbiano d'Abruzzo

Campania

Capri (Bianco, Rosso)
Fiano di Avellino
Greco di Tufo
Ischia (Bianco, Bianco Superiore, Rosso)
Solopaca (Bianco, Rosso)
Taurasi

Apulia

Aleatico di Puglia
Brindisi (Rosso, Rosato)
Caccé Mmitte di Lucera
Castel del Monte (Bianco, Rosso, Rosato)
Coperatino (Rosso, Rosato)
Leverano (Bianco, Rosso, Rosato)
Locorotondo
Martina or Martina Franca
Matino (Rosso, Rosato)
Moscato di Trani
Ostuni (Bianco, Ottavianello)
Primitivo di Manduria
Rosso Barletta
Rosso Canosa
Rosso di Cerignola
Salice Salentino (Rosso, Rosato)
San Severo (Bianco, Rosso, Rosato)
Squinzano (Rosso, Rosato)

Basilicata

Aglianico del Vulture

Calabria

Cirò (Classico, Bianco, Rosso, Rosato)
Donnici
Greco di Bianco
Lamezia
Melissa (Bianco, Rosso)
Pollino
Sant'Anna di Isola Capo Rizzuto
Savuto

Sicily

Bianco Alcamo or Alcamo
Cerasuolo di Vittoria
Etna (Bianco, Rosso, Rosato)
Faro
Malvasia delle Lipari
Marsala
Moscato di Noto
Moscato di Pantelleria
Moscato di Siracusa
Moscato Passito di Pantelleria

Sardinia

Campidano di Terralba
Cannonau di Sardegna
Carignano del Sulcis
Girò di Cagliari
Malvasia di Bosa
Malvasia di Cagliari
Mandrolisai (Rosso, Rosato)
Monica di Cagliari
Monica di Sardegna
Moscato di Cagliari
Moscato di Sardegna
Moscato di Sorso-Sennori
Nasco di Cagliari
Nuragus di Cagliari
Vermentino di Gallura
Vernaccia di Oristano

Source: Anderson, Burton, *The Simon and Schuster Pocket Guide to Italian Wines* (1982), Hazan, Victor, *Italian Wine* (Knopf, 1982).

D.O.C.G. Wines of Italy

Barbaresco	Piedmont
Barolo	Piedmont
Brunello di Montalcino	Tuscany
Chianti	Tuscany
Vino Nobile di Montepulciano	Tuscany

Principal Grape Varieties of Italy

Dark Grapes

Grape	Regions Where Grown*	Wines
Aglianico	Basilicata	Aglianico del Vulture
	Campania	Taurasi
Aleatico	Latium	Aleatico di Gradoli
(Muscato Nero)	Apulia	Aleatico di Puglia
Barbera	Piedmont	Barbera d'Alba
		Barbera d'Asti
		Barbera del Monferrato
	Lombardy	Botticino
		Cellatica
		Franciacorta
		Oltrepò Pavese
		Riviera del Garda
	Emilia-Romagna	Gutturnio dei Colli Piacentini
Bombino Nero	Apulia	Castel del Monte
Bonarda	Piedmont	Boca
		Fara
		Ghemme
		Sizzano
Brachetto	Piedmont	Brachetto d'Acqui
		Brachetto d'Asti
Brunello di Montalcino	Tuscany	Brunello di Montalcino
Cabernet Sauvignon	Veneto	Breganze Cabernet
or Cabernet Franc	Trentino-Alto Adige	Trentino Cabernet
	Friuli-Venezia-Giulia	Grave del Friuli Cabernet
		Colli Orientale del Friuli Cabernet

*These are the regions where the grapes are most important. Many of these grapes are grown elsewhere in Italy in smaller amounts.

Grape	Regions Where Grown*	Wines
Calabrese	Sicily	Cerasuolo di Vittoria
Canaiolo Nero	Tuscany	Chianti
		Vino Nobile di Montepulciano
Cannonau	Sardinia	Cannonau di Sardegna
Cesanese	Latium	Cesanese del Piglio
		Cesanese di Affile
Corvina Veronese	Veneto	Bardolino
		Valpolicella
Dolcetto	Piedmont	Dolcetto d'Acqui
		Dolcetto di Ovada
Freisa	Piedmont	Freisa d'Asti
Girò	Sardinia	Giro di Cagliari
Grignolino	Piedmont	Grignolino d'Asti
Gropello	Lombardy	Gropello Amarone
		Riviera del Garda
Lagrein	Trentino-Alto Adige	Trentino Lagrein
Lambrusco (several varieties)	Emilia-Romagna	Labrusco Reggiano
		Lambrusco di Sorbara, etc.
Merlot	Friuli-Venezia-Giulia	Colli Orientale del Friuli Merlot
		Grave del Friuli Merlot
	Trentino-Alto Adige	Trentino Merlot
	Veneto	Breganze Rosso
	Abruzzo	Montepulciano d'Abruzzo
Montepulciano	Marches	Rosso Conero
		Rosso Piceno
Nebbiolo (called Spanna around Gattinara)	Apulia	San Severo
	Piedmont	Barbaresco
		Barolo
		Boca

Grape	Regions Where Grown*	Wines
		Carema Fara Gattinara Ghemme Sizzano
(here called Chiavennasca)	Lombardy	Grumello Inferno Sassella Vagella
Negroamaro	Apulia	Brindisi Copertino Leverano Matino Salice Salentino Squinzano
Perricone	Sicily	Corvo Rosso
Pinot Nero	Friuli-Venezia-Giulia	Colli Orientale del Friuli Pinot Nero Collio Pinot Nero
	Lombardy	Oltrepò Pavese Pinot
	Trentino-Alto Adige	Trentino Pinot Nero
	Veneto	Breganze Pinot Nero
Primitive	Apulia	Primitivo di Manduria
Refosco	Friuli-Venezia-Giulia	Colli Orientali del Friuli Refosco Aquilea Refosco Grave del Friuli Refosco Latisana Refosco
Rondinella	Veneto	Bardolino Valpolicella

Grape	Regions Where Grown*	Wines
Sangiovese	Emilia-Romagna	Sangiovese di Romagna
(several varieties)	Latium	Sangiovese di Aprilia
	Marches	Sangiovese dei Colli Pesaresi
	Tuscany	Chianti
		Elba Rosso
		Vino Nobile di Montepulciano
	Umbria	Torgiano Rosso
	Veneto	Riviera del Garda
Schiava	Lombardy	Botticino
(several varieties)		Cellatica
	Trentino-Alto Adige	Caldaro
		Santa Maddalena
Uva di Troia	Apulia	Castel del Monte Rosso
		Rosso Barletta
		Rosso Canosa
Vespolina	Piedmont	Boca
		Fara
		Ghemme
		Sizzano

Light Grapes

Grape	Regions Where Grown*	Wines
Albana	Emilia-Romagna	Albana di Romagna
Ansonica (Inzolia)	Sicily	Corvo
		Marsala
	Tuscany	Parrina Bianco
Biancolella	Campania	Ischia Bianco
Bombino Bianco	Abruzzo	Trebbiano d'Abruzzo
	Apulia	San Severo Bianco

Grape	Regions Where Grown*	Wines
Catarratto	Sicily	Alcamo Corvo Etna Bianco Marsala
Cortese	Lombardy Piedmont	Oltrepò Pavese Cortese Cortese di Gaul
Erbaluce	Piedmont	Caluso Passito Caluso Passito Liquoroso
Fiano	Campania	Fiano di Avellino
Garganega	Veneto	Gambellara Soave
Greco	Calabria Campania Latium	Cirò Bianco Greco di Tufo Frascati
Grillo	Sicily	Marsala
Malvasia (several varieties)	Latium	Colli Albani Est! Est!! Est!!! Frascati Marino
	Tuscany	Chianti Vin Santo
	Umbria	Orvieto
	Marches	Verdicchio
	Sardinia	Malvasia di Bosa
Moscato Bianco	Piedmont Sardinia	Asti Spumante Moscato di Cagliari
Müller-Thurgau	Trentino-Alto Adige	Trentino Riesling

Grape	Regions Where Grown*	Wines
Nuragus	Sardinia	Nuragus di Cagliari
Picolit	Friuli-Venezia-Giulia	Colli Oriental del Friuli-Picolit
Pinot Bianco	Friuli-Venezia-Giulia	Collio Pinot Bianco Colli Orientale del Friuli Pinot Bianco Grave del Friuli Pinot Bianco
	Trentino-Alto Adige	Trentino Pinot Bianco
	Veneto	Berganze Pinot Bianco
Pinot Grigio	Friuli-Venezia-Giulia	Collio Pinot Grigio Colli Orientale del Friuli Pinot Grigio Grave del Friuli Pinot Grigio
	Trentino-Alto Adige	Trentino Pinot Grigio
	Veneto	Breganze Pinot Grigio
Prosecco	Veneto	Prosecco di Conegliano-Valdobbiadene
Riesling Italico	Friuli-Venezia-Giulia	Colli Orientale del Friuli Riesling
Riesling Renano	Lombardy	Oltrepò Pavese Riesling
	Trentino Alto Adige	Trentino Riesling
Tocai Friulano	Friuli-Venezia-Giulia	Colli Orientale del Friuli Tocai
	Lombardy	Collio Tocai
	Veneto	Tocai di San Martino della Battaglia Tocai di Lison Breganze Bianco Piave Tocai
Traminer Aromatico (Gewürztraminer)	Friuli-Venezia-Giulia	Collio Traminer Aromatico
	Trentino-Alto Adige	Trentino Traminer Aromatico

Grape	Regions Where Grown*	Wines
Trebbiano (several varieties)	Emilia-Romagna	Trebbiano di Romagna
	Latium	Est! Est!! Est!!!
		Frascati
	Lombardy	Lugana
	Tuscany	Chianti
		Elba Bianco
		Montecarlo
		Vin Santo
	Umbria	Orvieto
		Torgiano Bianco
	Veneto	Lugana
		Soave
Verdicchio (several varieties)	Marches	Verdicchio dei Castelli di Jesi
		Verdicchio di Matelica
Verduzzo Friulano	Friuli-Venezia-Giulia	Colli Orientale del Friuli Verduzzo
		Grave Del Friuli Verduzzo
	Veneto	Piave Verduzzo
Vernaccia (several varnishes)	Sardinia	Vernaccia di Oristano
	Tuscany	Vernaccia di San Gimignano
Vespaiolo	Veneto	Breganze Vespaiolo
Zibibbo (Moscato di Alessandria)	Sicily	Marsala
		Moscato di Pantelleria
		Moscato Passito di Pantelleria

Source: Pier Giovanni Garoglio, *Enciclopedia Vitivinicola Mondiale* (Milan: Unione Italiana Vini, 1973).

APPENDIX F

Caloric Values of Alcoholic Beverages

Wines	**Calories per ounce (approx.)**
Light wine	less than 18
Red table wine	25
Dry white table wine	25
Champagne (brut)	25
Champagne (extra dry)	29
Catawba (sweet)	30
Madeira (dry)	35
Porto	50
Sherry (dry)	35
Sherry (sweet)	50
Vermouth (dry)	35
Vermouth (sweet)	46
Malt beverages	**Calories per 8 ounces**
Light Beer	75
Beer	100
Ale	150
Spirits	**Calories per ounce (approx.)**
Vodka, gin, whiskies, etc.	65-85
Liqueurs	**Calories per ounce (approx.)**
Bénédictine, Chartreuse, Drambuie, and other proprietary and generic liqueurs	100-120
Bitters	**Calories per teaspoon**
Aromatic bitters	10

APPENDIX G

Conversions for Weights and Measures in the United States, England, and All Other Countries Using the Metric System

Conversion Tables Between U.S. and Metric Systems

	To Change	To	Multiply by
Length	centimeters	inches	0.394
	inches	centimeters	2.540
	meters	feet	3.281
	feet	meters	0.305
	kilometers	miles	0.621
	miles	kilometers	1.609
Area	square centimeters	square inches	0.155
	square inches	square centimeters	6.451
	square meters	square feet	10.764
	square feet	square meters	0.093
	hectares	acres	2.471
	acres	hectares	0.405
	square kilometers	square miles	0.386
	square miles	square kilometers	2.590

	To Change	To	Multiply by
VOLUME	cubic centimeters	cubic inches	0.061
	cubic inches	cubic centimeters	16.387
	cubic meters	cubic feet	35.315
	cubic feet	cubic meters	0.0283
LIQUID CAPACITY	centiliters	fluid ounces	0.338
	fluid ounces	centiliters	2.957
	liters	gallons	0.264
	gallons	liters	3.785
	hectoliters	gallons	26.418
	gallons	hectoliters	0.0378
WEIGHT	grams	ounces	0.035
	ounces	grams	28.35
	kilograms	pounds	2.205
	pounds	kilograms	0.454
	metric ton	long ton	0.984
	long ton	metric ton	1.016
	metric ton	short ton	0.907
	short ton	metric ton	1.102

Conversion Tables Within Each System

For most purposes the modern units used for measures and weights in the United States are the same as those used in Great Britain. The major exception is in the measurement of capacity. In the following tables, therefore, there are three systems for liquid capacity—U.S., British, and metric—instead of the two major systems— U.S.-British combined and metric.

The S.I. system (*Système Internationale*), a refinement of the long-used metric system, will in time become the universal system of measurement. Britain is already committed to a complete transfer to this system, and the United States has approved transfer on a voluntary, industry-by-industry, basis.

United States, Great Britain	Metric or S.I.
	Length
12 inches = 1 foot	10 millimeters = 1 centimeter
3 feet = 1 yard	10 centimeters = 1 decimeter
1,760 yards = 1 mile	10 decimeters = 1 meter
5,280 feet = 1 mile	10 meters = 1 dekameter
6,080 feet = 1 nautical mile	10 dekameters = 1 hectometer
	10 hectometers = 1 kilometer
	Area
144 square inches = 1 square foot	100 square centimeters = 1 square decimeter
9 square feet = 1 square yard	100 square decimeters = 1 square meter (centare)
4,840 square yards = 1 acre	100 square meters = 1 square dekameter (are)
43,560 square feet = 1 acre	10,000 square meters = 1 hectare
640 acres = 1 square mile	100 hectares = 1 square kilometer
	Volume and Dry Capacity
1,782 cubic inches = 1 cubic foot	1,000 cubic centimeters = 1 cubic decimeter
27 cubic feet = 1 cubic yard	1,000 cubic decimeters = 1 cubic meter

1 dry pint = 33.6 cubic inches

1 dry quart (2 pints) = 67.201 cubic inches

1 peck (8 quarts) = 537.6 cubic inches

1 bushel (4 pecks) = 2,150.42 cubic inches

1,000 cubic meters = 1 cubic dekameter

1,000 cubic dekameters = 1 cubic hectometer

1,000 cubic hectometers = 1 cubic kilometer

United States, Great Britain
(avoirdupois weight)

437.5 grams = 1 ounce

16 ounces = 1 pound

100 pounds = 1 cental

2,000 pounds = 1 short ton

2,240 pounds = 1 long ton

(Also in Great Britain)

14 pounds = 1 stone

2 stones = 1 quarter

4 quarters = 1 hundredweight

20 hundredweights = 1 long ton

Metric or S.I.

WEIGHT

1,000 milligrams = 1 gram

1,000 grams = 1 kilogram

100 kilograms = 1 quintal

1,000 kilograms = metric ton

Liquid Capacity

United States	Great Britain
16 fluid ounces = 1 pint	20 fluid ounces = 1 imperial pint
2 pints = 1 quart	2 imperial pints = 1 imperial quart
4 quarts = 1 gallon	4 imperial quarts = 1 imperial gallon*
5 fifths = 1 gallon	
1 fluid ounce = 1.8 cubic inches	1 fluid ounce = 1.735 cubic inches
1 pint = 28.88 cubic inches	1 imperial pint = 34.68 cubic inches
1 quart = 57.75 cubic inches	1 imperial quart = 69.35 cubic inches
1 gallon = 231 cubic inches	1 imperial gallon = 277.4 cubic inches

Metric or S.I.

10 milliliters = 1 centimeter

100 centiliters = 1 liter

100 liters = 1 hectoliter

10 hectoliters = 1 kiloliter

1 milliliter = 1 cubic centimeter

1 liter = 1,000 cubic centimeters

1 hectoliter = 100,000 cubic centimeters

*1.2 American gallons = 1 imperial gallon